JESUS IN GENESIS

MICHAEL ESSES, D.H.L.
JESUS IN GENESIS

Logos International
Plainfield, New Jersey

Jesus in Genesis
Copyright © 1974 by Logos International
185 North Avenue
Plainfield, N.J. 07060
All Rights Reserved
Printed in the United States of America
Library of Congress Catalog Card Number: 73-92248
International Standard Book Number:

0-88270-093-6 (hardcover)
0-88270-100-2 (paper)

EDITOR'S NOTE

Like Esses' *The Phenomenon of Obedience*, the text of this book has been prepared from tapes of Michael Esses' live—and lively—teaching sessions at Melodyland Christian Center in Anaheim, California. The reader will find Esses' own literal, scholarly translations—direct from the Hebrew Masoretic text —thoroughly intermingled with his inimitable paraphrases and often hilarious amplification, without the encumbrance of scholarly separation and specific chapter and verse citations. General Scripture references are given at the head of each chapter, however, to guide the reader wishing to consult parallel passages in his own Bible.

It is our prayer that the result has been the preservation in print of the captivating uniqueness of Esses' ultra-personal Bible studies, and that God will be glorified as the Holy Spirit quickens His word to you throughout these pages.

Irene Burk Harrell

To my dear precious wife, Betty Lee,
who stood on the promise of God in Acts 16:31 for years, claiming me for salvation, saying to Jesus, "If You have to break every bone in his body to save him, I'm praising You for his salvation."

CONTENTS

PREFACE

It has been a journey of many years, a journey that began in an obscure, dusty little synagogue nearly fifty years ago, with an intense little boy leaning over the Scriptures, trying to grasp the teaching that was poured into him daily.

He was the last in the line of scores of rabbis who had gone before him—father, grandfather, great grandfather, great-great grandfather, as far back as can be remembered. All this tradition had culminated into one small boy whose head was full of knowledge far beyond his years and comprehension.

Genesis, the beginning. How could one little mind understand the magnitude of the creation? How could a human being fathom a God who can create something from nothing, a God who can take a fistful of stars, fling them into a void, and make a universe, a God who can breathe His spirit into a handful of clay and make man?

These thoughts, these truths, are too much for man to understand, much less a little child, and the boy was left with knowledge but without understanding.

And the boy grew and became a man—full of knowledge. But there was a missing ingredient that kept the man from perceiving what he had been taught.

Finally, one day, God in His mercy revealed to him the missing ingredient, Jesus. Yes, it is Jesus who makes Genesis the revelation that it is. It is Jesus who steps out of every page of the Bible to show the love of God to His people. It is indeed Jesus who puts us in touch with His Father and gives us the knowledge that the reason for Genesis is love, God's love.

And now I understand.

1
In the Beginning, God . . .
(Genesis 1—2)

Genesis is the book of beginnings. The first word in Genesis is the word *bereshith* in the Hebrew. Translated literally, it means, "In the beginning *of* God's creation—" Creation isn't confined to the earth. The LORD may possibly have created life elsewhere in the universe in His own image and in His own likeness. It's very possible. Don't be at all surprised when our astronauts land on some planet and find life there in the image and in the likeness of Jesus Christ.

The second word in the Hebrew is *bara*. This word tells us that God took absolutely nothing and made something out of it. In the beginning, God took nothing and made something out of it—the heavens and the earth. Now the earth was unformed, void, chaotic, and darkness was upon the face of the deep.

Unformed, void, chaotic—that's how it was in the beginning of God's creation. Some theologians will tell you that between verse 1 and verse 2 of Genesis, Satan came in and destroyed God's perfect creation, and the earth *became* void and chaotic, with darkness upon the face of the deep. But the Scripture doesn't tell me that at all. The LORD made the earth void in the beginning for a purpose—that He might send His Holy Spirit, the Spirit of God, to hover over the face of the waters. And the Holy Spirit brought order out of chaos.

The Holy Spirit still takes that which is unformed, which is void—your life and my life—and forms it, fills it, and makes it complete. He takes a chaotic life and makes a perfect life out of it by His very Holy Spirit.

God sent His Holy Spirit to brood upon, to hover over, the face of the waters, to bring forth order out of chaos. Imagine a hen that just laid an egg. She cackles and she broods and she sits upon the egg until it hatches. In the beginning of the creation of the earth, God sent His Holy Spirit to brood upon the creation and to bring it forth in His perfection.

In verse 3 we read that God said, "Let there be light." In Hebrew, the word used for God is Elohim. It is not the singular name *El*, as in Beth-*el* which means "house of God," or the singular name *Yahweh*, but it is *Elohim*, the plural of *El*. The same word was used in the first verse—Elohim created the heavens and the earth. The Father, the Son, and the Holy Spirit did the creating. The trinity is in the very first verse of Genesis.

Elohim said, "Let there be light," and there was light. Where did the light come from? Darkness was upon the face of the deep. The sun, the moon, and the stars were not called into being until the fourth day. And yet God, Elohim, said, "Let there be light," and there was light, in perfect response to His will. Who was the light? Jesus was the light. At this point, the entire creation was turned over to Jesus Christ. The confirmation of this is in the New Testament, in Colossians 1:16-17, which says that all things were made by Him and for Him. From this point on, you will not see again the word *bara* with *bereshith*, which we found in the first verse, where God took nothing and made something out of it. From this point on, all further creation will be done by the Word.

God saw the light, that it was good, and God divided the light from the darkness. That there was a division between light and darkness tells us symbolically that there's good and bad. We can stay in the light, we can live in the light, we can move in the light, or we can choose the darkness. We're not puppets on a string. The LORD says, "I have put a division between the light and dark, and it is for you to decide this day whom you will choose."

And God called the light day and the darkness He called night, and there was evening and there was morning—one day. According to Hebrew custom, most Jews still consider that the day begins at evening and not in the morning, because the LORD said, "There was evening and morning, one day." God started His day in the evening. This explains why the sabbath is ushered in on Friday evening.

And God, Elohim, said, "Let there be a firmament in the midst of the waters; let it divide the waters from the waters."

There were two sets of waters, the waters above the firmament—these are the mists and the clouds, that come down to earth in the form of rain—and the waters under the firmament—the waters found on earth—the rivers and the seas and the oceans.

And God called the firmament heaven. It is above everything. It does not touch the earth. It is not earthbound. When
we move in our flesh, we are earthbound, and we have no part
of heaven. It is only when we move in the Spirit that we become fit for heaven.

When He called the waters to be gathered together into one
place, He commanded the oceans to come into existence. The
waters were there, and He said, "Pacific Ocean, you go here;
Atlantic Ocean, you go there." And then He said, "Let the dry
land appear."

When the LORD commanded the dry land to appear, immediately, in perfect response to His will, it was so. And God called
the dry land Earth, and the gathering together of the waters
He called Seas, and God, Elohim, saw that it was good. And
God said, "Let the earth put forth grass, and herb yielding
seed, and fruit trees bearing fruit after its own kind wherein is
the seed thereof upon the earth." The LORD specified that from
that point on, everything was to have its own seed, to reproduce
itself. He gave the earth the power to bring forth what He had
called into being. He gave fruit the power to reproduce itself
after its own kind. The LORD said, "Don't try to tamper with My
creation. Don't mess it up. Don't fool with it. I made it perfect.
I gave it power to reproduce itself. Don't start mixing, because
this would be the great adultery, adulterating My creation.
Thou shalt not commit adultery. I made everything just the
way I want it in My perfect will. Don't mix it; don't contami-
nate it. I'll hold you guilty if you do."

And there was evening and morning, a third day. And God
said, "Let there be lights in the firmament of the heaven to

4

divide the day from the night, and let them be for signs, for seasons, for days, and for years."

How long are the spans of time that we have just covered? The Scripture tells us that with God a day is as a thousand years. If a day is as a thousand years, it could be a thousand eons, it could be a thousand generations. We have no idea how long the first three days were, because until we come to verse fourteen, when the Lord calls into being lights in the firmament of the heaven to divide the day from the night, the first three days could have been three billion years or thirty billion years. There was no twenty-four-hour day as we know it, until God called into being the sun, the moon, and the stars.

And God made two great lights, the greater light to rule the day, the lesser light to rule the night, and He made the stars also. And God set them in the firmament of the heaven to give light upon the earth, and to divide the light from the darkness; and God saw that it was good. Jesus was the light until then. When Jesus called forth into existence the sun and the moon, He delegated authority to these two luminaries, to rule over the day and the night, and to divide the light from the darkness.

And there was evening, there was morning, a fourth day. And Elohim said, "Let the waters swarm with swarms of living creatures. Let fowl fly above the earth in the open firmament of the heavens." God created the great sea monsters and every living creature that moves, wherewith the water swarmed after its own kind, every winged fowl after its own kind, and God saw that it was good.

Now God blessed those that He called forth into being, and He said, "Be fruitful and multiply and fill the waters in the

5

seas, and let the fowl multiply in the earth." And there was evening, there was morning, the fifth day.

And God said, "Let the earth bring forth the living creature after its own kind, cattle, and creeping thing, and the beast after its own kind," and it was so. And God made the beast of the earth after its own kind and the cattle after their kind, and everything that creeps upon the ground after its own kind, and God saw that it was good.

God went to a great deal of trouble to specify that everything was made after its own kind. If you and I take a mare and a jackass and we breed them together, we come up with a mule. The mule cannot reproduce himself. He's an abomination to the Lord. We have adulterated God's creation. He said, "I have made everything after its own kind — don't mess with it!"

And God said, "Let us make man in our image after our likeness, and let them have dominion over the fish of the sea, over the fowl of the earth, over the cattle, over all the earth, over every creeping thing that creepeth upon the earth." Notice He said, "Let *us* . . ." This was Jesus calling everybody into being, into existence. This was Jesus speaking in agreement with the Father and the Holy Spirit.

If we were made in the image and in the likeness of Jesus Christ, we were made perfect, absolutely perfect. Later, when sin and death came into the world through the enemy, Satan, something happened to that image, that likeness. It became imperfect, defective. Man fell away from God and no longer reflected His image.

God created man in His own image. He called him into being in the image of God. Male and female made He them. And God blessed them, and God said unto them, "Be fruitful and multi-

6

ply and *fill* the earth and subdue it." (If your Bible says either "*re*fill" or "*re*plenish," it's not translated correctly from the Hebrew.) And God gave man dominion over the fish of the sea, over the fowl of the air, over every living thing that creeps upon the earth.

Then God said, "Take a look — behold — I have given you every herb yielding seed which is upon the face of all the earth, and every tree in which is the fruit of a tree yielding seed. To you, it shall be for food. And to every beast of the earth and to every fowl of the air, and to everything that creeps upon the earth, wherein there is the breath of life, I have given every green herb for food." In the beginning, God limited us to herbs, fruits, and vegetables. We were not allowed to eat any meat at this time. If we killed an animal to eat an animal's flesh, that would be murder. At this point, the LORD said, "You are vegetarians. You are without sin; you cannot eat flesh."

And God saw everything that He had made, and behold it was very good, and it was evening and it was morning, the sixth day. So on the sixth day, man and woman were made in the image and the likeness of God.

If God made man in the image of Himself, therefore, man has the very same dignity that God Himself has. The message to you and me in this is, "Don't ever do anything against your fellowman that would lessen his dignity, because the LORD would not do it." He will never lessen the dignity of any human being made in His image and in His likeness. In Leviticus 19:18, God says, "You shall not hold a grudge or resentment against your neighbor, but you shall love your neighbor as yourself."

When I look in the mirror, I see absolute perfection, and the Lord says, "When you look in that mirror and see absolute perfection, look in the very same mirror and see your neighbor as absolute perfection also. Rationalize for him as you do for yourself. Make excuses for him as you do for yourself. He's perfect, because he's made in the image of Jesus."

The Scripture represents God as deliberating over the making of the human species. It does not say, "Let man be created," but the Scripture says, "Come, let Us make man in Our image and in Our likeness, that man will think on a higher level, that man by the Spirit of God will think as God does. Let him have the power, the ability, to pull himself up out of the earth and move up out of the dust, and the earth, and the mire, and the clay, and the flesh, and move in the Holy Spirit of God, the Spirit of the LORD."

The LORD — Jesus — called everything into being. And it was very good. Everything that He called into being was good in itself, and when combined and united together in Him, it was proclaimed by Him to be *very* good. Everything in the universe was as the Creator, Jesus, willed it. Nothing was lacking, everything was in perfect harmony, bearing witness to the fact that Jesus planned the unity of nature.

In the second chapter of Genesis, we see that the heaven and the earth were finished, and all the host of them. And on the seventh day, God finished His work which He had made, and He *desisted* on the seventh day from all His work which He had made. If it says, "He rested," in your Bible, please change it to "desisted." This word means He stopped His creative activity. It doesn't mean that God was so tired that He had to rest.

Later, God tells us that we are to desist one day a week from all further generating of that green stuff that we tend to wor-

8

ship, the old American "el bucko." He says, "If you trust Me and believe Me, that I am who I am, that I am the LORD your God who will take care of all your needs, on the first six days and on the seventh day, or whatever day you dedicate to Me as your day of desistance, I will honor you, I will bless you, I will take care of every need that you have. You won't have to worry about that day."

The LORD Himself desisted from all further creative activity on one particular day. For Him, this happened to be the seventh day, our Saturday, the day of seven. But the word *sabbath* means "the day of desistance," not "the seventh day." Later on, God says in the Ten Commandments, "Remember to keep the *sabbath* day holy." He doesn't say, "Remember to keep the *seventh* day holy," but, "Keep the sabbath day holy, your day of desistance unto Me." He says, "You're to worship Me, praise Me, have your mind focused on Me, and not be out chasing after the buck on the day of desistance." God Himself desisted from any more creating on the seventh day.

And God blessed the seventh day and hallowed it because in it, He desisted from all His work. The LORD's day, as far as the Hebrew people are concerned, is Saturday, the sabbath day. But Jesus came into the world, and He said, "I am your sabbath rest. I am your rest of desistance. You are to rest in Me. You are to desist in Me." And if we rest in Jesus, we are freed from that day, and we can dedicate to the LORD any day we choose. If we have to work on Saturday and Sunday and Monday, making Tuesday our day of desistance, we can dedicate that day unto the Lord. He will accept it.

Jesus came into the world and freed us, and Jesus fulfilled

all Scripture for us. We're free in Him. And as we're free in Him, we rest in Him.

These are the generations of the heavens and of the earth, when they were created, in the day that the LORD *God* made earth and heaven. LORD *God?* What does that mean? In order to understand it, we need to look at the life of Moses.

The first five books of the Bible are known as the Five Books of Moses. How could they have been written by Moses? Although he wasn't even alive at the time the world was made, the LORD divinely inspired him, gave him every fact necessary to write an accurate account in the Books of Genesis, Exodus, Leviticus, Numbers, and Deuteronomy. Then Joshua took up the account at Moses' death.

In the Book of Exodus, the LORD tells Moses, "By My name Jehovah—Yahweh—I did not reveal Myself to any of the patriarchs, to any of mankind, but I am revealing this name unto you." And we see Moses using this name in Genesis 2:4. These are the generations of the heaven and of the earth when they were created in the day that the LORD *God*—"LORD God" in Hebrew is *Yahweh*—or *Jehovah—Elohim*, the singular name of God followed by the plural name of God. Moses, writing the Book of Genesis, referred to God by the name familiar to him, Jehovah Elohim. Moses knew Him by His singular name; he knew Him by His plural name. He spoke to the Father, the Son, and the Holy Spirit. He knew all three of them. He wrote, "These are the generations of the heaven and the earth when they were created in the day that Jehovah Elohim made earth and heaven." Moses knew God intimately; he spoke to Him face to face, mouth to mouth. He knew Him well enough to write down His name. In the New Testament, we see Jesus calling His Father in heaven, *Abba*. In Aramaic, *Abba* is "Daddy," not "Father." Jesus knew God intimately, so He could call Him "Daddy." I praise the Lord because I can call Him "Daddy," too.

No shrub of the field was yet in the earth, no herb of the field had yet sprung up, for Yahweh Elohim had not caused it to rain upon the earth, and there was not a man to till the ground.

But there used to go up a mist from the earth and water the whole face of the ground. The mist would not cause the seeds to spoil, and would not cause them to grow, but would keep them for just the right time for God's will when He would say, "Now grow."

God worked the same way with Moses. When Moses was born, Pharaoh issued a command saying all the male children were to be killed. But the Scripture tells us that when Moses was born, he was hidden for three months. He was a goodly child—that means the Lord zipped up his Jewish mouth and said, "Moses, keep quiet. When I stick you in the water when you're three months old, and I tell you to cry, that's the time to holler out, because I'll have Pharaoh's daughter standing by the water, and she will hear you. In the meantime, you're to be a good boy." So they were able to hide him for three months, because he never cried.

And so the Lord caused a mist to go up to water the ground so the seeds would be preserved until the Lord would say, "It's time to grow." Then, the Lord God formed man of the dust of the ground. He took the dust, He took this earth, and made man. Then He breathed into his nostrils the breath of life of His Holy Spirit, and man became a living soul the minute he

11

received that breath of life from God.

And the LORD God planted a garden eastward in Eden, and there He put the man He had formed. And out of the ground made the LORD God to grow every tree that is pleasant to the sight, and good for food; the tree of life also in the midst of the garden, and the tree of knowledge of good and evil.

And a river went out of Eden to water the garden; and from there it parted, and became four heads. The name of the first was Pishon. This river is lost to us. We don't know where it was. It was the river which compassed the whole land of Havilah, where there was gold. And the gold of that land was good; there was bdellium and the onyx stone. And the name of the second river was Gihon; the same it was that compassed the whole land of Cush. This river is lost to us also. But the third river was the Hiddekel, and that was the river which went toward the east of Asshur or Assyria. It is better known to us as the Tigris River. The fourth river was the Euphrates, and we know where that river is, too. Two of the rivers we know, but the other two are lost to us, so we can never find the Garden of Eden.

God would not want us to find the Garden of Eden. He fixed it so we could never find our way back in, because He wants us to worship the Creator and not the creation. He has already prepared a Savior, a deliverer, a healer, a salvager, who is Jesus Christ, and we can find our Eden in Him. Our everlasting life is in Jesus, not in the Garden of Eden.

And the LORD God took the man. He put him into the Garden of Eden to dress it and to keep it. He gave him a little job. He said, "See this little garden? Just take care of it and keep it.

That's all I want you to do. You don't have to punch a clock. You can come and go as you please."

And the LORD gave him a commandment, saying, "Man, Adam, you who were made of the dust, of every tree of the garden you may freely eat. But of the tree of the knowledge of good and evil, you shall not eat of it; for in the day that you eat thereof you shall surely die."

The LORD gave Adam a commandment, but He didn't tell him why He gave him the commandment. If I had been Adam, I would have asked the question, "Why?" And when the enemy appeared upon the scene, he would supply a reason. The enemy will always supply a reason. God may not give us one. He will say, "I command you to do this. I want you to be obedient unto Me. Obedience is better than sacrifice." You don't have to have a reason from the LORD. The minute you start asking "Why?" "Wherefore?" and "How?" the LORD says, "Forget it. All I want is your obedience." But when the enemy supplies the reason, you know you are in trouble.

And the LORD God—Jehovah Elohim—said, "It is not good that man should be alone." This still applies to you and me today. Leave a man alone, without his wife, and he will always get in trouble. If it wasn't for our wives, hardly any of us men would be saved. It's through the faithfulness of our wives standing with us, praying for us, putting up with us, committing us to the LORD constantly over and over again, that the LORD is able to work. So God said, "It is not good that man should be alone. I'll make a help meet for him."

And out of the ground, the LORD God formed every beast of the field, and every fowl of the air, and brought them unto the man to see what he would call them; and whatsoever the man called every living creature, that was the name thereof. Man alone has language and can give birth to language, and in giving names to earth's creatures, he established his dominion over them.

And the man gave names to all the cattle, all the fowl of the earth, to every beast of the field, but for Adam there was not found a help meet for him. Such a helper would be a wife, and a wife is not a man's shadow or his subordinate; she is his other self. She is his helper, in a sense in which no other creature on the face of the earth can be. When she is his helper, she matches him. The Hebrew term means that she is always at his side, that she is fit to associate with, that she is always over against him, corresponding to him. She stands with him side by side. When he gives up, she'll remain standing.

So the LORD said, "I will make a help meet for him, one who matches him and will stand with him."

And the LORD caused a deep sleep to fall upon the man, and he slept. The LORD anesthetized him and took one of his ribs, and He closed up the place with flesh. And the rib which the LORD God—Jehovah Elohim—had taken from the man, made He a woman, and brought her unto the man.

And the man looked at her and said, "This is now bone of my bones, flesh of my flesh. She shall be called a woman because she was taken out of man." Therefore, a man shall leave his father and his mother, and he shall cleave unto his wife, and they shall be one flesh. The Lord never said that a man should leave his father and his mother and should cleave unto his number one, number two, number three, and number four wives and that they would become four fleshes. He said a man should leave his father and his mother and should cleave unto

14

his *one* wife and they, together, should be one flesh in Jesus Christ.

This verse was not spoken by Adam, it was given by the Holy Spirit; these words were spoken by Jesus. Moses wrote them down. It was a revelation unto him as he wrote them.

Marriage is sacred, it is holy, it is an estate given by God. When a man gets married, the minister says, "Therefore, those whom God hath put together, let no man put asunder." This is ordained by God, that a man is to leave and to forsake everything and everybody, and to cleave unto his wife as Jesus cleaves unto His bride, the Church. As He gave His life to His bride, the Church, so a man is to cherish his wife, love her, respect her, honor her. She's not his subordinate. She is his other self.

In the day that they were made, God called both of them Adam because they were equal in His sight. They were both naked, the man and his wife, and they were not ashamed. The creation was perfect, as God had planned it.

2
Now the Serpent ...
(Genesis 3—6:7)

In Genesis chapter three, we see the trial of man's freedom
and the fall of man. God had spoken to Adam. He did not speak
to the woman, He spoke to the man. Today, the Lord speaks to
the man, who is the prophet and priest in his home. If the man
fails to convey God's message to his wife, the man is going to
be held accountable. The LORD held Adam guilty, responsible,
accountable for his failure to impress upon his wife the vital
importance of God's command when he left her alone. He said,
"Honey, I'm going to be out working in my little garden, doing
my little job. You take care of the house."

Adam went away, and Satan appeared upon the scene. Now
the serpent was more subtle than any beast of the field which
the LORD God had made. And he said unto the woman, "You
really mean to tell me that God spoke to you? Are you trying
to tell me that you shall not eat of any tree in the garden?" The
woman was immediately put on the defensive, and she said
unto Satan, the serpent, "Of the fruit of the trees of the garden,

we may eat, but of the fruit of the tree which is in the midst of the garden, God has said, 'You shall not eat of it, neither shall you touch it, lest you die.' " The woman took God's word and she added to it. The LORD said, "You shall not eat of any fruit of the tree," but He didn't say anything about not touching it. The woman expounded on God's word, and the minute she did, Satan had her trapped.

And the serpent said unto the woman, "No way. You're not going to die. It's all a lie." Remember, the woman was guileless, she was totally unsuspecting, and she fell into the trap as she enlarged on God's word. Her exaggeration trapped her and caused her to fall. Satan boldly denied the truth of God's threat. He said, "You shall not surely die in the day that you touch it."

Then Satan suggested a reason for God's command. He told the woman that when God gave His order not to eat of the fruit, it was not for man's benefit, but because God was envious of what man would become if he ate the forbidden fruit. He said, "God knows that in the day that you eat thereof, your eyes shall be opened. You shall be as God, knowing good and evil." And Satan made the forbidden fruit seem very tempting to the woman, very beautiful to her. But he didn't tell her to eat it.

And when the woman saw that the tree was good for food, and that it was a delight to the eye, and that the tree was to be desired to make one wise, she took of the fruit thereof, and she did eat. And as she ate, Adam came from his little job in the garden, and she gave also unto her husband with her, and he did eat. She had been arguing with Satan, the serpent, all afternoon long before she ate, but when Adam came running home, the minute she saw him, and she gave him of the fruit, he immediately took of the fruit and he ate, because he was afraid she knew a little more than he did at this point. He didn't argue as she had argued with the enemy. He immediately took of the fruit, because he wanted to be as wise as she was. It's tough to live with a woman who is smarter than you are.

And the eyes of them both were opened, and they knew that they were naked, and they sewed fig leaves together, and they made themselves girdles. And they heard the voice of the LORD God—Jehovah Elohim—walking in the garden in the cool of the day, and the man and his wife hid themselves from the presence of the Holy Spirit among the trees of the garden. And the LORD God called unto the man and said, "Where are you?" Of course God knew where he was, but He asked him in order to bring him salvation. He said to Adam," At what point of sin are you? Where are you in your relationship to Me? Are you still saved? Do you want to confess to Me that which you have done and repent of it?" He was asking him for a confession, for repentance, offering salvation, deliverance. If Adam had acknowledged his sin and said, "Yes, LORD, I have sinned," the LORD would have forgiven his sin.

The LORD God called unto the man and said unto him, "Where art thou?"

And Adam said, "I heard Thy voice in the garden, and I was afraid, because I was naked, and I hid myself."

And again the LORD called him to salvation and repentance, saying to him, "Adam, who told you that you were naked?" At this point, Adam should have said, "I ate of the fruit of the tree," but he didn't say a word. And the LORD confronted him again and said, "Have you eaten of the tree whereof I commanded you that you should not eat?"

And the man turned around, and he said to the LORD, "You see that dumb female that You gave me? She gave me of the fruit, and I ate. It's Your fault, because You insisted that I have a helper. It's her fault, and it's Your fault. The woman whom You gave to be with me, she gave me of the tree and I did eat." Adam passed the buck. And we've been passing the buck to our wives ever since.

And the LORD God said unto the woman, "What is this that you have done?" The woman answered truthfully, saying, "Satan, the serpent, tricked me and beguiled me, and I did eat." She confessed. She did not pass the buck. She did not put the blame on somebody else. She acknowledged her own weakness, that she was tricked, that she was fooled.

And God said unto the serpent, unto Satan, "Because you have done this, you are cursed above all cattle, and above all beasts of the field. Upon your belly you shall go, and dust you shall eat all the days of your life."

Man had fallen. Adam, who was of the earth, had arrogantly answered the LORD when He tried to call him back to repentance and salvation. But immediately, we see the love, and the grace, and the mercy of God, as He promised salvation to all of mankind, through another Adam who would come into the world. As sin and death came into the world by the first Adam, grace, salvation, and eternal life would come into the world by the second Adam who would be Jesus Christ.

In Genesis 3:15 is the promise of salvation. The Lord was still speaking to Satan, and He said, "I will put enmity between thee and the woman, between your seed and her Seed. He shall bruise your head and you shall bruise His heel."

Have you ever heard of a woman having a seed of her own?

No. It takes a man to impregnate the woman. The promise was that the woman who would be coming into the world would have a seed of her own, and that Seed would be the Savior, the Messiah, Jesus, the Christ. And God promised that Jesus would be victorious. He would bruise the head of Satan, and all Satan could do would be to nip at the heels of the followers of Jesus Christ.

Remember, Satan can't get to you, because Jesus is your protection and my protection, and nothing can penetrate His shed Blood, not even the enemy.

And the LORD said unto the woman, "I will greatly multiply your pain and your travail, and in your pain, you shall bring forth children, and your desire shall be to your husband, and he shall rule over you." This was not a curse that God brought upon the woman. The LORD never cursed the woman. He never found her guilty. Adam failed to communicate to his wife the importance of what the LORD said to him. He was the prophet and priest in his home, just like I am, just like every man is supposed to be.

The LORD cursed the ground for Adam's sake, but not for the sake of the woman. God only reminded her, "Much, much will I make your pain and your travail. In pain will you bring forth children, and your desire will be unto your husband, and he will rule over you." This was not a sentence upon the woman. It did not contain the term "cursed." Moreover, God Himself pronounced the fruitfulness of man a blessing, and therewith, woman's pain and travail are bound up, being part of a woman's physical being. These words addressed to the woman were just a reminder. In effect, the LORD was telling the woman, "You, I do not need to punish, because when I asked you the question,

20

'What is this that you have done?' you answered me honestly, faithfully, in sincerity. You said, 'I was tricked, I was beguiled, and I sinned.' " She acknowledged her sin, and so God did not need to punish her. A sufficiency of woe and suffering was hers already, because of her own physical being, the way God made her. And God said, "Despite the pain and the travail that you have in giving birth, the longing for motherhood will remain in the woman the most powerful instinct that I could possibly give any woman."

Then the LORD spoke to Adam, and He said unto him, "Because you listened unto the voice of your wife—"

There's nothing wrong with listening to your wife—except when it takes precedence over the voice of the LORD. The voice of the LORD comes first, above everything and everybody else.

The LORD said, "Adam, you listened to your wife before you listened to Me. Because you have done this, and you have eaten of the tree which I commanded you, saying, 'You shall not eat of it,' cursed is the ground for your sake; in toil you shall eat of it all the days of your life. Thorns also and thistles shall it bring forth to thee, and you shall eat the herb of the field. In the sweat of your face, you shall eat bread, till you return unto the ground, for out of it you were taken; for dust you are and unto dust you shall return."

And the man called his wife's name Eve, because she was the mother of all living. The Hebrew name for Eve is *Hawwah*, meaning "the mother of all living."

It was Adam's duty from the very beginning to till the ground, but now the work would become much more laborious. The soil would henceforth yield its produce only as a result of unceasing hard toil. As long as Adam lived, the earth was under a curse.

And the Lord said, "Whereas, you do eat the herb of the field—I have told you, you cannot eat any flesh—the spontaneous growth of the soil will be weeds from this point on. Weeds will grow among the herbs, because the ground is cursed for your sake, Adam. And these weeds are unsuitable for human consumption. Therefore, a man's only food is the herb which he can acquire only by hard toil." And the Lord said, "In the sweat of your brow, the necessity of laboring, you're going to have to toil, to produce. It's not going to be easy, as it was before you sinned. Before you sinned, all you did was to cultivate the soil and say, 'In the name of the Lord, grow,' and it grew. It was as simple as that. Now you're going to have to work for it." And the necessity of labor has proved to be man's greatest blessing from the Lord, the cause of all progress and improvement.

The Lord will still take a bad thing and make a good thing out of it, and all things work together for good to those who love God. Even something like this.

Then the Lord God made for Adam and for his wife garments of skin, and He clothed them. They had just sinned, and the Lord covered them. God Himself shed the first blood, the blood of animals, to show Adam and Eve that they still had His love and His grace and His mercy. He hated the sin, but He loved the sinner. He made them garments of skins; He clothed them with His grace.

And the Lord God said, "Behold, the man has become as one of Us, to know good and evil." Jesus was speaking to the Father and to the Holy Spirit. "And now what if he put forth his hand and take also of the tree of life, and eat, and live forever?"

If Adam touched Jesus, he would live forever. But it was not yet time for man to have everlasting life. He was still in a sinful state. Therefore, the LORD God—Yahweh Elohim—sent him forth from the Garden of Eden to till the ground from which he was taken.

He drove out the man; and He placed at the east of the Garden of Eden the Cherubim, and a flaming sword which turned every way to guard the way to the tree of life. These Cherubim were mighty angels. Our rabbis say that the Cherubim stood at least thirty feet high, and they had a flaming sword, turning every which way, so that if man, Adam, ever tried to enter back into the garden, he could not. There's only one way back in for any of us—and that is through the body and blood of Jesus. No man would ever come to the Father again except through Jesus Christ. Nobody would ever have a relationship again like Adam had before he sinned. The sin that Adam caused, we inherited. The sin of Adam has been passed on from father to son, ever since, the sin of rebellion.

Now the man knew his wife, and she conceived and bore Cain and said, "I have gotten a man with the help of the LORD." "With the help of the LORD" means that it was a blessing.

When Adam and Eve got kicked out of the Garden of Eden, Adam said to the woman, "Lady, it's your fault. I even told the LORD it was your fault. I blamed Him, and I blame you." He pouted and he sulked. "If it wasn't for you, lady, I'd still be back in that Garden of Eden. I would have a nice little job, just walking around, touching the flowers, the shrubs, the bushes, the herbs, and telling them to grow, and they would grow. Now

I really have to work." He came home tired every day, and he griped and complained to his wife, blaming her. Then he knew his wife intimately. She conceived, and she bore a son, and she said, "This was the love, and the grace, and the mercy of the LORD. With the help of the LORD, I have been reinstated into good standing with my husband, because I have now given him a son." She praised God for the blessing that had come to their family.

Adam was grateful, too, and Eve conceived again and bore Abel. Abel was a keeper of sheep, but Cain was a tiller of the ground. And in the course of time, it came to pass that Cain brought of the fruit of the ground an offering unto the LORD. From the earliest times, man knew that he was to bring an offering unto the LORD in praise and thanksgiving for what God had done for him. Abel brought of the firstlings of his flock —the best sheep that he had—and of the fat thereof.

The LORD *tells us over and over again in the Old Testament that we're not to eat the fat. The fat is His. The Lord, looking far into the future, realized that in our days, the medical profession was going to say, "We have just discovered that if you eat fat, the cholesterol is going to kill you." And the* LORD *knew the physicians would know what they were talking about. So he commanded men not to eat of the fat thereof, because it might kill them. He was showing us love, grace, and mercy clear back then.*

And the LORD had respect unto Abel and to his offering. But unto Cain and to his offering, He had not respect. This Scripture tells us the importance of the blood, and the importance of obedience. Cain knew exactly what he was supposed to do. Abel knew exactly what he was supposed to do.

From the beginning, God had made it plain to the family of Adam that there were two conditions that had to be present before a sacrifice was acceptable.

First, the person making the sacrifice had to have a clean heart, and be found righteous in the eyes of God. Second, the sacrifice itself had to be a blood sacrifice.

Cain tried to negate the blood sacrifice by sacrificing the produce that had come from the ground which God had cursed. It was Cain's way of saying, "I want to do this *my* way." He failed to recognize that God's word is not just an option, God's word is *law*.

What should Cain have done? If he was truly trying to be right with God, to bring a proper offering to the LORD, he would have gone to his brother Abel, his younger brother, and he would have said, "Kid, I want to bring an offering to the LORD. I want to trade you these fruits and vegetables for a sheep, so I can bring a right offering to God." That would have been an act of humility, but Cain did not want to humble himself before his kid brother. He wasn't about to do that. He was going to bring second best to God and hope to get blessed anyway. That's the story of mankind. We think we can bring to God second best and get away with it, but we never do.

The LORD did not have respect unto Cain and his offering. He rejected his offering. But He accepted the offering that Abel brought. So a resentment for Abel was born in Cain's heart.

And Cain was very wroth; he was very angry with the LORD. How dare God reject his offering! Didn't the LORD know he had worked for those lousy fruits and vegetables for three days? He could have eaten them himself. Here he did God a favor and

25

brought them to Him as an offering, and He rejected it. God sure had a lot of nerve!

And Cain's countenance fell. He was walking around feeling sorry for himself. Again we see the love, and the grace, and the mercy of the LORD as He spoke to Cain and said unto him, "Why are you angry? Why is your countenance fallen? What is it that you're feeling sorry about?" The LORD was divinely intervening to arrest the progress of the evil taking place in the heart and mind of Cain.

And the LORD told him, "If you do well, shall it not be lifted up from you? If you want to get rid of this grudge, this resentment, this hatred that you have for Me, the LORD your God, and this grudge and this resentment and hatred that you have for your brother Abel, shall I not lift it for you? All you have to do is surrender it unto Me, and I'll take it from you."

The LORD was really telling him, "Shall I not accept you? I will accept you, if you turn to Me." The LORD continued to speak to him, because there was still no answer. "If you do not do well, sin couches and lurks at your door, and unto you is its desire, but you may rule over it. You have the power to rule over the sin which couches at the door of your heart ready to come in and to eat you up." The LORD compared sin to a ravenous beast lying in wait for its prey. It crouches at the entrance of the house, the door of a man's heart, to spring upon the victim as soon as the door of his heart is opened by a small grudge, a small resentment, a small hatred.

By harboring feelings of vexation, Cain opened the door of his heart to the evil passions of envy, anger, and violence, which eventually ended in murder, because he would not listen to the LORD. He still wanted to do his own thing.

Passion and evil imagination are ever assaulting the heart of man. Yet you can conquer them in Jesus Christ. You can conquer them in the LORD, if only you stand in the LORD and resist with determination. Say, "Get away from me, Satan, I stand in the LORD Jesus Christ. He that is within me is greater than he that is outside." The LORD says, "The desire of sin is always to overtake you, but you may rule over it in Me. There's power in My name of Jesus. If you call upon My name, I will deliver you."

Cain did not answer the LORD at all. This was sheer arrogance. Instead, he turned to his brother Abel as if the LORD couldn't hear what he was saying, as if the LORD couldn't see what he was doing. Cain spoke unto Abel, his brother, and he told him, "Let us go out into the field."

And it came to pass, when they were in the field, that Cain rose up against Abel, his brother, and slew him. He wouldn't get rid of that grudge, that resentment, that envy, that hatred, and he killed his brother. The LORD tried to stop him, but he wouldn't stop.

God will give us enough rope to hang ourselves if we want to. But before He does that, He will speak to you and me over and over and over and over again, trying to stop the process of our sin. That's the love of God. That's the love of Jesus. That's the grace and the mercy of the LORD.

Cain had killed his brother. And the LORD divinely intervened in his life again and spoke to him once more. And the LORD said unto Cain, "Where is Abel your brother?" Of course God knew where Abel was. But the LORD was giving Cain an opportunity to turn to Him and say, "LORD, I didn't listen to You. I'm sorry. I killed my brother in anger. Forgive me." If he had done that, the LORD would have forgiven him. But instead, Cain answered the LORD, "I don't know where Abel is. Am I my brother's keeper? What did You do, put me in charge of him now? I could care less where he is."

He answered arrogantly to the LORD, falsely and insolently. Only a murderer altogether renounces the obligation of brotherhood, and he just renounced it, saying indignantly, "Am I my brother's keeper? It's between You and him. I don't know anything about him."

And the LORD spoke to him again, still calling him to salvation. And the LORD said, "What is this that you have done? What is it that you have done, Cain?" No answer.

And the LORD continued to speak, and He said, "The voice of your brother's blood cries unto Me from the ground. The voice of your brother's blood is crying for vengeance. And now, cursed are you from the ground which has opened her mouth to receive your brother's blood from your hand. Therefore, from this point on, when you till the ground, it shall not henceforth yield unto you her strength. Your dad had herbs, fruit, and vegetables; he had weeds, but he was able to live. But with you, from this point on, nothing. Cain, you're going to be a fugitive and a wanderer over all the face of the earth. You're going to have to beg for your food. You're going to have to ask for a handout to have anything to eat. Whatever you touch—anything that you do—will turn into dust."

Finally Cain decided to speak to the LORD. "LORD, my punishment is greater than I can bear." The Hebrew words mean he's asking the LORD, "LORD, is my iniquity too great to be forgiven? Can I still be forgiven, LORD?"

Cain continued to speak, and he said, "Behold, take a look

at what You've done, LORD. You have driven me out this day from the face of the land, and from Your face shall I be hid, and I shall be a fugitive and a wanderer in the earth. And it shall come to pass that whosoever finds me will slay me." He complained to the LORD that he'd be banished into the desert to share the fate of an outlaw.

And he reminded the LORD that he'd be hidden from the face of the LORD, and he said, "To be hidden from Your face, God, is to forfeit divine protection." He thought he had passed from grace into judgment. He was finally crying a cry of anguish, and this revealed him as a man not totally bad, one to whom banishment from God's divine presence was a distinct ingredient in his cup of misery.

Again, the LORD intervened in his life and said unto him, "Whosoever slays Cain, vengeance shall be taken upon him sevenfold." And the LORD set a sign for Cain, lest anyone finding him should smite him.

What was the sign that the LORD set for Cain, the mark of Cain? Did God take out His great big heavenly rubber stamp and stamp Cain on the forehead? Was that the mark of Cain? The color of his skin? The cross? A hardened heart? There are many different opinions about it, but I believe the mark of Cain was that he was going to have to live as a beggar, a fugitive, a wanderer. Anyone would recognize Cain when he came up and said, "So maybe you can spare a little food?"

Whatever the outward visible sign, all who saw him would know who he was—and that the divine protection of God was upon him, that God Himself would take vengeance upon anyone who harmed him.

Cain went out from the presence of the LORD, and he dwelt

in the land of Nod on the east of Eden. Having forfeited God's favor, Cain withdrew from the neigborhood of Eden, which was the special abode of God's Holy Spirit and His divine presence. This is the rabbinical interpretation of this verse of Scripture which we have just studied.

And Cain knew his wife, and she conceived and bore Enoch, and he built a city. By Hebrew oral tradition, Cain married one of his sisters. According to *Halley's Commentary*, Adam and Eve had 33 sons and 27 daughters.

And Cain knew his wife intimately; she conceived and she bore a son Enoch. And Cain built a city; and called the name of the city after the name of his son, Enoch. Unto Enoch was born Irad. Irad begat Mehujael. Mehujael begat Methusael. Methusael begat Lamech.

Lamech took unto himself two wives; the name of one was Adah, and the name of the other Zillah. And Adah bore Jabal; he was the father of such as dwell in tents and have cattle. And his brother's name was Jubal; he was the father of all such as handle the harp and the pipe. And Zillah, she bore Tubal-cain, the forger of every cutting instrument of brass and iron, and the sister of Tubal-cain was Naamah.

The entire genealogy is placed here leading up to Naamah, because Naamah, a descendant of Cain, would be found on the ark with Noah. She would be Noah's wife. Their son, Ham, would sin later on, because the sin of Cain was still present.

Lamech turned to his two wives, Adah and Zillah, and told them, "Hear my voice, you wives of Lamech. Listen unto my speech, for I have slain a man for wounding me. One man wounded me, and I killed him; and I killed another young man for just bruising me." The arrogance that was in Cain was found in this descendant, who said, "If Cain will be avenged by the LORD sevenfold, I, Lamech, will now avenge anybody who comes against me seventy and sevenfold." This is pure, sheer arrogance, a triumphal song of arrogance upon the invention of weapons mentioned in the preceding verse. Lamech had killed two people, and he boasted to his wives, "See! I have taken two men's lives, though they inflicted only a bruise on me, and should necessity arise, I feel able to lay low any assailant who crosses my path.

"If Cain, who was unarmed, was promised a sevenfold vengeance on a foe by the LORD, I, equipped with weapons invented by Tubal-cain, will be able to exact a vengeance much greater than the LORD was ever able to exact. In my arrogance, I can do that which is greater than what the LORD can do."

This heathen song (4:23-24) marks the growth of the spirit of Cain.

And Adam knew his wife intimately again, and she bore a son and called his name Seth, which means "compensation," "For God," said she, "has appointed me another seed instead of Abel, whom Cain slew." And to Seth also there was born a son; and he called his name Enosh: then men began to call upon the name of the LORD. Now Enosh is another name in Hebrew for "man," a man who is not born of the earth, but a man who is born of the spirit. This Enosh would not be like his father, Adam, who was earthbound. Enosh would walk in the Spirit of the LORD, standing upright in the Spirit of God.

Genesis, chapter five, is the book of the generations of Adam. In the day that God created man, in the likeness of God made He him. Jesus made him in His own likeness. Male and female made He them, and He blessed them, and He called them Adam in the day that they were created. And Adam lived 130 years and begat a son in his own likeness, after his image, and he called his name Seth.

And the days of Adam after he had begotten Seth were 800 years, and he begat sons and daughters. And all the days that Adam lived were 930 years; and he died.

And Seth lived 105 years and begat Enosh. And Seth lived after he begat Enosh 807 years, and begat sons and daughters. And all the days of Seth were 912 years, and he died.

And Enosh lived 90 years, and begat Kenan. Enosh lived after he begat Kenan 815 years, and he begat sons and daughters. And all the days of Enosh were 905 years, and he died.

Now this entire genealogy was kept orally from father to son. It was also handed down on a staff. The eldest in the family, who received the birthright and the blessing, would have the entire genealogy on his staff. They all carried a staff in their hand, just like the one Moses had. It was their birth certificate, their genealogy. They could prove who they were.

Kenan lived 70 years and he begat Mahalalel. Kenan lived after he begat Mahalalel 840 years, and he begat sons and daughters. All the days of Kenan were 910 years, and he died. And Mahalalel lived 65 years, and he begat Jared. And Mahalalel lived after he begot Jared 830 years, and he begat sons and daughters. And all the days of Mahalalel were 895 years, and he died.

And Jared lived 162 years, and he begat Enoch. And Jared lived after he begat Enoch 800 years, and he begat sons and daughters. And all the days of Jared were 962 years, and he died.

And Enoch lived 65 years, and he begat Methuselah. Enoch walked with God after he begat Methuselah 300 years, and he begat sons and daughters.

What does it mean that Enoch walked with God? He was a spiritual man. He walked uprightly in heart. Enoch walked in the fear of God, and he served the LORD in spirit and in truth. Other men merely existed and preserved the race physically, but Enoch led a life of intimate companionship with God. He had a personal relationship with the LORD. That he walked with God means that he was on a righteous course with his life, accompanied by God, His Creator, and His Maker. And all the days of Enoch were 365 years. And Enoch walked with God; and he was not, for God took him. God translated him into heaven. His 365 years corresponds to every day of every year in our lives.

If we really want to walk with God, it has to be a day-by-day experience with the LORD. Each day that the LORD has made, we must rejoice and be glad in it, and commit that day unto Him and walk with Him. If we walk with Him, that day belongs to us in the LORD Jesus Christ. And He becomes one with us as we walk obediently with our Jesus, 365 days of every year of our lives.

And Methuselah lived 187 years, and he begat Lamech. And Methuselah lived after he begat Lamech 782 years; he begat sons and daughters. And all the days of Methuselah were 969 years, and he died.

Methuselah was the longest living man on the face of the earth. And the LORD kept him alive for 969 years for one purpose. His lifespan overlapped that of Adam by 243 years, and Adam carried a firsthand report of the Garden of Eden.

33

Adam told it to Methuselah personally, and Methuselah personally told it to Shem, who would be upon the ark and in the post-flood period, and Shem told it to Abraham, the father of the Hebrew people, from whom would be coming Jesus Christ the Messiah. And all mankind would know that the Garden of Eden was real.

And Methusaleh died, and Lamech lived 182 years and begat a son, and he called his name Noah, saying. "This same shall comfort us in our work and in the toil of our hands which comes from the ground which the LORD hath cursed."

As long as Adam lived, the earth was under a curse, and according to the chronology of this chapter, Noah was the first man born after the death of Adam, and his birth became the heralding of a new age for mankind. Noah would give us rest— Hebrew oral tradition tells us that Noah invented the plow which helped mankind immeasurably.

So Lamech lived after he begat Noah 595 years, and he begat sons and daughters. And all the days of Lamech were 777 years, and he died. And Noah was 500 years old, and Noah begat Shem, Ham, and Japheth from his wife, Naamah.

And it came to pass that when men began to multiply on the face of the earth, and daughters were born unto them, the *sons of God* saw the daughters of men that they were fair, and they took them wives, whomsoever they chose.

These sons of God were not fallen angels, because Jesus tells us that the angels neither marry nor are given in marriage. The accurate translation from the Hebrew shows that the sons of God, the righteous sons of Seth, departed from God and took up the idolatry of the daughters of Cain.

And the LORD said, "My Spirit shall not strive with man

forever, for he also is flesh; therefore, his days shall be 120 years." God brought judgment against man because man had turned his back against God. The sons of *the* God were worshipping other gods.

Man had been living for many years, but now God would start decreasing his lifespan, and man would reach a maximum age of 120 years.

At the same time, God would commission Noah, and give him 120 years to build an ark so mankind would have 120 years to repent from that which they had done.

In Genesis 6:4 we read that *Nephilim* appeared in the earth in those days, and also after that, when the sons of God came unto the daughters of men, and they bore children to them. And they became mighty men which were of old, men of renown—renowned for their terrible wickedness. The Hebrew world *Nephilim* means those who have fallen and are backslidden; no giants are mentioned.

And the LORD saw the wickedness of man was great in the earth, and that every imagination of the thoughts of man's heart was evil continually. And it grieved the LORD that He had made man on the earth; it hurt Him at His heart. And the LORD said, "I will blot out man whom I have created from the face of the earth, both man and beast, creeping things and fowl of the air, for it grieves me that I have made them."

Why would the animals be destroyed? Because man was using the animals, corrupting the animals for his own pleasure, for his own vice, for his own abomination. That's the reason judgment was brought upon the animals. Such evil was not within their power, but it was within man's power, and God would remove every corrupt thing from off the face of the earth.

3
But Noah...
(Gen. 6:8—Gen. 9:17)

But Noah found grace in the eyes of the LORD. And these
are the generations of Noah. Noah was in his generations a
man righteous and wholehearted. Noah walked with God, and
Noah begat three sons, Shem, Ham, and Japheth. Noah was
in a righteous relationship, not only with God, but also with
his fellow human beings.

The earth we see was corrupt before God, and the earth
was filled with violence. And God saw the earth and behold,
it was corrupt, for all flesh had corrupted his way upon the
earth. Every abomination, every evil imagination of man had
been brought into play. Sexual relationships between men and
animals, between animals and women, homosexuality, drunken-
ness, immorality, drugs—anything evil you could think of,
man did.

Jesus was asked the question, "When will the end be? Give

*us a sign. When will be the end of days? When will Your Second
Coming be?"*

*He said, "No man knows the time, the place, and the hour,
but I tell you this, that the conditions in the earth will be as
they were in the days of Noah." And we have these days with
us today, these very same conditions with us right now. The
time is very short. The* LORD *is on His way back. He's returning
very soon. Praise God, because we're going to look up very
shortly, and see that our redemption draweth nigh.*

All flesh had corrupted its way upon the earth, and God
spoke to Noah and said, "The end of all flesh is come before
Me; for the earth is filled with violence through them; and,
behold, I will destroy them with the earth."

And God gave Noah a commission: "Make you an ark of
gopher wood. Rooms you shall make in the ark, and you shall
pitch it within and without with pitch. And this is how you
shall make it. The length of the ark three hundred cubits. I
don't want you to make just a small rowboat. This ark is to be
a ship of great stature." Three hundred cubits is 450 feet, the
length of the largest luxury ship the United States has, the
United States. Four hundred fifty feet long—that's a pretty
big rowboat.

And the LORD said, "The width of it shall be 75 feet and the
height of it 45 feet. A light you shall make to the ark, and to a
cubit you shall finish it upward." A cubit is a foot and a half.
He's going to need light, because there was going to be darkness; there was going to be rain forty days and forty nights.
There was going to be a seismic upheaval, a tidal wave. The
sun would not shine.

The LORD showed Noah where to find a luminous mineral

substance, and He said, "I want you to put this all around the ark and finish it eighteen inches high, and this will give you light."

And God said, "After you finish this light, you shall put the door of the ark in the side thereof; with lower, second, and third stories you shall make it. And I, behold, I will bring a flood of waters upon the earth to destroy all flesh, wherein is the breath of life, under heaven. Everything that is in the earth shall perish. But I, the LORD, will make and establish My covenant with you. You shall come into the ark, you, your sons, your wife, your sons' wives. And of every living thing of all flesh, two of every sort you shall bring into the ark, male and female."

The LORD didn't tell Noah to go out and gather these animals; He would send them by His Holy Spirit to the ark, and as He sent them to the ark, Noah would bring them in. He saved whom He chose to save. He chose to save Noah, his wife Naamah, his sons—Shem, Ham, and Japheth—and their wives, and the animals He sent to the ark.

And God said, "I will establish My covenant with you. And as I send you these animals, bring them into the ark, keep them alive with you. They shall be male and female. Of the fowl after their kind, of the cattle after their kind, of every creeping thing of the ground after its kind, two of every sort shall come unto you. Don't go out and gather them, Noah. I will send them by My Holy Spirit. They will come unto you, and you will keep them alive. And take you unto you of all food that is eaten, and gather it to you; and it shall be for food for you and for them." Thus did Noah. According to all that God commanded him, so did he.

Praise the LORD. Noah was obedient unto the LORD. And the animals were obedient, too. They came to the ark, and they waited upon the LORD. The LORD tells you and me to stand and see the salvation of the LORD, to be still and know that He is God, and even the animals could understand that by His Holy Spirit He had sent them.

And the Lord spoke unto Noah and said, "Come you and all of your house into the ark, for you have I seen righteous before Me in this generation." Noah found grace in the eyes of the LORD. That Noah was righteous, that he was blameless, was spoken by the LORD.

From this, our rabbis have deduced that the Lord in His love, in His grace, in His mercy, can say about a man, "You, I have seen righteous; you, I have seen blameless." But as people in the LORD, we ourselves should not flatter a man too much. We can say to a man, "We know that you are walking with the LORD; we are praising God for your faithfulness." But only the LORD can make the statement, "You have I seen righteous before Me, and blameless in this generation."

And God said to Noah, "Of every clean beast, you shall take unto you seven and seven, each with his mate, and of the beasts that are not clean, two, the male and his mate. Of the fowl also of the air, seven and seven, male and female, to keep seed alive upon the face of all the earth."

How was Noah going to determine which were the clean animals and which were the unclean? As they came to him, those who came seven by seven were clean. Those who came to him two by two were unclean. It was a miracle of the LORD.

And then God said to Noah, "You still have another seven days' time to carry out all the last-minute instructions that I have given you. For yet seven days, and I will cause it to rain upon the earth forty days and forty nights; and every living substance that I have made will I blot off the face of the earth."

And Noah did according unto all that the LORD commanded him. And Noah was 600 years old when the flood of waters was upon the earth. And Noah went in, and his sons, his wife, and his sons' wives with him, into the ark, because of the waters of the flood. Of the clean beasts, and of the beasts that are not clean, of the fowls, and of everything that creeps upon the ground, there went in two and two unto Noah into the ark, the male and the female, as God commanded Noah. And it came to pass that the Lord kept His word—after exactly seven days, the waters of the flood were upon the earth.

And in the six-hundredth year of Noah's life, in the second month on the seventeenth day of the month, on the same day were all the fountains of the great deep broken up, and the windows of heaven were opened. There was total, complete destruction.

The earth was not destroyed by the floods and the rains— that was called "the water from above." But the great fountains of the deep were opened; there was a great seismic upheaval and huge tidal waves, hot scalding water from beneath, cold water from above.

After everything had gone into the ark, the LORD shut them in. Literally, God fastened the door so that it could withstand the violence of the storm. Divine protection encompassed Noah as he was about to be sent out in that ark into the midst of the floods, the tidal waves, and the earth's crust being broken.

The divine mercy of the LORD *works in your life and my life as He shuts us in, in Jesus Christ. He seals us in Jesus, and if*

*we're sealed in Him, what could possibly come against us?
Nothing. No storm. No circumstance. Nothing. All we need to
do is stand and say, "LORD, I know You have sealed me in
Jesus. I know You have placed Him in me, and me in Him, the
Father in all of us." How could we possibly be defeated?*

The LORD sealed them in; He fastened the door, and shut
them in. And the flood was forty days upon the earth. The
waters increased and bore up the ark, and it was lifted up
above the earth. And the waters prevailed and increased greatly
upon the earth. The ark went upon the face of the waters, and
the waters prevailed exceedingly upon the earth. Fifteen cubits
upward did the waters prevail, and all the high mountains that
were under the whole heaven were covered. The LORD brought
the flood only twenty-two and a half feet higher than the highest mountain. That wiped out all living creatures upon the face
of the earth.

All flesh perished that moved upon the earth, both fowl,
cattle, beast, every swarming thing that swarms upon the
earth and every man, all in whose nostrils was the breath of the
spirit of life. Whatsoever was in the dry land died, and God
blotted out every living substance which was upon the face of
the ground, both man and cattle, creeping thing, fowl of the
heaven. And Noah only was left, and they that were with him
in the ark. And the waters prevailed upon the earth a hundred
and fifty days; they dominated the earth. After the forty-days'
downpour, the waters reached their highest point and remained
there for a period of a hundred and ten days. And after the
hundred and fifty days had passed, from the beginning of the
flood, the waters began to diminish, to go down.

There is a set time with the LORD, the LORD never forgets,

but the Scripture shows us that God will take a situation, and He will shelve it. He will hold it in abeyance until the proper time. And at the proper time, God remembered Noah and every living thing, all the cattle that was with him in the ark. And God made a wind to pass over the earth, and the waters subsided. God had been righteously indignant, but now His anger subsided, too, and the waters grew calm after the fury of the storm.

The fountains of the deep and the windows of heaven were stopped, and the rain from heaven was restrained. And the waters returned from off the earth continually; and after the end of a hundred and fifty days, the waters decreased.

And the ark rested in the seventh month on the seventeenth day of the month upon the mountains of Ararat. Ararat is 17,500 feet high. That ark is still there today.*

The waters decreased continually until the tenth month, and in the tenth month on the first day of the month were the tops of the mountains seen. And it came to pass at the end of forty days that Noah opened the window of the ark which he had made, and he sent forth a raven. A raven is a scavenger. The raven would be able to sustain himself by feeding on carrion which would abound if the earth was dry. Noah sent out a good scout, the raven. It went to and fro until the waters were dried up from off the earth.

And Noah sent forth from him a dove to see if the waters were abated from off the face of the ground. But the dove found no rest for the sole of her foot, and she returned unto him into the ark, for the waters were still on the face of the whole earth.

---

*Fernand Navarra, *Noah's Ark: I Touched It* (Plainfield, New Jersey: Logos International, 1974).

The dove is a symbol of the Holy Spirit. Noah was moving by the Spirit of the LORD, so he sent forth a symbol of the Holy Spirit of God, knowing the message would come back to him by the Holy Spirit as to whether or not it was time to go out. He was going to stay sealed in in the Lord until the Lord told him, "Okay, now it's time to get up."

Noah put forth his hand. He brought the dove back into the ark, and he stayed another seven days, and again he sent forth the dove out of the ark, and the dove came in to him at evening and behold, in her mouth was an olive leaf freshly plucked. And Noah knew that the waters were abated from off the face of the earth.

Where did the olive leaf come from? How would an olive tree live? It was a miracle of the LORD. The LORD gave that sign to the dove to bring back to Noah. By herself, a dove would never pick up an olive leaf, because an olive leaf is bitter. The message to Noah was that it is far better to receive that which is bitter from the hands of the LORD than to receive the sweetest thing from the hands of men.

That was the message to Noah. It is also the message to you and me and to all mankind. It is far better for us to receive that which is bitter from the LORD than the sweetest thing from the hand of man.

And Noah waited another seven days, and he sent forth the dove again, and she returned not unto him anymore. Noah knew it was safe to go forth.

And it came to pass in the six hundred and first year in the first month, the first day of the month, the waters were dried up from off the face of the earth; and Noah removed the covering of the ark, and looked, and, behold, the face of the ground was dry. And in the second month, on the twenty-seventh day of the month, was the earth dried.

Remember, Noah was waiting upon the Lord. The Lord had sealed him in. Noah was going to wait until he got a message from the Lord. If the Lord never spoke to him, he was going to stay in that ark forever. He was waiting upon the Lord. He knew where his salvation was. He knew where his source of life was. It was in the Lord. He was going to wait until the Lord told him, "Okay, Noah, go." And when He told him to go, he would go.

And God spoke unto Noah, saying, "Go forth from the ark, you, your wife, your sons, your sons' wives with you. Bring forth with you every living thing that is with you of all flesh, both fowl and cattle, every creeping thing that creeps upon the earth, that they may swarm in the earth, be fruitful, and multiply upon the earth."

And Noah, in obedience to the Lord, went forth, and his sons and his wife and his sons' wives with him. Every beast, every creeping thing, every fowl, whatsoever moved upon the earth, after their families, went forth out of the ark. Noah did not lead them out, but they went from the ark as the Lord moved them by His Holy Spirit, letting them know it was time to move out of the ark.

And Noah built an altar unto the Lord, and took of every clean beast and of every clean fowl and offered burnt offerings on the altar. That was why he had taken seven and seven of clean beasts into the ark—to have some to sacrifice to the Lord. They were not used for food, because at this point, mankind was not permitted to eat flesh.

The Lord smelled a sweet savour, the sacrifice of obedience.

The sacrifice offered by Noah was agreeable unto the LORD. The LORD accepted with pleasure the obedience of Noah's heart.

Much later, God spoke to the people of Israel through Isaiah, Jeremiah, and Ezekiel, and He said, "You have piled the altars high with sacrifices. You have brought Me all the sacrifices you can think of, but I detest, I abhor, I reject your sacrifices because you have dirty hearts. While you bring Me your sacrifice, you're hoping to buy Me, you're hoping to bribe Me. You have connived a plan to kill somebody for his money, you have cheated a widow, or an orphan. I don't want Your sacrifices. All I want is Your love and Your obedience."

Because Noah's sacrifice of obedience was agreeable unto the LORD, God made a covenant with all of mankind and with every living creature upon the face of the earth. And the LORD said, "I will not again curse the ground any more for man's sake. Even though I am the LORD his God, and I know that from his youth on up, man's imagination and his heart is evil, yet, I did promise that I would send him a Redeemer, a Savior. I did promise that I would send him the true Adam, the One who would make him right with Me, by His body, by His blood, and by His sacrifice." That One would be Jesus Christ, the Messiah, the Savior of the world. And the LORD said, "Neither will I smite anymore everything living as I have done. While the earth remains, seedtime and harvest, and cold and heat, and summer and winter, and day and night shall not cease."

And God blessed Noah and his sons and said unto them, "Be fruitful, and multiply, and refill the earth." God's command to Adam was, "Be fruitful, and multiply, and *fill* the earth." Now this command to Noah, after the earth had been destroyed with the flood, was "Be fruitful, and multiply, and refill, replenish

45

the earth. And the fear of you, the dread of you, shall be upon every beast of the earth, upon every fowl of the air and upon all wherewith the ground teemeth, and upon all the fish of the sea. Into your hand they are delivered."

The LORD gave Noah dominion over everything upon the face of the earth.

Then God gave Noah the first seven commandments given to mankind.

The LORD said, "Every moving thing that lives shall be for food for you, even as the green herb have I given you all." Up until this point, man was restricted to eating herbs, fruit, and vegetables. Now the LORD said every living thing was given to man for food. Now he could kill and eat flesh. "Only—" and here is the commandment—"only flesh with the life thereof, which is the blood thereof, shall you not eat." God gave us this commandment because the life is in the blood. He wasn't speaking against eating rare meat after the life blood has already been drained out of it, and only the natural juices remain.

In the Talmud, we have the rabbinical laws which tell us how to kosher meat. We must take any piece of meat and pour kosher salt upon it to suck all the blood out of it. But there's no blood in that meat, just its natural juice. We do this for six hours, and after you cook it, my shoe tastes better. It becomes so tough—but this is not what the LORD spoke about. He was speaking against the heathen practice of drinking blood, which was supposed to make them virile, and strong. And yet, the LORD said, "If there's any disease in that blood, the minute you drink or eat that blood, it's going to be carried on to you."

Our teenagers today get hepatitis when they are on drugs;

the minute they inject that dirty needle into their arms, they are infected, because it goes into the bloodstream. The LORD *said, "Stay away from the blood." There's only one blood that He will allow you and me to partake of and participate in, and that is the blood of Jesus Christ. When Jesus picked up the cup at the Passover, and instituted the Last Supper and the New Covenant, He said, "This is My blood, which is shed for you for the remission of your sin."*

In His second command to man at this time, God said, "Surely, your blood of your lives will I require." This is a commandment, a prohibition against suicide. "You shall not kill yourself. I made you in My image and in My likeness. If you destroy that image, you are destroying the image of God. And surely, your blood of your own life will I require of you. You're going to have to answer to Me if you take your own life."

And then He said, "At the hand of every beast will I require it. If an animal kills a man, it must be put to death." Later on, in Exodus 21:28, God commanded that an ox which gored a man should be killed. And then He said that if you have an ox, and you know he has the habit of goring, and you don't restrain him, and he gores somebody else and kills him, not only will the ox be killed, but you'll also be killed. You're responsible. The principles underlying these laws have passed into our laws in the United States.

Let's say you have a swimming pool and you have a fence around it. A child climbs over your fence, gets into your pool and drowns. You are responsible. The law calls your swimming pool an attractive nuisance. You have to take every precaution to protect that child who is innocent and doesn't know what he is doing. From the Ten Commandments, in the United

States of America today, we have not three thousand, not three million, but an endless number of laws that have been enacted and are being added to daily, just to uphold the Ten Commandments given by God.

The next commandment: "At the hand of man, even at the hand of every man's brother, will I require the life of man." If God seeks the blood of a man at the hand of a beast which kills him, how much more will He exact vengeance from a human being who murders his brother man. This is a commandment against murder.

The next commandment provides for capital punishment: "Whosoever sheddeth man's blood, by man shall his blood be shed." God gives a reason for this commandment, "For in the image of God made He man." Jesus made man in the image of God, with a dignity that he receives as a gift from the love, and the mercy, and the grace of the LORD, regardless of race, or creed, or denomination. This tells us that we're all the same. We are all descended from one man, and there's only one head above us and that is Jesus Christ. Because man was created in the image of God, He can never be reduced to the level of a thing or a chattel. He is a human being, and each human being has his own personality.

When we pastors counsel with people about to be married, we tell them, "Don't start changing each other. You fell in love with the person you met, with their personality. You love them the way they are." We often end up in divorce because we all start working to change the other person into our image and our likeness instead of letting him remain in the image in which we married him, the image of God. We foolishly try to make our mate over into a duplicate of ourself.

Once again the Lord said to Noah, "Be fruitful and multiply, swarm in the earth, and multiply therein." And God spoke unto Noah and to his sons with him, saying, "As for Me, behold I establish My covenant with you and with your seed after you, with every living creature that is with you, the fowl, the cattle, every beast of the earth with you, and of all that go out of the ark, even every beast of the earth. And I will establish My covenant with you; neither shall all flesh be cut off any more by the waters of a flood; neither shall there any more be a flood to destroy the earth."

God not only made a covenant with man, but with every living creature. And God said, "This is the token of the covenant which I make between Me and you and every living creature that is with you, for perpetual generations. I have set My bow in the cloud, and it shall be for a token of a covenant between Me and the earth. And it shall come to pass that when I bring clouds over the earth, and the bow is seen in the cloud, that I will remember My covenant which is between you and Me and every living creature of all flesh. And the waters shall no more become a flood to destroy all flesh."

The Lord said, "I have set My bow in the cloud." This is the rainbow. And the Lord said, "When I look upon the rainbow, I will remember My covenant. I am a God who is a just God, I am a God who is a holy God. When justice comes before me and says, 'Take a look at those You made in Your image and in Your likeness, Lord. They're sinning again,' I will look upon the token of this covenant that I made with man and with beast, and I will remember My covenant, saying, 'I will no longer destroy him from off the face of the earth.' My grace and My mercy will temper My justice."

Later on, Moses found out about God's attribute of mercy. Israel was about to be destroyed because she had made a golden calf in order to worship it as a god. And they bowed down to the golden calf saying, "This is the LORD our God which brought us up out of the land of Egypt." And Moses appealed to the mercy of the LORD: "LORD, grant mercy now for Your people Israel." And he received mercy as he interceded for all of Israel. The LORD listened to him.

The LORD has given us the gift of intercessory prayer. He says, "I will permit myself to be entreated of you, and I will spare you, but you first have to step out by faith and ask. If you're not going to ask, you're not going to receive." How did Jesus put it? "Ask the Father in My name, presenting all that I am to you, and you shall receive." There are no ifs, ands, or buts—you shall receive. Knock and it will be opened unto you. Ask, seek, and knock, and keep on asking, seeking, and knocking, and you will receive. The LORD says, "I have given it to you all. I did it upon the cross, and if I did it, don't worry. It's all taken care of."

We are healed. All we have to do is stay in that healing. We can refuse the attack of Satan. Many a time I've gotten up in the morning when I was supposed to preach to two or three thousand people, and I had a 104° temperature. Now there were two things I could do. One was to lie down and say, "I feel terrible," and just not go do it. The other thing I could do was to arise, as the LORD says, "Arise, have I not commanded you? Be of good courage and of good cheer. Get up out of your bed, and go preach and teach, and I will go before you." And by the time I'd get in the pulpit, I wouldn't have any fever. That's not mind over matter; that's standing on the promises of God. The

LORD *says, "I have healed you. By My stripes, you were healed. You are healed and you will remain healed." We can refuse the attack of Satan. We can say, "Get thee behind me, Satan. I don't want the sickness. I refuse to accept it, in the name of Jesus. I don't have to have it."*

When He says, "By my stripes you are healed," remember He had thirty-nine stripes on His back. By Jewish law, it was illegal for anyone to receive more than thirty-nine lashes. If you check with a medical doctor, he will tell you there are thirty-nine major illnesses that can kill mankind. And those stripes on the back of Jesus Christ healed every major illness of mankind. And I say, "Praise God that He took those stripes upon Himself, that I don't have to bear them, that He bore them for me."

The LORD made a covenant with Noah. It was for perpetual generations, an *everlasting* covenant between God and every living creature of all flesh that is upon the earth.

4
And the Sons of Noah
(Gen. 9:18—Gen. 11)

And the sons of Noah that went forth from the ark were Shem, and Ham, and Japheth; and Ham was the father of Canaan. And these three were the sons of Noah, and of these was the whole earth overspread. And Noah, the husbandman, began and planted a vineyard. And being a dumb-dumb, he drank of the wine, and he was drunk. He did not realize the power of the fruit of the vine. He was really naïve. He was loaded, and he passed out. And he was uncovered within his tent.

And Ham, the father of Canaan, saw the nakedness of his father, and he told his two brethren without. And Shem and Japheth took a garment, and laid it upon their shoulders and went backward, and they covered the nakedness of their father, and their faces were backward, and they did not look upon their father's nakedness.

When Noah awoke from his wine, he knew what his youngest son had done unto him. And he cursed Ham's son, his own grandson, Canaan.

A grandfather loves his grandson, but Noah cursed Canaan instead of Ham. And the LORD would honor his curse. And he said, "Cursed be Canaan; a servant of servants shall he be unto his brethren." In the genealogies recorded in the Bible, all the descendants of Canaan are servant people.

Then Noah blessed Shem. He said, "Blessed be the LORD God of Shem, and let Canaan be his servant. May God enlarge Japheth, and he shall dwell in the tents of Shem, and Canaan shall be his servant."

In this prophecy given by the Holy Spirit, we learn that God will enlarge Japheth. All the Indo-European races are descended from Japheth. The descendants of Shem, the Shemites or Semites would become very small. And the descendants of Japheth would go out and bring forth the Word of God, and preach the Gospel to all the peoples of the earth. And they would dwell in the tents of Shem, knowing the everlasting Father through Jesus Christ.

And Noah lived after the flood 350 years. And all the days of Noah were 950 years, and he died.

In the tenth chapter of Genesis, we see the family of the nations, and exactly where all the nations came from. All came from three brothers, of one father, so we're all related, and we all came from one father. But there are the different generations, the different peoples. Now these are the generations of the sons of Noah—Shem, Ham, and Japheth—and unto them were sons born after the flood.

The sons of Japheth—the Indo-European races—are Gomer,

Magog, Madai, Javan, Tubal, Meshech, and Tiras. Gomer became the Cimmerians on the Caspian Sea. This is within the boundaries of Russia. Magog became the Scythians whose territory lays on the borders of the Caucasus. Magog became Russia itself. Madai became the Medes. Javan became the Greeks, or the Ionians, in the older language.

The sons of Gomer were Ashkenaz, Riphath, and Togarmah. The Ashkenaz lived in the neighborhood of Ararat in Armenia. Later in Hebrew literature, we find the Ashkenazic Jews who lived in Germany.

There are two groups of Jews—Sephardic Jews and Ashkenazic Jews. Sephardic Jews are those who lived and stayed in and around the Holy Land, and the Ashkenazic Jews are those who migrated to Europe and lived in and around Germany and Russia, Lithuania, and Poland. Ashkenazic Jews are the most brilliant of all Jews. They are the mathematicians, the scientists, the nuclear physicists. The Sephardic Jews have completely different customs and traditions. The Sephardic Jews, my people, stayed in and around the Holy Land and stayed grounded in the Scriptures. They never went out and appropriated the wisdom and knowledge the LORD promised them. Today these people are still living according to the commandments and customs recorded in The Bible.

When Israel became a nation in fulfillment of the prophecy of Isaiah 66:8 that a nation would be born in one day, it was the Zionists, the Ashkenazic Jews, the brilliant European Jews, who came forth as the ruling power in Israel. Then, as all the rest of the Jews migrated to Israel, the balance of power began to shift, because Jews who lived in and around the Holy Land came back, and today they, the Sephardic Jews, far outnumber the European or Ashkenazic Jews. And the two kinds of Jews don't even speak the same language. Sephardic Jews speak Hebrew, Arabic, Aramaic, and Chaldean, but never Yiddish. Yiddish vocabulary is mostly derived from the German language, although a few words come from Russian.

There's a conflict, because the Sephardic Jews say, "Let's go back to the Bible. Let's live exactly as the Bible teaches." And the Ashkenazic Jew, the European Jew, says, "We are a modern state; we are a modern nation. We are going to live as all the rest of the nations live." The controversy will never be resolved, just as the situation between the Jew and the Arab will never be resolved, until the King of Peace Himself comes back, who is Jesus Christ.

And in the prophecy of Zechariah, as the LORD spoke by the Holy Spirit, we read that when Christ stands on the Mount of Olives, and they look upon Him whom they have pierced, only one-third will accept Him. Two-thirds will reject Jesus, even in the end-time when they behold Him in His glory and full majesty.

I would have expected my God, my Jesus, to come in full majesty when He came the first time. It is a great miracle that He came as a babe in a manger, a humble, helpless baby. And this is why most Jews today don't accept Jesus. But the day is coming when every knee shall bow and every tongue shall confess that Jesus Christ is Lord! Praise God.

And the sons of Javan are the Greeks—Elishah, Tarshish, Kittim, and Dodanim. From the name of Elishah in Hebrew, we get the name of southern Sicily, Sicily itself, and Cyprus. Tarshish was "the farthest seaport" in ancient Spain, the one to which Jonah was escaping. Kittim was the race inhabiting part of the island of Cyprus, of Phoenician extraction. Dodanim was the island of Rhodes, in the Hebrew, *Rodanim*. We still have some of these names with us today.

By these were the isles of the nations divided in their lands, every one after his tongue, after their families in their nations. The sons of Ham were Cush, Mizraim, Phut, and Canaan. The most ancient name for Egypt is Ham or Kem, in the Hebrew meaning "black," alluding to the dark color of the people, and also to the dark color of the Egyptian soil. Cush was Ethiopia, Mizraim was the most common name for Egypt itself, and Phut was Libya. We have all these nations with us today. The Canaanites first occupied the land of the Philistines. The name afterward was extended to the whole of western Palestine. According to this verse, Mizraim and Canaan were brothers, and Palestine and Egypt were provinces of the same empire. And the sons of Cush were Seba, Havilah, Sabtah, Raamah, Sabtechah; and the sons of Raamah, Sheba and Dedan.

Cush was Ethiopia, Sheba was descended from Cush. In our Hebrew rabbinical laws, Sheba was not descended from Cush, because Solomon could not have married an Ethiopian.

In the *Talmud*, Sheba is considered to be the southern part of the Arabian peninsula, and the Queen of Sheba was not an Ethiopian, but an Arab queen who came to meet with Solomon. But we know where Sheba really is. And Haile Selassie in Ethiopia is entitled to fly a flag which says, "The lion of Judah," which he truly is, because he is descended from my ancestor Solomon and Sheba.

And Cush begat Nimrod. This Nimrod was an Ethiopian, descended from Ham and Cain. And Nimrod began to be a mighty one in the earth. He acquired dominion and ascendancy by conquest, and by the terror that he inspired. He was a mighty hunter before the Lord. He placed himself above and beyond the LORD. He said, "I come before the LORD. The LORD God is not who He says He is, but I am the only one on the face of the earth. And I come before the LORD." The minute anyone places himself before God, the whole thing is going to crumble, the whole thing is going to come falling down. In history, when they want to describe somebody who is arrogant in his own power, in his own arrogancy, they say, "He is like Nimrod— before the LORD." And the beginning of Nimrod's kingdom was Babel, meaning Babylon.

When he began to reign, his dominion extended over the cities of Babel, and Erech, and Accad, and Calnah. Babel, or Babylon, was the center of the ancient Orient, and for many centuries, the mistress of the world. Today the word is used as a symbol for spiritual wickedness. In the Book of Revelation, we see Jesus Christ destroying the spirit of Babylon once and for all, the spirit of the Antichrist, the spirit of wickedness, the spirit of idolatry, the spirit of abomination.

Erech is the Babylonian city called Uruk, now called Warka, which is on the left bank of the lower Euphrates. Accad is the city of Agade, and the land of Accad in the northern part of Babylon. Shinar itself is the old biblical Hebrew name for the whole of Babylon. Shinar was also identified with the land of the Sumerians.

Out of Babylon came Asshur, Assyria, whose capital was Nineveh, and Rehoboth, and Calah, and Resen between Nineveh and Calah; the same is a great city. These were the suburbs of Nineveh. And Mizraim, Egypt, begat Ludim, Anamin, Lehabim, Naphtuhim, Pathrusim, Casluhim, and Caphtorim from whom the Philistines came forth.

And Canaan begat Sidon, his firstborn, and Heth, and the Jebusite, the Amorite, the Girgasite, the Hivite, the Arkite, the Sinite, the Arvadite, the Zemarite, the Hamathite, and afterward were the families of the Canaanites spread abroad. These are the seven nations that later on, God commanded the people of Israel to drive out from before them, to kill every last man, woman, and child. He said, "You're not to leave any of them alive."

Is this the same LORD *that we find in the New Testament? Is this the same Jesus? Is this the Jesus of love that we have in beautiful pictures, carrying the lamb in His arms? Is this the Jesus you can step all over, do anything you want to Him, as long as you come back and say, "I'm sorry"? Yes, He's the same Jesus as the One who commands us to go in and take the Promised Land, saying, "I have held out salvation to these people for hundreds of years. They have refused to accept salvation. They have been disobedient. They have sacrificed their little babies to the false fire god, and if you permit them to live, you will do the very same thing. And if you don't obey Me, what I thought to do to them, I will do to you." It is the same Jesus, but My people, Israel, refused to believe God for His word. And He did to us what He thought to do to the Jebusites, the Hivites, the Hittites, the Amorites, because we did mix with them, we did sacrifice our children, we did burn our children up alive to the heathen gods. And all this came to pass. The* LORD *keeps His word; whether it's grace or judgment, He keeps His word. He never changes. He's the same yesterday, today, and forever.*

And the border of the Canaanites was from Sidon, as you go toward Gerar as far as Gaza, as you go toward Sodom and Gomorrah, Admah, Zeboim, and even unto Lasha. These are the sons of Ham, after their families, after their tongues, in their lands, in their nations.

And unto Shem, the father of all the children of Eber, the elder brother of Japheth, to him also were children born. The sons of Aram: Uz, and Hul, Gether, Mash. Arphaxad begat Salah; Salah begat Eber. And unto Eber were born two sons: the name of one was Peleg, for in his days was the earth divided.

One part of Peleg's family went one way, one part went the other way. They were scattered all over the face of the earth, later on, at the tower of Babel.

And Peleg's brother's name was Joktan. And Joktan begat Almodad, Sheleph, Hazarmaveth, Jerah, Hadoram, Uzal, Diklah, Obal, Abimael, Sheba, Ophir, Havilah, Jobab; all these were the sons of Joktan. And their dwelling was from Mesha, as you go toward Sephar unto the mountain of the east.

These are the sons of Shem, after their families, after their tongues, in their lands, after their nations. These are the families of the sons of Noah, after their generations, in their nations: and from these, the nations spread out on the earth after the flood.

And the whole earth was of one language and of one speech. They had a small vocabulary. And it came to pass, that as they journeyed from the east, they found a plain in the land of Shinar, which is in the land of Babylon, and they dwelt there. (Shinar today is becoming more and more to be regarded by our scientists and archaeologists as the cradle of the earliest civilization.) And they said one to another, "Come, let us make brick and burn them thoroughly [their clay bricks were usually sun-dried, but these were burned in fire to increase their durability], and let us build us a city and a tower with its top in heaven, and let us make us a name, lest we be scattered abroad upon the face of the whole earth."

They didn't want to be scattered all over the face of the earth, so they were going to build a tower so high it would reach up into heaven. They were going to try to bring themselves up to the same level as God. And by their own pride, by their own arrogance, what they feared the most happened to them.

And the Lord came down to see the city and the tower, which the children of men builded. And the Lord said, "Behold, they are one people, they all have one language, and this is what they begin to do. And now, nothing will be withholden from them which they have purposed to do."

The Lord Jesus Himself spoke, saying, "Come, let us"— here we have the trinity again—"go down and there confound their language that they may not understand one another's speech." In the Talmud, in our rabbinical tradition and rabbinical writings, we have it that a man would ask for brick, or he'd call for mortar, or for slime, and nobody understood him. Nobody understood anybody else. Everybody had a different language. The Lord confounded all the languages of the people who were building the tower in defiance, in arrogance, to the Lord.

And the Lord scattered them abroad from there upon the face of all the earth, and they left off building the city. Therefore, the name of it was called Babel, a word which has been carried over into English, signifying a confusion of speech or languages. There was babbling; nobody could understand anybody else, because the LORD did there confound the language of all the earth.

And these are the generations of Shem. Shem was 100 years old and begat Arphaxad two years after the flood. And Shem lived after he begat Arphaxad 500 years, and begat sons and daughters.

And Arphaxad lived 35 years and begat Salah. And Arphaxad lived after he begat Salah 403 years, and begat sons and daughters.

And Salah lived 30 years and begat Eber. And Salah lived after he begat Eber 403 years, and begat sons and daughters.

And Eber lived 34 years, and begat Peleg. And Eber lived after he begat Peleg 430 years, and he begat sons and daughters.

And Peleg lived 30 years, and begat Reu. And Peleg lived after he begat Reu 209 years, and he begat sons and daughters.

And Reu lived 32 years and begat Serug. And Reu lived after he begat Serug 207 years, and begat sons and daughters.

Notice what's happening. When the LORD spoke to Noah, He gave him a hundred and twenty years to build the ark, and He said, "My Spirit shall not strive or abide in man. I will destroy man, for I regret that I made man. I will limit his days. I will give him a hundred and twenty years to repent, but I will limit his lifespan to a hundred and twenty years." In this genealogy, we see man's lifespan is getting shorter.

And Serug lived 30 years, and he begat Nahor. And Serug

lived after he begat Nahor 200 years, and he begat sons and daughters.

And Nahor lived 29 years, and he begat Terah. And Nahor lived after he begat Terah 119 years, and begat sons and daughters. And Terah lived 70 years, and begat Abram, Nahor, and Haran.

5
And the LORD Said unto Abram . . .
(Genesis 12—17:4)

Now these are the generations of Terah: Terah begat Abram, Nahor, and Haran; and Haran begat Lot. And Haran died in the presence of his father Terah in the land of his nativity, in Ur of the Chaldees.

My father, Abram, is descended from Shem, and he came from Ur of the Chaldees. He was a Chaldean, a Babylonian, of the tribe of the Habiru. This is where we get the name "Hebrew." The Hebrew letters, the Hebrew symbols, are the Chaldean alphabet. The Chaldean language is very close to Hebrew.

Abram and Nahor took to themselves wives; the name of Abram's wife was Sarai; the name of Nahor's wife, Milcah, the daughter of Haran, the father of Milcah, and the father of Iscah.

And Sarai was barren; she had no child. And Terah took

Abram his son and Lot the son of Haran, his son's son, and
Sarai his daughter-in-law, his son Abram's wife, and went forth
with them from Ur of the Chaldees to go into the land of
Canaan, and they came unto Haran and they dwelt there. And
the days of Terah were 205 years, and Terah died in Haran.

The reason why Terah left Ur of the Chaldees has been
handed down to us by oral tradition. He was not commanded
by God to leave. Terah did not know the LORD. He was an idol
worshiper; in fact, he was an idol manufacturer. As Terah was
an idol manufacturer, he had his warehouse full of these idols
that he sold for a living. He would make them, and then he
would go into the marketplace and sell them.

And Abram had a burden upon him from the LORD. He had
the feeling that there must be something else besides that
which his father made with his own hands. There must be
some power, somebody in the universe greater than the things
that his father made.

So one day, Abram got up very early in the morning and fell
down and worshiped the sun. In the evening, when the sun disappeared, he said, "Surely, this cannot be God, because it disappeared." And the moon came up, and he worshiped the moon.
Pretty soon, at dawn, the moon disappeared. Another time, he
saw the stars and worshiped the stars, and then they disappeared. And he said again, "Surely, this cannot be God."

Abram was searching, seeking for God. One day, his father,
Terah, went into the marketplace, and he wrote up a whole
bunch of orders for idols. And before Terah got back home,
Abram went into the storehouse, and he took a sledgehammer
and broke every idol, except one big idol standing over in the
corner. When his father, Terah, came in, ready to fill his orders,

64

he found everything broken. And he said, "Abie, what happened?"

And Abram told him, "You see that big idol standing in the corner? He took the hammer and broke them all."

And Terah said, "How could something I made with my own hands break all the rest of the idols?"

Then Abram, through the power of the Holy Spirit, the LORD being upon him, asked his father, "How can you fall down on your knees and worship what you made with your own hands?"

Then the king kicked Abram and Terah out of Ur of Chaldees, and Terah went into Haran and dwelt there until he died. But the LORD touched Abram, because He saw the desire of his heart. He was seeking, he was searching to know the living God, the true God. He would not worship any idols, but he would worship the Lord.

And the LORD appeared to Abram and spoke to him and commanded him, saying, "Get yourself out of your country from your kindred, from your father's house, unto the land that I will show you, and I will make of you a great nation. I will bless you. I will make your name great, and you, yourself, will be a blessing. I will bless them that bless you, and him that curses you will I curse, and in you shall all the families of the earth be blessed."

We inherit every one of these promises today in Jesus Christ. As Christians, we have the same Abrahamic covenant that God made with Abraham. There has never been a nation able to withstand, to flourish, to grow, that has persecuted us Christians or us Jews, because that promise still holds true. The LORD says, "I will bless those who bless you, and I will curse those who curse you." Anytime anybody curses you, don't feel sorry for yourself; start praying for them, because the LORD *keeps His word.*

And Abram went as the LORD had spoken unto him; and Lot went with him. And Abram was seventy-five years old when he departed out of Haran. But he made a mistake. The LORD had commanded him to go by himself, to leave his kindred, leave his family. He didn't say, "Take your nephew Lot with you," but Abram took his nephew Lot with him. That was Abram's first departure from the command of the LORD. Abram would be called the friend of God. God would speak about him saying, "He is my friend." The LORD would judge him righteous. He would grant him everlasting life and salvation. But sin carries a consequence, and because Abram took Lot, problems would arise later on.

And Abram took Sarai, his wife, and Lot, his brother's son, and all their substance that they had gathered, all the souls that they had gotten in Haran, and they went forth to go into the land of Canaan, and into the land of Canaan they came.

And Abram passed through the land unto the place of Sichem, unto the terebinth of Moreh. And the Canaanite was still then in the land.

And the LORD appeared unto Abram—Abram saw Jesus face to face—and the LORD said, "Unto thy seed will I give this land," and Abram built there an altar unto the LORD, who appeared unto him. And he removed from there unto the mountain on the east of Beth-el, and he pitched his tent, having Beth-el on the west, and Ai on the east, and he built there an altar unto the LORD, and he called upon the name of the LORD.

What was the name of the LORD that Abram called upon?

Not Jehovah. Later on, in Exodus 6:3, we see God speaking to Moses, saying, "By My name Jehovah—or Yahweh—Abraham, Isaac, Jacob did not know Me, but by My name El Shaddai they did know Me." Abram did not know the name Yahweh.

Scripture says that the LORD appeared to Abram face to face. But Scripture also tells us that no man has ever seen God and lived. So Abram must have spoken to Jesus. And if he spoke to Jesus, he called upon the name of Jesus. He knew the name of the LORD.

And Abram continued to journey in the power of the LORD, by His Holy Spirit, going on still toward the south.

And there was a famine in the land, and Abram went down into Egypt to sojourn there, intending to stay there for just a short while until the famine was gone from the land of Canaan. For the famine was sore in the land. And it came to pass that when he was come near to enter into Egypt, that he said unto Sarai, his wife, "I know you're a fair woman to look upon. And when the Egyptians see you, they'll desire you. They'll tell Pharaoh about you, and he'll want you for his harem."

Although Sarai was barren, and at sixty-five years of age, she had already gone through the change of life, the menopause, and although Abram was seventy-five, the LORD had promised him offspring through Sarai. He was going to have to wait on that promise for twenty-five years, but it would come.

Meanwhile Abram was afraid that when they went down into Egypt, those who looked upon her would desire her. He was holding the promises of God in his hand, but he didn't trust God to take care of them. He said to his wife, "Sarai, I want you to lie for my sake. Of course, it's not really a whole lie, it's just a half a lie. I want you to tell them you're my sister, because truly you are my half-sister. That's slightly kosher. We might get away with that with the LORD. Otherwise, it'll come to pass, when the Egyptians shall see you, they will say, 'This is his wife,' and they will kill me, but you, they will keep alive."

Abram took his trust, and his faith, and his refuge, and put it in his wife instead of letting it rest in the LORD. The LORD had just given him every possible promise He could give him. "I will bless those who bless you. I will curse those who curse you." Nobody could possibly come against Abram, but he reverted back to his flesh temporarily; momentarily, he forgot about the LORD. He forgot about the promises that God gave him.

We have seventy-seven hundred promises in the Bible that belong to us. There are fifteen hundred promises from Jesus Christ that tell us that by His stripes we were healed, and yet, we're still sick. We forget who Jesus is. We fail to appropriate and receive the promises that God gave us. We forget all about the LORD.

And it came to pass—exactly what Abram was afraid of—that when Abram came into Egypt, the Egyptians did behold the woman that she was very fair. And the princes of Pharaoh saw her, and they praised her to Pharaoh, and the woman was taken and put into Pharaoh's harem. And he dealt well with Abram for her sake. Now Abram was not feeling too bad. Pharaoh was dealing very kindly with him, giving him gold, silver, cattle. Abram was doing all right—he was getting sheep, oxen, menservants, maidservants, he asses, she asses, and camels. The Pharaoh was very much enraptured with Sarai. She didn't look her age. The LORD was rejuvenating her, working a miracle in her life, because from her would come the son of the promise, and from that son of the promise would come Jesus Christ, the One who would fulfill the promise, fulfill the Old Covenant, and *be* the New Covenant. But Abram was out of the LORD's will.

The LORD has His perfect will, and He has His permissive will. Anytime you or I want to step out of the LORD's perfect will, He will let us step out into His permissive will, and if we want to go hang ourselves, He'll let us. Abram was hanging himself, stepping out into the permissive will of the LORD. He was not moving in the perfect will of God.

We are not puppets. We're not attached to a string. The LORD has given us free will and free choice. Joshua said, "As for me and my house, we will choose the LORD." We can use our free will and our free choice to choose Jesus. This day will I choose Jesus. This day is the day of salvation.

Because Abram was disobedient, the LORD had to step in. He divinely intervened, because from Sarai was to come the son of the promise. So the LORD plagued Pharaoh and his house with great plagues because of Sarai, Abram's wife. And Pharaoh inquired by his sorcery and witchcraft to discover the truth. According to our rabbis, according to Hebrew oral tradition, the plague was of a nature to safeguard Sarai's honor. The LORD sealed shut all of the women in Pharaoh's harem.

And now Pharaoh called Abram and said, "What is this that you have done unto me? Why did you not tell me that she was your wife? Why did you say that she is your sister so that I took her to be my wife? Now therefore, behold your wife—take a look at her. I have not touched her. She's still your wife; she's still with her honor. Take her and go your way." And Pharaoh gave men charge concerning him, and they brought him on the way, and his wife and all that he had. And he kept all the gifts that Pharaoh had given him.

Abram went up out of Egypt, he, and his wife, and all that he had, and Lot with him, into the south. In Egypt, Abram had become very rich in cattle, in silver, and in gold. And he went on his journeys from the south even to Beth-el, unto the place where his tent had been at the very beginning, between Beth-el and Ai, unto the place of the altar which he had made there at the first. And Abram there called on the name of the LORD.

And Lot also, which went with Abram, had flocks, and herds, and tents. And the land was not able to bear them, that they might dwell together: for their substance was great, so that they could not dwell together. And there was a strife between the herdsmen of Abram's cattle, and the herdsmen of Lot's cattle. The problem arose because the LORD never told Abram to take Lot with him. And the Canaanites and the Perizzites dwelled in the land.

And Abram decided to trust God. Abram had repented of his disobedience, and he said to Lot, "Let there be no strife, I pray you, between me and thee. Take a look at the land that is before you. Whichever part of the land you want, take it. It's yours. If you want to go to the left, I'll go to the right. If you want to go to the right, I'll go to the left."

And Lot lifted up his eyes and beheld all the plain of the Jordan, that it was well watered everywhere before the LORD destroyed Sodom and Gomorrah, like the garden of the LORD, like the land of Egypt, as you go unto Zoar. He lifted up his eyes and saw the circle of the Jordan. A large part of the valley is very fertile, and wherever water comes in the Middle East, flowers rise as far as your knees, and the herbs grow to the height of your shoulder. Lot looked and he saw a very fertile valley, and he said, "That's what I want."

So Lot chose him all the plain of the Jordan. And Lot journeyed east, and they separated themselves one from the other. And Abram dwelled in the land of Canaan, and Lot dwelled in the cities of the plain, and moved his tent as far as Sodom.

Now the men of Sodom were wicked and sinners against the LORD exceedingly.

And the LORD spoke unto Abram, after that Lot was separated from him, and renewed His assurance to Abram, by giving him the divine promise once again, when he was back in His proper will, when Lot had left him.

And the LORD said unto Abram, after that Lot was separated from him, "Lift up your eyes, and look from the place where you now are, northward, southward, eastward, and westward. For all the land which you see, to you will I give it and your seed forever. And I will make your seed as the dust of the earth, so that if a man can number the dust of the earth, then shall thy seed also be numbered."

The LORD was not referring only to the Jewish people. He was referring also to the Christians, because Abraham would be the father of all nations, and all those who would come to know God would be called the children of Abraham through Jesus Christ. In the Gospel of Matthew, the genealogy of Jesus is from Abraham and the son of Abraham.

We have here another story from Hebrew oral tradition. When the LORD said, "Lift up your eyes," we are told by our

71

rabbis that the LORD took Abram by His Holy Spirit up into outer space. There He showed him all the stars of the universe, and He said, "Abram, do you believe that your descendants will be as numerous as these stars?" And Abram said, "I believe." And the LORD accounted it unto him for righteousness, because he believed the Word of the LORD.

And God said to Abram, "Arise, get up, and walk through the land in the length of it and the breadth of it, for unto thee will I give it." And Abram moved his tent and came and dwelt by the terebinths of Mamre, which are in Hebron, and there he built an altar unto the LORD, which is still there today.

And it came to pass in the days of Amraphel, king of Shinar, Arioch, king of Ellasar, Chedorlaomer, king of Elam, and Tidal, king of Goiim, that they made war with Bera, king of Sodom, and with Birsha, king of Gomorrah, Shinab, king of Admah, and Shemeber, king of Zeboiim, and the king of Bela, which is the same as Zoar. All these came as allies unto the vale of Siddim, which is the salt sea, the Dead Sea. Twelve years they served Chedorlaomer, and in the thirteenth year they rebelled. And in the fourteenth year came Chedorlaomer, and the kings that were with him and smote the Rephaims in Ashteroth Karnaim, and the Zuzims in Ham, and the Emims in Shaveh Kiriathaim, and the Horites in mount Seir, unto El-paran, which is by the wilderness.

And they turned back and came to Enmishpat, the same as Kadesh, and they smote all the country of the Amalekites, and also the Amorites, that dwelt in Hazezon-tamar.

And there went out the king of Sodom, and the king of Gomorrah, the king of Admah, the king of Zeboiim, the king of Bela (the same as Zoar), and they set the battle in array against them in the vale of Siddim; against Chedorlaomer, the king of Elam, Tidal, king of Goiim, Amraphel, king of Shinar, Arioch, king of Ellaser; four kings against the five.

The vale of Siddim was full of slimepits. The pits hampered the flight of the defeated army, and the kings of Sodom and Gomorrah fled, and they fell there. And they that remained fled to the mountains. And they took all the goods of Sodom and Gomorrah, all their victuals, and they went their way. And they also took Lot, Abram's brother's son, who dwelt in Sodom, and his goods, and they departed.

And there came one that escaped and told Abram, the Hebrew. (This is the first time Abram is called a Hebrew.) Now there dwelt by the terebinths of Mamre the Amorite, brother of Eshcol, brother of Aner, and these were confederates with Abram. And when Abram heard that his nephew Lot was taken captive, he led forth his trained men born in his house, 318 of them, and pursued as far as the territory of Dan.

He was going to fight an entire army with 318 men. He was going in the will of the LORD, by the direction of the LORD.

And he divided himself against them, by night, he and his servants, and smote them. He formed his men in several bodies which attacked the enemy in the dark from different directions. The suddenness of the onslaught, and the attack and the assault in several places simultaneously enabled the small bands of men to throw a far larger force into panic. The same strategy was given to Gideon by the LORD later on (Judg. 7:16).

And the LORD delivered the enemy into his hands. He pursued them unto Hobah on the left hand of Damascus, and he brought back all the goods, his nephew Lot, his goods, and the women also, and the people.

And the king of Sodom went out to meet him after his return from the slaughter of Chedorlaomer and the kings that were with him at the vale of Shaveh, the king's dale.

And Melchizedek, king of Salem, brought forth bread and wine, and he was the priest of God, the most high. And He blessed him, and said, "Blessed be Abram of the most high God, maker of heaven and earth. And blessed be the most high God, who has delivered your enemies into your hand." And he, Abram, gave Melchizedek a tenth of all that he possessed.

In Hebrews 7:2, the Holy Spirit says that Melchizedek is King of peace, King of righteousness. Abraham gave him a tithe because he knew who He was. The LORD had appeared to him once before. He knew the Priest of God most high. And this Melchizedek, King of Salem and Priest of the most high God, met Abraham returning from the slaughter of the kings, and blessed him. And Abraham gave to Him a tenth portion of all the spoils.

Now observe and consider how great a personage this was to whom even Abraham, the patriarch, gave a tenth, the topmost, the pick of the heap of the spoils. And it is true that those descendants of Levi, who are charged with the priestly office, are commanded in the law to take tithes from the people, which means they are to take tithes from their brethren, though these have descended from Abraham. But this Melchizedek, who had not their Levitical ancestry, who was not of the tribe of Levi, received tithes from Abraham himself, and He blessed him, Abraham, who possessed the promises of God. The lesser person, Abraham, was blessed by the greater one, Melchizedek. A person might even say that Levi, the father of the priestly tribe himself, who received tithes, paid tithes to Melchizedek through Abraham. The tribe of Levi had never paid a tithe, but the LORD, being gracious, had them giving a tithe to Melchizedek while they were still in the loins of Abraham.

Levi was still in the loins of his forefather Abraham when Melchizedek met Abraham. Now, if perfection, that is, perfect fellowship between God and the worshiper, had been attainable by the Levitical priesthood (for under it the people were given the law), why was it further necessary that there should arise another and a different kind of priest, one after the order of Melchizedek rather than one appointed after the order and rank of Aaron?

What did Aaron do? When Moses was up on the mount forty days, the people came to Aaron and they said, "Make us a god that we can see."

And he said, "Give me your gold," and he melted the gold and made the golden calf. He engraved it in bold Hebrew letters, "This is your god, O Israel, which brought you up out of the land of Egypt."

And when Moses came down from the mount and saw what was taking place, he broke the stone tablets on which the commandments of God were written, and he said, "Aaron, you are the high priest of Israel! How did you cause the people of Israel to sin?"

Aaron said, "I didn't do anything. They came to me and they said, 'Make us a god,' and I just told them to give me the gold, and they gave me the gold, and I put it in the fire, and out came the golden calf." Aaron made everything worse by lying about it. And Moses had to intercede with the LORD to spare Aaron's life. And the LORD honored Moses' intercessory prayer.

Jesus was one appointed after the order of Melchizedek

rather than after the order and rank of Aaron. And when there is a change in the priesthood, there is of necessity an alteration of the law concerning the priesthood as well. Our LORD, Jesus Christ, sprang from the tribe of Judah, no member of which had officiated at the altar. Moses mentioned nothing about priests in connection with that tribe.

And it was not without the taking of an oath that Christ was made priest. Those who formerly became priests received their office without its being confirmed by the taking of an oath, but Jesus was designated, and addressed, and saluted with an oath. The LORD hath sworn and will not regret or change His mind. "You are a priest forever according to the order of Melchize-dek" (Ps. 110:4). In keeping with the oath's greater strength and force, Jesus has become the guarantee of a better and a stronger agreement and a more excellent and more advantageous covenant.

The former successive line of priests was made up of many individuals, each prevented by death from continuing perpetually in office. They died, and then came another high priest. But He, Jesus, holds His priesthood unchangeably, because He lives forever. Therefore, He is able to save to the uttermost, completely, perfectly, finally, and for all time and eternity those who come to God through Him. He is always able to make petition to God and intercede with Him and intervene for us.

This high priest was perfectly adapted to our needs as was fitting—holy, blameless, unstained by sin, separated from sinners, and exalted higher than the heavens. He had no day-by-day necessity, as did each of the other high priests, to offer sacrifice, first of all, for His own personal sins and then for those of the people, because He met all the requirements once and for all when He brought Himself as a sacrifice which He offered up. The law had set up men in their weakness, frail sinful, dying human beings, as high priests. But God's oath, which was spoken later, after the institution of the law, chose and appointed as priest One whose appointment was permanent and complete, a Son who has been made perfect forever, your Jesus, and my Jesus. Praise God.

And the king of Sodom spoke unto Abram, and said, "Give me the persons, and take the goods for yourself."

And Abram said to the king of Sodom, "I have lifted up my hand unto the Lord, unto the Lord God most high, maker of heaven and earth, that I will not take a thread, nor a shoe-latchet, nor aught that is yours, lest you should say, 'I have made Abram rich.' It is God who supplies all my needs, and I won't take anything from you except what the young men have eaten, and the portion of the men which went with me, Aner, Eshcol, and Mamre; let them take their portion."

After these things, the Word of the Lord came unto Abram in a vision, saying, "Fear not, Abram. I am your shield, and your reward shall be exceedingly great." This was the first *mogen*, promise, that the Lord made to Abram.

Mogen David was the promise that God made to King David saying, "I am your mogen, I am your shield. I am the wall of fire surrounding you. Nobody will ever come against you all the days of your life, because I am your shield." And if the Lord is your shield and my shield, of whom do we have to be afraid? Whom shall we fear? The Lord is my shield, the Lord Jesus Christ. His shed blood is my shield.

Abram was becoming a little more courageous. He was learning how to speak to the Lord. Moses had the courage to speak

77

to the LORD. *The* LORD *wants you and me to speak to Him. And He doesn't want us, when we speak to Him, to say, "Oh* LORD, *if it be Thy will." He doesn't want us to use "Thee" and "Thou" and all the fancy language we can dig up. The* LORD *has revealed His will in the Word. His revealed will is to bless us. He says, "I have come into the world to give you life and to give it more abundantly." So why say, "If it be Thy will"? We know what His will is. All we need to do is to be obedient to His will and not our own.*

Abram again received this reassurance from God, and he turned around and said, "O LORD God, what would You give me, seeing that I go childless and he that shall be possessor of my house, my heir, is Eliezer of Damascus?" And Abram said, "Behold, to me You have given no seed. You made me a promise, and I've waited, but so far, nothing has happened. And lo, one born in my house is my heir, this Eliezer of Damascus."

And behold, the Word of the LORD came unto him, saying, "This man shall not be your heir, but he that shall come forth out of your own bowels shall be your heir." And He brought him forth abroad, and said, "Look now toward heaven. Count the stars, if you are able to count them." And He said unto him, "So shall your seed be." Abram believed in the LORD, and the LORD counted it unto him for righteousness. And He said unto him, "I am the LORD that brought you up out of Ur of the Chaldees. I am the same LORD." Later on, the LORD would say to the people of Israel, "I am the LORD thy God that brought you up out of the land of Egypt, out of bondage, out of slavery."

God was reminding Abram that He was the same LORD, and then He said, "I brought you from Ur to give you this land to inherit it."

And Abram said, "Oh Lord God, whereby—how—shall I know already yet that I'm going to inherit it?"

And He said unto him, "Take me a heifer of three years old, and a she goat of three years old, and a ram of three years old, and a turtledove, and a young pigeon." And he took unto him all of these, and he divided them in the midst, and he laid each half over against the other, but the birds he divided not. The birds were not divided, because they represented the Holy Spirit, and you can never divide the Holy Spirit.

The ancient method of making a covenant was to cut an animal in half, and the contracting parties who made the covenant would pass between the portions of the slain animals, thereby uniting themselves by the bond of the blood shed by the animal.

The Lord was going to deal with Abram on his own level, to demonstrate to Abram that He would keep His part of the covenant He was about to make.

And the birds of prey came down upon the carcasses, and Abram drove them away. And it came to pass that when the sun was going down, a deep sleep fell upon Abram, and lo, a dread, even a great darkness fell upon him. The Lord put Abram into a deep sleep just as He had put Adam in a deep sleep when He removed the rib from His side and made the woman.

And He said unto Abram, "Know for a surety that your seed shall be a stranger in a land that is not theirs, and there they shall serve them, and there they shall afflict them four hundred years. And also that nation, whom they shall serve, will I judge; and afterward, they shall come forth with great substance." The gifts of the Egyptians would be the great substance they would bring forth from Egypt. "But you shall go to your fathers in peace, and you shall be buried in a good old age."

And God said, "And in the fourth generation, your descendants shall come back here, for the iniquity of the Amorites is not yet full. I'm still holding out My love, grace, mercy, and salvation to these people. If they will repent of their abominations, I will forgive their iniquity, their sin, their transgression."

Now, it came to pass, that when the sun was going down, there was a thick darkness, and behold a smoking furnace, and a flaming torch that passed between these pieces. God's Holy Spirit was the flaming torch, the smoking furnace, that passed between the pieces of the sacrifice.

And in that day, the LORD made a covenant with Abram, saying, "Unto your seed have I given this land, from the river of Egypt unto the great river, the river Euphrates. The Kenites, the Kenizzites, the Kadmonites, the Hittites, the Perizzites, and the Rephaims, the Amorites, the Canaanites, the Girgashites, and the Jebusites. They're all yours."

I'm sure at this point, Abram said, "Praise God!"

Now Abram's wife, Sarai, was barren, she had borne him no children, and she had a handmaid, an Egyptian whose name was Hagar. The LORD had given Abram a promise that his seed would be as numerous as the stars and the sand, and said, "Abie, do you believe?" And he had said, "I believe, LORD." And He had said, "I have counted it unto you for righteousness, because you believed My word."

And Sarai came unto Abram, and she said, "Behold now, take a look, in case you haven't noticed—" Every time we see the word *behold*, in the Hebrew, it means, "Take a look."

"Behold, take a look, look very closely, because the LORD has restrained me from bearing." She knew from whose hands a child comes, that it's from the LORD. She said, "I don't know what's happened to me that I can't have any children, but the LORD has restrained me from having children."

And Sarai said to Abram, "Go in, I pray thee, unto my handmaid. It may be that I shall be builded up through her."

Abram listened to the voice of Sarai. He had the promises of God in his hand, and he should have listened to the LORD, but he listened to Sarai, his wife, as she said, "Perhaps I may be builded up through Hagar."

And Sarai took Hagar, the Egyptian, her handmaid, after Abram had walked ten years in the land of Canaan, and she gave her to Abram, her husband, to be his wife.

And he went in unto Hagar, and she conceived. And when Hagar saw that she had conceived, her mistress was despised in her eyes. Hagar was walking around with a nice, cute, little belly because she had conceived. And she looked at Sarai, and she said, "Behold—take a look at me. The LORD hasn't restrained me, but He has restrained you. There must be something wrong with you. I know I'm right with the LORD, because I'm going to have a child, but you are not going to have any children."

Her mistress was despised in her eyes. And Hagar the handmaid, the Egyptian, flaunted herself above her mistress. She figured she was in a better situation than Sarai was.

So Sarai turned to Abram, and she said unto him, "Abram, my wrong be upon thee. Who told you to listen to me instead of listening to God? Who does the talking with you, me or the LORD? Who's the prophet and the priest in this house? You are. How come you listened to me instead of listening to the LORD? The LORD gave you a promise, and said He's going to multiply you. He's going to make your seed and your descendants as numerous as the stars and as the sand. And now let my wrong, the condition I find myself in, despised by my handmaid, be upon you, because you listened to me instead of listening to God.

"I gave my handmaid unto your bosom, and when she saw that she had conceived, I was despised in her eyes, and now the LORD judge between me and thee, who's right and who's wrong."

Abram *was* wrong. He should have listened to the LORD. If he'd listened to the LORD, we wouldn't have the situation we have today. All the Arab nations have descended from Hagar's son Ishmael, and the Arab and the Jew have been at constant war from that day till this day. And it will never be resolved until the King of Peace, Jesus Christ, comes back.

The Arabs say that it was Ishmael and not Isaac that Abraham laid on the rock for a sacrifice to the LORD. And since Ishmael was the oldest son of Abraham, therefore, the promises given to Abraham rightfully pass on to him. Therefore, the Promised Land belongs to my brother, the Arab, and not to me, the Jew. You can see how both sides have reasoned as they do. But God is the authority. God speaking to Abram, said, "Your seed, your descendants, will pass through the promised son, Isaac, not through Ishmael, not through Eliezer, your servant, but through Isaac, the son of the promise."

And Abram now turned unto Sarai, his wife, and he said, "Behold, your maid is in your hands; do to her what is good in your eyes. She is your handmaid, she is in your power." From his knowledge of Sarai, Abram thought she would aim merely to bring Hagar back to proper behavior, because Sarai was a kind, generous, compassionate woman. But Sarai dealt harshly with Hagar, and she fled from before her face. Sarai imposed heavy tasks upon Hagar, who was pregnant. Maybe Sarai figured if she imposed heavy tasks on Hagar, she would miscarry and no longer be arrogant toward her.

Sarai, our mother, acted sinfully in ill-treating Hagar, and Abram stood by and said nothing. They both sinned.

And Hagar fled from Sarai. And the Angel of the LORD found Hagar by a fountain of water in the wilderness on the way to Shur. And He said, "Hagar, Sarai's handmaid, where do you come from? And where do you go?"

And she said, "I flee from the face of my mistress, Sarai."

And the Angel of the LORD said unto her, "Return to your mistress, and submit yourself under her hand."

Doesn't that sound like Jesus? When He came in the flesh, what did He tell us if we were running away from a wife, a husband, a neighbor, anybody who was ill-treating us? He said, "Go back and submit, and by your love, and by your witness, and by your testimony, you can win them to Me. Never return evil for evil, but return love for evil." In the same way, the Angel of the LORD said unto Hagar, "Yes, Sarai dealt very harshly with you. She imposed heavy burdens upon you, but now go back and submit to her."

And the Angel of the LORD said unto her, "I will greatly multiply your seed, and this seed shall not be numbered for multitude. Behold, you are with child, and you shall bear a son, and you shall call his name Ishmael, because the LORD has

heard your affliction." In Hebrew, the name *Ishmael* means
"God is hearing." God has heard Hagar's affliction and groan-
ing. And then the Angel of the LORD gave the description of
the Arab that is still true today:

"And he shall be a wild ass of a man. His hand shall be
against every man, and every man's hand shall be against him;
and he shall dwell in the presence of all his brethren." This is
true today, as we see Jews and Arabs dwelling side by side.

Abram had taken the situation into his own hands; he
couldn't wait upon God's promise. He couldn't wait upon
God's Word. And God gave him a circumstance to deal with.
Abram brought it on himself.

And Hagar called the name of the LORD that spoke unto her,
"Thou art a God of seeing." For she said, "Have I also here
looked after Him that seeth me?" Wherefore the well where
she was when the Angel of the LORD appeared unto her was
called Beer-lahai-roi, meaning, "well of the Living One who
appeared to me." It is located between Kadesh and Bered.

And Hagar bore Abram a son, and Abram called the name
of his son whom Hagar bore unto him, Ishmael. And Abram
was 86 years old when Hagar bore Ishmael to Abram.

Now, when Abram was 99 years old, the LORD again appeared
to him to make a covenant with him, and to remind him that
he still had a covenant existing. And the LORD said unto Abram,
"I am God Almighty." In the Hebrew, the words are, "I am
El Shaddai."

As El Shaddai, the LORD revealed Himself as a heavenly,
gracious, loving Father. When God the Father reached a point
where He was about to wipe us out, when His attribute of
justice would come before Him, saying, "Your children have

sinned and deserve to be destroyed," His attribute of mercy would come before Him, and instead of wiping us out, He would take us to His bosom, and He would nurture us and would pour out His love, and His grace, and His mercy.

When God appeared to Abram, He said, "I am El Shaddai. You can stake your life upon My mercy."

When we study the Psalms, we see that the people of Israel later on constantly confess, as David is led by the Holy Spirit, that "His mercy endureth forever," that in spite of our sinning, the LORD's *mercy would prevail. Whenever we come to Him with a sincere and a repentant heart, and ask for forgiveness, He is just and faithful to forgive us our sin.*

6
Thy Name Shall Be Called Abraham . . .
(Genesis 17:5—25:10)

And God said to Abram, "I am El Shaddai. Walk before Me. Be thou wholehearted, and I will make My covenant between Me and thee, and I will multiply thee exceedingly." And Abram fell on his face, and God talked with him, saying, "As for Me, behold, My covenant is with you, and you shall be the father of a multitude of nations.

"Neither shall your name anymore be called Abram, but your name shall be Abraham." The LORD took an "h" out of His unpronounceable name, YHWH, and He put it in the name of Abram. By changing His name from Abram to Abraham, He made him the father of all nations, and He also made him a part of the LORD. He was signifying to Abram, "From this point on, you are part of Me, and I am part of you."

What do we say to somebody when they ask us what we are? We say we are Christians. We have the name of Jesus in our name, the name of Christ, the Messiah. We have Christ in us, and we are in Him. Jesus said, "Father, I pray that as You and I are one, that they may be one with Us." We are one with Him. When the Lord *took the "h" letter out of His name, and placed it in the name of Abraham, He made him forever part of Himself.*

And He said, "The father of a multitude of nations have I made you, and I will make you exceedingly fruitful, and I will make nations of you, and kings shall come out of you—a multitude of kings. And I will establish My covenant between Me and thee and your seed after you throughout their generations for an everlasting covenant. And I will be a God unto you and to your seed after you."

Here is the covenant: "I will be your God, and you shall be My people. No matter how much you sin, I will still love you, because I have given you My word that I will be your God. You're going to get spanked once in a while, but I will still be your God. Even if I put you in exile, put you in bondage, put you in affliction, I will be with you in that affliction. I give you My word I will never leave you nor forsake you. While you are in bondage," the Lord says, "I am in bondage also, because I'm right there with you.

"This covenant is not only with you, Abraham, but with your seed [plural] after you for all generations. And I will give unto you and to your seed after you the land of your sojourning, all the land of Canaan for an everlasting possession, and I will be their God, the God of future generations. They will know me as a living God." In the New Testament, we see God is not ashamed to be called the God of Abraham, the God of Isaac, and the God of Jacob. He's not ashamed to be called their God, because He's not the God of the dead, but of the living. By this we know that Abraham, Isaac, and Jacob are with Him, because they looked into the distant future, and they saw the coming Messiah, and by their faith and by their trust in Him, in Jesus, the LORD accounted it unto them for righteousness.

And God said unto Abraham, "As for thee, you shall keep My covenant, you and your seed after you throughout their generations. And this is My covenant which you shall keep between you and Me and your seed after you—every male among you shall be circumcised." And God told Abraham, "Don't ask Me why. This is what I want you to do. I want you to be obedient. Don't ask me, 'Why should I be circumcised?' " You and I might have the tendency to ask the LORD, "Well, why?" But the LORD says, "Don't ask. If I tell you to do something, do it." We saw the obedience of Abram when the LORD said, "Leave your kindred, leave your homeland. Go, and when you get there, I'll tell you that you're there." Now He commanded him to be circumcised. And Abraham was ninety-nine years of age.

And the LORD said, "You shall be circumcised in the flesh of your foreskin. It shall be a token of a covenant between you and Me. By doing this act, you will confirm your covenant relationship with Me."

We enter into the New Covenant by the circumcision of the heart which is accomplished when we are baptized into Jesus Christ.* This is the sign of the New Covenant as we enter and

---

*For an in-depth study of the scriptural basis of the New Covenant circumcision of the heart in water baptism, see James Beall's, *Rise, to Newness of Life* (Grand Rapids, Mich.: Evangel Press, 1974).

die with Christ Jesus in the waters of baptism and rise with Him into a new life. We do it out of love. Jesus said, "If you love Me, you will keep My commandment." He was without sin, but he was baptized nonetheless. He said, "I am doing it to fulfill all righteousness, that you may enter in with Me into an everlasting life."

And the LORD specified that he that is eight days old shall be circumcised, "every male among you throughout all of your generations, he that is born in your house or bought with money or any foreigner that is not of your seed. If he lives in your house, he is to be circumcised."

Why did the LORD say, "eight days"? Why didn't He say seven, or nine, or three, or two?

Medical doctors have just found out in the last few years that the safest time to circumcise a child is in the eighth day because the coagulant in the bloodstream reaches its highest level on the eighth day, and it starts to decline thereafter for the rest of that person's life.

And the LORD said, "He that is born in your house, he that is bought with your money, needs to be circumcised, and My covenant shall be in your flesh for an everlasting covenant. And the uncircumcised male who is not circumcised in the flesh of his foreskin, that soul shall be cut off from his people. He has broken My covenant." If anyone refuses circumcision, the LORD says he has broken the covenant, and the LORD casts him aside, because he refuses to enter into a contract with the LORD.

And God said unto Abraham, "As for Sarai, thy wife, thou shalt not call her name Sarai, but Sarah shall her name be."

The LORD took the other "h" out of His YHWH, and He put it in the name Sarai. "Sarah" means "princess." Sarah became a princess with God, and she would become the ancestress of Jesus Christ. He would remove that grudge, that resentment, that hatred from her heart for Hagar, the Egyptian, the mother of Ishmael, because He was convicting her by His Holy Spirit. And He gave her a new name, a name written down in glory.

And God said, "Sarah shall her name be. And I will bless her, and moreover, I will give you a son of her. Yes, I shall bless her, and she shall be a mother of, not just one nation, but of many nations. Kings of people shall come of her, kings of many people and of many nations shall come of her."

Then Abraham fell upon his face and he laughed. And he said in his heart, "Shall a child be born unto him that is a hundred years old? And shall Sarah, that is ninety years old, bear?" And Abraham said unto God, "O, that Ishmael might live before thee." He loved the boy very much. Even today, every Arab reveres Abraham more than even the Hebrew people revere Abraham. He is their father.

And Abraham was speaking to the LORD face to face. He said, "O would it be, LORD, in Your will that Ishmael would be my heir, and that this covenant that you made with me would pass through him?" Abraham loved Ishmael so much that he prayed, "Oh, that Ishmael would be my heir."

But God said, "No, but Sarah, your wife, shall bear you a son, and you shall call his name Isaac, and I will establish My covenant with him for an everlasting covenant and with his seed after him. And as for Ishmael, I have heard you. And behold, I have already blessed him. Don't worry about him; he's well taken care of. I will make him fruitful; I will multiply him exceedingly. Twelve princes, twelve nations of Arabs, shall he beget, and I will make him a great nation, but My covenant will I establish with Isaac, whom Sarah shall bear unto you at this set time in the next year."

The LORD left off talking with him, and God went up from Abraham. And Abraham took Ishmael, his son, and all that were born in his house, and all that were bought with his money, every male among the men of Abraham's house; and he circumcised the flesh of their foreskin in the very same day that God had commanded him.

Abraham was not a procrastinator. When the LORD spoke to him, he was obedient unto the LORD. He didn't say, "Gee, I'm ninety-nine, almost a hundred years old. I'm going to put it off till maybe I feel a little better, maybe till I get a little stronger, maybe till I get a little older, maybe just before I die." No, he was obedient unto the LORD. The very same day that God commanded him, he carried out the commandment of the LORD. That's obedience. Abraham fathered the son of the promise *after* he was obedient to God's command to be circumcised.

And Abraham was ninety-nine years old when he was circumcised in the flesh of his foreskin. And Ishmael, his son, was thirteen years old when he was circumcised in the flesh of his foreskin.

The Arabs of today circumcise their children at the age of thirteen because their father, Ishmael, was circumcised at the age of thirteen. My father, Isaac, was circumcised at the age of eight days, as God commanded Abraham.

And again, the LORD appeared unto Abraham by the terebinths of Mamre as he sat in the tent door in the heat of the day three days after his circumcision. And he lifted up his eyes and he looked and lo, there were three men which stood over against him. And when he saw tnem, he ran to meet them.

And as he ran to meet the three men, he bowed down to the earth, and he worshiped the LORD, and he said, "My LORD—" He recognized that one of the three was the LORD. He'd met Him on two previous occasions, and he said, "My LORD, if I have found favor in Your sight, pass not away, I pray Thee, from Your servant. Let a little water be fetched, and wash Your feet and recline Yourself under the tree. And I will fetch a morsel of bread and stay You Your heart, and after that, You shall pass on, forasmuch as You are come to Your servant."

And they said, "So do as you have said." There were three, the LORD and two servants of the LORD, two angels.

And Abraham hastened into the tent unto Sarah and he said, "Make ready quickly three measures of fine meal, knead it, and make cakes." It was the time of the future Passover, so she made unleavened bread.

And Abraham ran unto the herd, and he fetched a calf tender and good, and he gave it unto his young man, his servant, and he hastened to dress it. And he took curd and milk and the calf which he had dressed, and he set it before them, and he stood by them under the tree, and they did eat. And they, the angels, said unto him, "Where is Sarah, your wife?" And Abraham was pleased to be able to say, "Behold, she is in the tent. She is exactly where she is supposed to be. Isn't that the job you gave her, LORD? She's in the tent, and she's not out running around somewhere."

Now, the way our rabbis put it in the Talmud, Abraham was praising Sarah with the highest excellence and the highest compliment he could pay—that she was in the tent where the LORD said she should be.

And the LORD said, "I will certainly return unto you when

the season comes around, and lo, Sarah, your wife, shall have a son." And Sarah heard in the tent door which was behind them. Sarah herself had never heard the promise from the mouth of the LORD, and she was eavesdropping to see what the three strangers had to say to Abraham. And she heard that next year, when the season came around again, she would have a son. And now Abraham and Sarah were old and well stricken in age, and it had ceased to be with Sarah after the manner of woman. She no longer had a period. She had gone through the menopause. She had had her change of life. She was ninety years of age, and it would really take a miracle for her to have a baby. God would have to work hard to bring such a thing to pass.

And Sarah did just what Abraham did when he heard the news. She laughed incredulously saying, "After I am that old, shall I have pleasure, my lord being old also? After I'm ninety years of age, and my husband is a hundred years of age, and he's as good as dead already yet, I am going to have pleasure from my lord, from my husband, and I'm going to have a son?"

And the LORD turned around and spoke to Abraham, the prophet and priest in the home.

There's the same chain of command in the New Testament that we see in the Old Testament. The LORD Jesus Christ speaks to the head of the house, the man in that house, and it is the wife's duty to help him be the prophet and priest in that house.

Without my wife's help, I wouldn't be where I am today, because the LORD used her—that Scotch Irish Presbyterian. If it wasn't for her, I'd be in some hellhole someplace. The LORD used her. The faithfulness of a woman is exceeded by none.

There is an old Hebrew saying that man is the first to run off, the minute things get tough. The minute he gets into any kind of adverse circumstance, he'll try to escape. But the woman stands and she stands, and she prays, and she prays, and constantly intercedes for her husband and for her family. In the churches today, you see, predominantly, faithful women praying for their families. The man is off watching a football game, playing golf, watching the baseball game. The wife is there worshiping the LORD.

The LORD turned around unto Abraham, and He said, "Wherefore did Sarah laugh saying, 'Shall I of a surety bear a child who am old?' " And the LORD *said* to Abraham, "Is anything too hard for Me? Can't I change this situation?" And He told him again, "At the set time that I told you about, at that very set time, I will return unto you when the season comes around, and Sarah shall have a son." God reaffirmed the promise and the covenant.

Then Sarah denied, saying, "I laughed not," for she was afraid. She suddenly realized that this was the LORD, and He meant business.

And He said, "No, but you did laugh."

And the men—the two with the LORD—rose up from the earth and looked out toward Sodom, and Abraham went with them to bring them on the way, to put them on the road, and the LORD said, speaking to Himself, "Shall I hide from Abraham that which I am doing, seeing that Abraham will surely become a great and mighty nation, and all the nations of the earth shall be blessed in him? For I have known Abraham to the end that he may command his children and his household after him, that they may always keep the way of the LORD to do righteousness and justice, to the end that the LORD may bring upon Abraham that which He has spoken of him." The LORD said, "For I have known him; I have regarded him; I have chosen him."

God's choice of Abraham was not an arbitrary election. He chose him before the beginning of time. He knew him from the beginning, to the end that Abraham would raise his children in the nurture and the admonition of the LORD, to do righteousness and justice.

An important doctrine is being taught here. Our rabbis put it this way. It is the sacred duty of every Israelite to transmit the Hebrew heritage to his Hebrew children after him. The last injunction of a true Hebrew father to his children is that they should walk in the way of the LORD, and do righteousness and justice. Even on his deathbed, he is to remind his children to walk in the way of the LORD, to do righteousness and justice. These injunctions are put in writing, and this custom has given rise to a distinct type of literary production which is called "the Jewish ethical will."

And the LORD said, "Verily, the cry of Sodom and Gomorrah is very great, and verily, their sin is exceedingly grievous. I will go down and see whether they have done altogether according to the cry of it, which is come up unto me; and if not, I will know."

The LORD was holding out His hand for salvation, giving them one more chance before total destruction. If they would repent, there was salvation; there was forgiveness.

And the men turned from there, and they went toward Sodom, but Abraham stood yet before the LORD. The two men went on their way. And they each had a mission. One of them was to rescue Lot, and the other one was to destroy Sodom and Gomorrah.

But the LORD was still speaking to Abraham, and Abraham was standing close to the LORD. And Abraham stood yet before the LORD, and Abraham drew near, and he said, "Would You indeed destroy the righteous with the wicked, You, the Judge of all the universe?" He knew his nephew Lot was in Sodom, and he was thinking about his nephew and his family. "Perhaps there are fifty righteous within the city. Will You indeed sweep away and not forgive the place for the fifty righteous therein? Far be it from You to do after this manner, to slay the righteous with the wicked. Shall not the Judge of all the earth do justly?"

And the LORD said, "If I find in Sodom fifty righteous within the city, then I will forgive all the place for their sake."

And Abraham answered and said, "Behold now, take a look. I have taken it upon myself to speak unto the LORD. I, who am nothing but dust and ashes. Perhaps there shall lack five of the fifty righteous; will you destroy all the city for lack of five?"

And He, the LORD, said, "I will not destroy it if I find there forty-five."

Abraham figured he was really outwitting the LORD, bringing Him down by five. And he spoke unto Him again and said, "LORD, perhaps there shall be found forty there." He was getting bolder, bringing Him down another five.

And the LORD said, "I will not do it for the forty's sake."

And Abraham said, "O let not the LORD be angry, and I will speak. Perhaps there will be thirty found there." He jumped ten that time, from forty down to thirty.

And He, the LORD, said, "I will not do it if I find thirty there."

And Abraham said, "Behold now, I have taken it upon myself to speak unto the LORD. Perhaps there shall be twenty found there." He took him down another ten.

And He said, "I will not destroy it for the twenty's sake."

And Abraham said, "O let not the LORD be angry, and I will speak yet but this once more. Peradventure ten shall be found there."

And the LORD said, "I will not destroy it for the ten's sake."

And the LORD went His way as soon as He had left off speaking to Abraham, and Abraham returned unto his place.

The two angels came to Sodom at eventide, and Lot sat in the gate of Sodom. And when Lot saw the angels, he rose up to meet them, and he fell down on his face to the earth. He recognized they were angels. And he said, "Behold, now my lords, turn aside, I pray you, into your servant's house. Tarry all night, and wash your feet, and you shall rise up early and go on your way."

This was the first time that the men were referred to as angels. And Lot asked them to come into his house, but they said, "No, we will abide in the broad place all night; we will stay in the city square."

And he urged them greatly, and they turned in unto him and entered into his house. He made them a feast. He did bake unleavened bread, and they did eat.

But before they lay down, the men of the city, even the men of Sodom, compassed the house round and about, both young and old, and all the people from every quarter. And they called unto Lot, and said unto him, "Where are the men that came in unto you this night? Bring them out unto us that we may know them intimately." The sin of Sodom and Gomorrah was homosexuality. That was the sin that went up before the LORD.

And Lot went out unto them and shut the door after him. The angels were inside, and Lot went out and he said, "I pray you, my brethren, do nothing so wickedly. Behold now, I have two daughters that have not known man. Let me, I pray you, bring them out unto you, and do you to them as is good in your eyes, only unto these men do nothing, forasmuch as they are come under the shadow of my roof."

They said, "This one fellow came in to sojourn among us— this guy Lot came in as a stranger among us—and now wants to judge us. Now we will deal worse with you than with them." And they pressed sore upon the man Lot, and they drew near to break the door. But the men, the angels, put forth their hand, and brought Lot into the house with them, and they shut the door. And they smote the men that were at the door of the house with blindness, both small and great, so that they wearied themselves to find the door. The angels blinded the men, the homosexuals, and they could not even find the door.

And the angels said unto Lot, "Do you have any others in your family besides those that are here? Sons-in-law, and your sons, and your daughters, and whomsoever you have in the city, bring them out of the place. For we will destroy this place, because the cry of them is waxed great before the face of the LORD; and the LORD hath sent us to destroy it."

And Lot went out, and spoke to his sons-in-law who married his daughters and said, "Up, get you out of this place, for the LORD will destroy the city." But he seemed foolish to them. When you speak about God to those who don't know God, it's always foolishness to them. And Lot's sons-in-law thought he was only joking.

And when the morning arose, then the angels hastened

Lot, saying, "Arise, take your wife and your two daughters that are here, lest you be swept away in the iniquity of the city." But still he lingered. He didn't want to go.

Remember the obedience of Abraham—the minute the LORD commanded him, he went. He moved. Right away. But Lot was lingering, thinking, "Maybe something will take place. Maybe the LORD is going to change His mind. Maybe this. Maybe that." He lingered, proscrastinated. He didn't want to go. He had a good business, making all kinds of money. Why give it all up? Maybe at the last minute—

And the men physically laid hold upon his hand and upon the hand of his wife, and upon the hand of his two daughters, the LORD being merciful unto him. And He took them physically by the hand and He said, "Come, I'm going to drag you out of this stinking city." The LORD was merciful unto Lot, because He had made a promise to Abraham, and God never breaks a promise.

So the LORD being merciful unto him, they brought Lot and set him outside the city.

And it came to pass, when they had brought him outside the city, that the angel who brought him said, "Escape for your life. Look not behind you, neither stay in all the plain. Escape to the mountains, lest you be swept away."

And Lot said unto him, "Oh not so, my lord." This guy really had nerve, didn't he? They physically took him out of the city to spare his life, and they told him to go to the mountain. And he argued with them, "Oh, not so, my lord. Why do I have to go all the way to the mountains? Behold, now, your servant has found grace in your sight, and you have magnified your mercy which you have shown unto me in saving my life, but I can't escape to the mountain, lest the evil overtake me and I die.

"Behold now, take a look, angel. This city is near for one to flee unto, and it is just a little city. O angel, let me escape there, and my soul shall live."

And the angel said unto him, "I have accepted you concerning this thing also, and I will not overthrow the city of that which you have spoken."

Notice the mercy of the LORD. The angel, who was commissioned to destroy Sodom and Gomorrah and six of the plain cities, said, "For your sake, I will not destroy the city of that which you have spoken. Now hurry, hasten! Escape there, for I can't do anything till you come there; otherwise, you're going to be destroyed with the overthrow."

Therefore, the name of that city was called Zoar. And the sun was risen upon the earth when Lot came to Zoar.

Then the LORD caused to rain upon Sodom and upon Gomorrah brimstone and fire from the LORD out of heaven; and He overthrew those cities, and all the cities of the plain, and all the inhabitants of the cities, and that which grew upon the ground.

But Lot's wife looked back from behind him, and she became a pillar of salt.

And Abraham got himself up early in the morning to the place where he had stood before the LORD, to the very spot where he stood conversing with the LORD, and he looked out toward Sodom and Gomorrah and toward all the land of the plain and beheld, and lo, the smoke of the land went up as the smoke of a furnace.

And God sent Lot out when He overthrew the cities in

which Lot dwelt. And Lot went up out of Zoar and dwelt in the mountain, and his two daughters with him. For he feared to dwell in Zoar; and he dwelt in a cave, he and his two daughters. In the beginning, the angel had told him to go up to the mountain, and not to go to Zoar. But Lot said, "Well, take a look at it. Zoar is just a little city yet. It's not a big city. Let me stay in a little city. Why should I take a thirty-mile hike up the mountain when I can just stay in the little city?" And the angels said, "All right, we will not overthrow the city. The LORD will honor His promise to Abraham. If you remain in that city, that city will not be overthrown."

So the angel did not overthrow that city. The city was not destroyed. But while Lot was in that city of Zoar, the spirit of fear came upon him, and he was afraid to stay there. Then he went to the mountain where the angel told him to go in the first place. He was being a little bit obedient, doing a little bit of what the LORD told him to do in the beginning. And he went to the mountain and dwelt in a cave, he and his two daughters.

And the firstborn daughter, the elder, said to the younger, "Our father is old, and there is not a man in the earth to come in unto us after the manner of all the earth." What kind of a statement was that, that there was not a man on all the face of the earth to come in unto them as man and woman are accustomed to doing? They had just left a populated city, Zoar, but the eldest told the youngest there was not a man left.

And she said, "Come, let us make our father drink wine, and we will lie with him that we may preserve seed of our father. Let's go to bed with him, let's have an incestuous relationship with our father, but let's get him drunk first. We will

101

commit the sin, but we don't want him to sin. After all, he is our father. If he's drunk, he will not know. It won't be his fault." From the time of Noah, they had learned the power of wine.

So they made their father drink wine that night. And the firstborn went in and lay with her father, and he knew not when she lay down, nor when she arose, because he was drunk. And it came to pass on the next day, that the firstborn said unto the younger, "Take a look, behold, I lay yesternight with my father. Let us make him drink wine this night also, and you go in and lie with him, that we may preserve seed of our father." And they made their father drink wine that night also. And the younger arose and lay with him, and he knew not when she lay down, nor when she arose, because he was drunk again. Thus were both the daughters of Lot with child by their father. And their offspring have given us problems, from that time until today. They have been a thorn in the side of Israel from then till now.

And the firstborn bore a son and called his name Moab, "from my father." He became the father of Moabites. The younger also bore a son, and she called his name Benammi, "son of my people." And the same is the father of the children of Ammon unto this very day. The Ammonites live in and around what is called Ammon Jordan till today.

We will see, as we continue to study the Bible, the conflict between the Israelites, the Moabites, and the Ammonites, but through it all, there is a great picture that emerges: God's love, His grace, and His mercy are available to anybody. We are all His children, every race, every nation, every color, every creed. The LORD chose a Moabitess by the name of Ruth to be the great-great-great-great grandmother of Jesus Christ. He chose a Canaanite by the name of Rahab, who was a prostitute, to be the great-great-great-great-great-great grandmother of Salmon, from whom would come Boaz, who would marry Ruth, and from these two would come King David, and from David would come forth the Lion of Judah, Jesus Christ Himself.

And Abraham journeyed from thence toward the lands of the south, and he dwelt between Kadesh and Shur and sojourned in Gerar. And Abraham said of Sarah, his wife, "She is my sister." He told the same lie that he had told in Egypt, where the LORD had performed a miracle to protect Sarah and where the Pharaoh sent him out with great wealth. Afterward, Abraham had gone back to the place where he had built the altar, and he had sought the LORD's face, and he had repented of the sin and the lie, but now he was going to move back into his flesh again. He was going to backslide just a little bit, thinking, "Boy, when I was down in Egypt, and I told that Pharaoh down there that Sarah was my sister, boy, I made out like a thief. I came out smelling like a rose, and maybe this trick will work again. I'm going to try pulling it on the king of Gerar, on good old Abimelech."

The LORD called Abraham His friend, but Abraham was a human being. He was not the LORD, he was not God, he was not a saint. He was going to sin, but the LORD would continue to work in his life, to convict him of sin, and to bring him back to the right path. Abraham was going to have to learn that he needed to be born again, not just once, but every day, every minute, every hour of his life. Being born again isn't something that happens one time and then we forget about it. God works with us constantly. Jesus works with us always.

So Abraham went, and he sojourned in Gerar, and he said of Sarah, his wife, "She is my sister." Remember, she was his half-sister, so he was only telling half a lie. So Abimelech took Sarah, and he put her in his harem. And God came to Abimelech in a dream of the night and said to him, "Behold, you are a dead man because of the woman you have taken in, for she belongs to another man. She's another man's wife."

Now Abimelech had not come near her; he had not touched her. He said, "LORD, will you even slay a righteous nation? Will you slay me and all my people who are righteous? I haven't sinned. As far as I know, this woman is that man's sister. Now you're telling me she is the man's wife. Did he not say himself unto me, 'She is my sister'? And she, even she herself said, 'He is my brother.' In the simplicity of my heart and the innocency of my hands have I done this thing."

And God said unto him in the dream, "Yes, I know that in the simplicity of your heart you have done this, and I, the LORD, have also withheld you from sinning, not against Abraham, or against Sarah, but from sinning against Me. I did not suffer you to touch her. Now, therefore, restore the man's wife, for he is a prophet, and he shall pray for you and you shall live. But if you do not restore her, you will die. But this prophet of Mine, this Abraham of Mine, this friend of Mine, he will pray for you if you humble yourself before him."

Sometimes when we go and ask somebody to pray for us, it's an act of humility, an act of humbleness. I'll never forget the night after my ordination at Melodyland. I had been a rabbi and had just been ordained a minister of the Gospel, and I had ulcers. The night after my ordination, Kathryn Kuhlman was at Melodyland to close our charismatic conference, and

I was standing right in front of the altar with several of the other ministers. As she started to pray, the Holy Spirit descended upon her, and she said, in the middle of her prayer, "Somebody was just healed of a stomach ulcer."

I had gotten home quite late that afternoon, about four-thirty, and the pastor had said that we should be in the auditorium by five-thirty, so I had gobbled my food like a turkey and rushed to make it by five-thirty. By that time I was having severe pain. Miss Kuhlman said, "Somebody was just healed. Would you come forth, the one who was healed of a stomach ulcer, and give witness and testimony unto the LORD *Jesus Christ?" I just stood there, about two feet away from her, and she continued to pray. In another few minutes, she said, "Would the person who was just healed of an ulcer, and your pain has been taken away from you, please come forward and witness to the* LORD *Jesus Christ." I was still standing there.*

In my mind, I was hearing the message, "Well, you're not going to stand up and tell all these people that you, a minister of the Gospel, have ulcers? Where's your faith?" It was the enemy talking to me. "Oh you of little faith. How could you possibly have ulcers if you're a minister?"

And Kathryn Kuhlman continued to pray, and as she was praying, the Spirit of the LORD *descended upon her, and she said, "You're about to grieve God's Holy Spirit. Come forth and witness to the* LORD *Jesus Christ. I will not continue any further until you do."*

Then I ran up to the pulpit and said, "I was just healed." And the miracle of the LORD *took place, and many others who had ulcers came forward and witnessed to the* LORD *Jesus Christ. He not only healed me, He healed each and every one*

of them. It took an act of humility to step forward and say,
"I'm such a bigshot that, really, I had an ulcer, but I wasn't
going to tell you about it." But the LORD *really healed me.*

And Abimelech rose early in the morning, called all of his
servants, and told all these things in their ears. The men were
sore afraid. They believed God. The fear of the LORD was
upon them.

And Abimelech called Abraham and said unto him, "What
is this that you have done unto us? Wherein have I sinned
against you that you have brought on me and my kingdom a
great sin? Why have you done these deeds unto me that ought
not to be done? What caused you to do it?"

And Abraham said, "Because I thought, surely, you are
a people who are heathen; you don't know the LORD. The
respect, the awe, the reverence, and the fear of the LORD is
not in this place. And I thought you would surely slay me for
my wife's sake. And moreover, I really didn't lie all that much.
She really is indeed my sister, my half-sister, the daughter of
my father, but not the daughter of my mother. I didn't really
tell you that big of a lie." Abraham was still protecting himself,
still on the defensive, rationalizing.

And Abraham said, "When God caused me to wander from
my father's house, I said unto my wife, 'This is the kindness
which you can show me in my heart. At every place where we
will come, say to the people of me, "He is my brother." ' "

And Abimelech took sheep, oxen, menservants, women-
servants, and gave them to Abraham and restored to him Sarah,
his wife. And Abimelech said, "Behold, my land is before you.
Dwell where it pleases you." The LORD had spoken to Abimelech. He had the fear of the LORD upon him. And unto Sarah

he said, "Behold, I have given your brother a thousand pieces of silver. That is for thee a covering of the eyes—to all that are with thee; and before all men, you are righted and righteous."

He said, "I have justified you, showing the world by giving the thousand pieces of silver to blind men's eyes to the wrong which has been done to you. But I did not touch you."

And Abraham prayed unto God as the LORD told Abimelech he would do for him. And God healed Abimelech, and his wife, and his maidservants, and they bore children. For the LORD had fast closed up all the wombs of the house of Abimelech because of Sarah, Abraham's wife. His whole harem had been sealed shut.

Now, the LORD had made a covenant with Abraham, with Sarah. He had said, "At the appointed time, at the set time in the following year in the spring, when I come back, Sarah is going to have a son, and his name shall be called Isaac."

And the LORD remembered his appointed time with Sarah as He had said, and the LORD did unto Sarah as He had spoken. And Sarah conceived and bore Abraham a son in his old age at the set time. The exact time the LORD said she would give birth, she gave birth, at the exact hour, the exact day.

The miracle of the LORD was made manifest to all mankind.

So Sarah conceived, and she bore Abraham a son in his old age at the set time of which God had spoken to him. And Abraham called the name of his son that was born unto him, whom Sarah bore to him, Isaac. And Abraham circumcised his son Isaac when he was eight days old, as God had commanded him.

And Abraham was a hundred years old when his son Isaac was born unto him. Sarah was ninety. And Sarah said, "God has made rejoicing for me. Everyone that hears of this will rejoice on account of me. God has given me joy, and all generations after me will rejoice with me when they hear the story of my son Isaac, how in my old age God kept His promise, how He shed His love, and His grace, and His mercy upon me."

And the child grew and was weaned. Usually, Orthodox Jews, Hebrews, don't wean their children until about two or three years of age. That's why we Jews are so healthy. And it's an occasion for a family feast. All the family gets together at the ceremony of weaning.

And Abraham and Sarah threw a great feast; they had a party on the day when they weaned Isaac. And Sarah said, "Who would have said unto Abraham that Sarah should give children suck?" She had only one child, but she said, "*children* suck," to be a living witness to the living God. As they held the weaning celebration, and people came into their tent to rejoice with them, Sarah nursed at her breast every baby that was present at that ceremony, to prove to them and to the world that she gave children suck, that her child was not adopted but that she did have milk in her breast. She said, "Who would have believed that Sarah would see such a miracle?"

And Sarah saw the son of Hagar, Ishmael, mocking, deriding Isaac in the feasting, the rejoicing over the child Isaac, inasmuch as he was the elder son, and he thought, the heir to his father's estate. And they were making a big thing out of this young kid.

When Sarah saw Ishmael mocking her son Isaac, she had a natural desire to drive him out of the house. She said unto Abraham, "Cast out this bondwoman and her son, for the son of the bondwoman shall not be heir with my son, even with

Isaac. The estate, the inheritance, the blessing, the birthright will go to my son Isaac, and not to Ishmael. Even though I took things in my own hands when I gave you my maid to be your wife, and Ishmael is your eldest son, he is not *my* son. And you shouldn't have listened to me in the first place; you should have listened to the LORD. I'm just a poor, stupid, weak woman. You got me in all this mess, Abie."

All this was very grievous to Abraham. He was a loving father; he loved his son Ishmael.

And God spoke unto Abraham and He said, "Abraham, let it not be grievous in your sight because of the lad and because of the bondwoman Hagar. In all that Sarah saith unto you, listen unto her voice, for in Isaac shall seed be called unto you."

So God said that Abraham might act upon Sarah's wish and send Ishmael away, to avoid any dispute later on concerning the inheritance.

Before Abraham died, he took another wife by the name of Keturah, and he had children by her, but he sent them all away also, so there would be no dispute about the inheritance, because God's blessing, God's promise, God's birthright was to pass to Isaac. And God told Abraham, "Of the son of the bondwoman, the slave, I will also make a nation, because he is your seed."

And Abraham rose up early in the morning, and took bread and a bottle of water, and gave it unto Hagar, putting it on her shoulder. She had the child with her, and he sent her away. "The child" was seventeen years old. He could be considered a child, a lad, as long as he lived in his father's house and was unmarried. With God, the age of accountability is the age of twenty.

When God commanded Moses to take a census of the people, He told him to count males from twenty years old and upward who were able to go to war. Males under twenty were teenagers —to stay at home with their mamas. They had not reached the age of accountability.

And Abraham sent Hagar and Ishmael away, and she departed and she wandered in the wilderness of Beer-sheba.

Beer-sheba is a desert, a wilderness area. Today they are building new apartment buildings there for Jews who are coming back to Israel from all parts of the world. And they have big mirrors, solar reflectors, on the roofs of the apartment houses to provide energy for all the heat and the hot water and the air conditioning that they want. It's in the middle of the desert, the middle of the wilderness.

Hagar strayed in the wilderness of Beer-sheba. And when the water in the bottle was gone, she cast the child under one of the shrubs, to protect him from the heat of the sun. She told him, "You stay there." And she walked away from him so she wouldn't have to look as he died of thirst and of the heat.

In Beer-sheba at certain times of the year, it can get up to 140°. I've been there when it's been that hot.

So Hagar put Ishmael under one of the shrubs to give him some protection from the heat, the sun, and the wind, and she went and she sat herself down over against him, a long way off, as though it were a bow shot, for she said, "LORD, let me not look upon the death of the child." And as she sat over against him, she lifted up her voice and she wept, and she cried unto the LORD. And God heard the voice of the lad. The lad was crying at the same time, because he was thirsty. He was already dehydrating.

And the Angel of the LORD, the same Angel who had appeared to Hagar once before and made a covenant with her, called unto Hagar out of heaven and said, "Hey, Hagar, what aileth thee? What are you sweating about? I know it's hot in the desert, but what are you sweating about? I made a covenant with you. I told you from this boy I'd bring forth twelve nations. Do you think I'm going to let him die in the wilderness, in the desert? No way."

And the Angel said to her, "Hagar, fear not. You have nothing to be afraid of, for God has heard the voice of the lad where he is. In the very circumstance that Ishmael is in, He has heard his voice."

The LORD *hears your voice and my voice in the circumstance we find ourselves in. All we have to do is cry out unto the* LORD *and say, "*LORD, *here I am. Now hear my voice. You said You would. I need Your help,* LORD, *I need it now." The* LORD *would hear your voice and my voice, and He would answer us.*

And God had heard the voice of the lad where he was. And He said, "Arise, get up, lift up the lad. Hold him fast by your hand, and I, the LORD your God, will make of him a great nation."

It's no accident that in Israel today we see more Arabs coming to know and to love the LORD Jesus Christ than my people Israel. Bethlehem is almost 100 percent Christian Arabs. Nazareth is almost 100 percent Christian Arabs. Practically all of Israel is Christian Arabs, with the exception of four Jewish cities, the new city of Jerusalem, Tel Aviv, Haifa, and Tiberias. They all know and love the LORD Jesus Christ. Some of them are third, fourth, and fifth generation Christians. Here is God's covenant, Jesus making the covenant: "I have heard the lad where he is. Hold him fast by the hand and let Me do the work, and I will make of him a great nation. You let Me be the LORD. You just hold him fast by the hand, and I'll do the rest."

And Jesus gives the same message to you and me with our kids. "You hold them fast by the hand, and I will make of them what I want them to be."

And God opened her eyes, and she saw a well of water. She went, and filled the bottle with water, and she gave the lad drink. And God was with the lad as He had promised He would be. And he grew and he dwelt in the wilderness, in the desert. And he became an archer, and he dwelt in the wilderness of Paran, and his mother took him a wife out of the land of Egypt, out of her people.

And it came to pass at that time, that Abimelech and Phichol, the captain of his host, spoke unto Abraham, saying, "God is with you in all that you do. We have no doubt about it; we have seen the miracle of God in your life, and in the way He has prospered you. Everything that you touch turns to good. Now, therefore, make an oath with us, swear unto me here, by God, that you will not deal falsely with me, nor with my son, nor with my son's son, but according to the kindness that I have shown you, you shall do unto me in the land wherein you have sojourned and you have been a stranger."

And Abraham said, "I will swear."

But Abraham reproved Abimelech because of the well of water which Abimelech's servants had violently taken away from him. And Abimelech said, "I didn't know, and I still don't know who has done this thing, neither had I heard of it until today."

So Abraham took sheep and oxen, and gave them unto Abimelech, and the two of them made a covenant. And Abraham set seven ewe lambs of the flock by themselves. And Abimelech said unto Abraham, "What do you mean by these seven ewe lambs which you have set apart by themselves?"

And Abraham said, "Truly, these seven ewe lambs you shall take of my hand, that it may be a witness unto me that I have dug this well."

Wherefore, the place was called Beer-sheba, which means "well of the oath." There an oath was taken in the name of the LORD, and a covenant was made between two parties, God being a witness to this covenant. God was dealing with Abraham for the lie he had told Abimelech about Sarah, and every well that he dug had contention with it, with the men of Abimelech.

So they made a covenant at Beer-sheba. Abimelech rose up and Phichol, the captain of his host, and they returned unto the land of the Philistines.

And Abraham planted a tamarisk tree in Beer-sheba and called there on the name of the LORD, the everlasting God. And Abraham sojourned in the land of the Philistines many days. He stayed there quite a while. Abraham's testing period was still in process.

Do you have a testing period that is still going on? You can praise the LORD that you have a testing period that is still going on in your life. Because God loves you enough that He's still testing you. He's still burning the dross and chaff out of your life.

Abraham's testing period was still taking place. The LORD was still speaking to him, still saying to him, "Abraham, I have called you My friend. I have accounted it unto you as righteousness that you believed Me by faith. You trusted Me. You believed My word, but now I'm going to test you one more time. And I'm going to ask you to do something that's going to stagger your imagination. You're not going to believe it. I'm going to give you a commandment which will sound to you like it's coming from the very devil himself. I'm going to command you to do exactly what the heathen do. I'm going to ask you to sacrifice your son alive to Me." This is what the idolaters, the heathen, did. They sacrificed their children alive to their idols.

Now the LORD God, the living God, was going to ask Abraham to do the very same thing. He was going to see if he would put his money where his mouth was. He was going to see if his heart was right—if his soul and his mind were right with God.

It came to pass after these things that God did prove Abraham, and said unto him, "Abraham," and again, Abraham said, "Here am I."

And He said, "Now, Abraham, take your son, your only son, whom you love, even Isaac, and get thee into the land of Moriah, and offer him there for a burnt offering upon one of the mountains which I will tell you of."

Again, Abraham rose up early in the morning. Even today, all Orthodox Jews rise up early in the morning to worship and praise God, because Abraham was obedient unto the LORD, and rose up early in the morning before the sun even came up. All Jews today, if they're not completed in Jesus Christ, rise up early in the morning, to worship, and thank, and praise God, just as Abraham did, who set the example for us by his obedience.

There's nothing wrong with getting up early in the morning to worship and praise God. I used to do this, but I used to gripe and complain about it. All my friends—the Christian kids— would be asleep till at least eight o'clock, but my father would wake me up at five-thirty in the morning to get up and go to the synagogue. And I used to say, "Can't we worship the LORD *at seven in the morning? Doesn't the* LORD *accept our worship at seven in the morning like He does at five-thirty?" But my father didn't change our routine. We followed the example of our patriarch, Abraham, who rose up early in the morning.*

And Abraham saddled his ass and took two of his young men with him and his son Isaac. He cleaved the wood for the burnt offering. And he rose up and went unto the place of which God had told him.

On the third day, Abraham lifted up his eyes and saw the place afar off. And Abraham said unto his young men, "Stay here with the ass, and I and the lad will go yonder, and we will worship, and *we* will come back unto you."

And Abraham took the wood of the burnt offering and laid it upon Isaac, his son, and he took in his own hand the fire and the knife, and they went, both of them together. The son of the Old Covenant was carrying the wood for his sacrifice upon his back.

And Isaac spoke unto Abraham his father and said, "My father," and he said, "Here am I, my son." And he said, "Dad, take a look. We have the wood and the fire, but where is the lamb for the burnt offering?"

And the Holy Spirit descended upon Abraham, and Abraham said, "God Himself will provide the lamb for the burnt offering, my son." According to tradition, two thousand years later, to the very day, just a few hundred yards away from where Abraham laid Isaac upon a rock to sacrifice him, God Himself provided the Lamb of God which taketh away the sin of all the world, His Son, Jesus Christ, on that very same mountain, Mount Moriah, where He carried His own cross, His own wood, upon His back to be sacrificed willingly for us. God Himself provided that sacrifice exactly as He said He would, on the very same mount, on the very same spot, the very same day.

So they went, both of them together, and they came to the place of which God had told them, and Abraham built an altar there, laid the wood in order, bound Isaac, his son, and laid him on the altar upon the wood. Notice the obedience of Isaac —no griping or complaining, no murmuring, not a word. Notice the obedience of Jesus Christ. He counted it as a joy. And Isaac permitted his father to bind him upon this altar. Isaac was thirty years of age.

And his father laid him upon the altar, upon the wood, and Abraham stretched forth his hand and took the knife to slay his son. And the Angel of the LORD, Jesus, the Redeeming Angel, called unto him out of heaven and said, "Abraham, Abraham." And he said, "Here am I." And He said, "Lay not your hand upon the lad. Neither do thou anything unto him, for now I know that you are a God-fearing man, seeing that you have not withheld your son, your only son, from Me. I have tested you; you have passed the test. I have tried you; you have passed the trial."

*There is going to come a time in your life and in my life when
the* LORD *is going to say, "I want your only son." Can we say
to the* LORD*, "As you sacrificed Your Son upon the cross of
Calvary for me,* LORD*, You can have everything that I have.
It's Yours"? This was the lesson I had to learn when my boy,
my youngest son, three and a half years of age, went home to
be with the* LORD *in a fire that destroyed our house. This was
the lesson I had to learn, that as Jesus Christ went to the cross
for me, I could say, "Thank You,* LORD*. I will praise You for
the circumstance. I will thank You. I will rejoice with You that
I know my son is with Your Son."*

And Abraham lifted up his eyes and looked, and behold,
behind him, there was a ram caught in the thicket by his horns.
And Abraham took the ram and offered him for a burnt offering instead of his son. So the burnt offering was accepted by
the LORD, and Abraham called the name of that place Jehovah-
jireh, as it is said to this day, "Jehovah will provide."

The LORD *reveals Himself to you and me in a personal and
in a real way, when we are obedient unto Him. Obedience is
better than sacrifice. God was demanding the obedience of
Abraham, not the sacrifice. "Do you love Me as I have loved
you, Abraham? Will you return the very same love that I have
given you?"*

And the Angel of the LORD called to Abraham out of heaven
the second time, and said "By Myself have I sworn, that
because you have done this thing, and you have not withheld
your son, your only son, in blessing I will bless thee, and in
multiplying I will multiply thee. I will multiply thy seed as
the stars of the heavens and as the sand which is upon the
seashore. And your Seed—" here is where it changes in the

Hebrew, to "your Seed," singular—"your Seed shall possess the gate of His enemies."

Abraham's Seed was going to defeat Satan upon the cross of Calvary. He was going to defeat him once and for all, to take away the sting of death. And God said to Abraham, "And all of your descendants who are called by His name, Christian, will not be afraid to go through that door of death, because they will know that My Son, Jesus Christ, will be there waiting for them. They'll have no fear. And in this Seed, who is coming into the world, shall all the nations of the earth be blessed, because you have been obedient to My voice."

So Abraham returned unto his young men, and they rose up, and they went together to Beer-sheba. And Abraham dwelt at Beer-sheba, and it came to pass after these things, that it was told Abraham, saying, "Behold, Milcah, she has also borne unto your brother Nahor, Uz, his firstborn, and Buz, his brother, Kemuel, the father of Aram, and Chesed, and Hazo, and Pildash, and Jidlaph, and Bethuel. And Bethuel begat Rebekah, and these eight did Milcah bear to Nahor, Abraham's brother. And his concubine, whose name was Reumah, she also bore Tebah, Gaham, Thahash, and Maachah.

This genealogy was placed here by the LORD to give us the genealogy of Rebekah, who would become the wife of Isaac, the son of the promise. Through them, Christ would be brought into the world. The son of the Old Covenant, Isaac, would never be permitted by the LORD to leave the Promised Land.

His son Jacob would go down into Egypt. His father Abraham went down into Egypt. Isaac tried to go down into Egypt, but the LORD said, "No. You are the son of the covenant; you are the son of the promise. You will stay in the

Promised Land." And the son of the Old Covenant never left the Promised Land. And Jesus, the Son of the New Covenant, never left the Promised Land except when Joseph and Mary took Him as an infant to Egypt to escape from King Herod. He never traveled two hundred miles in either direction, and yet He turned the world right side up.

Praise the LORD.

The life of Sarah was 127 years, and these were the years of the life of Sarah. And Sarah died in Kirjath-arba; the same is Hebron in the land of Canaan: and Abraham came to mourn for Sarah and to weep for her.

And Abraham rose up from before his dead and spoke unto the children of Heth, saying, "I am a stranger and a sojourner with you. Give me a possession of a burying place with you, that I may bury my dead out of my sight."

Abraham was among the heathen Hittites, seeking a place to bury his wife. He had come to mourn for Sarah and to weep for her. "Mourning" in the Hebrew indicates loud wailing and crying, which is still the custom with all Orthodox Jews today. It's a manifestation of grief.

He spoke to the Hittites, saying, "I am a stranger, a sojourner with you, and it is far better if I bury my dead out of my sight." This is the first reference in the Bible to burial. And the reverential concern which Abraham had for Sarah showed his love for her. He was seeking a place of honor to bury her, and from this evolved the Jewish law that it is good for a person to bury his dead.

Abraham asked the children of Heth for a place to bury his dead out of his sight. And the children of Heth answered Abraham, saying unto him, "Hear us, my lord. You are a mighty prince among us. In the choice of all our sepulchers, bury your dead. None of us shall withhold from you his sepulcher, but that you may bury your dead."

So, Abraham bowed down to them, saying, "If it be your mind that I should bury my dead out of my sight, hear me and entreat for me to Ephron, the son of Zohar, that he may give me the cave of Machpelah, which he has, which is in the end of his field, for the full price. Let him give it to me in the midst of you for a possession of a burying place."

Now Ephron was sitting in the midst of the children of Heth, and Ephron, the Hittite, answered Abraham in the hearing of the children of Heth, even all of them that went in at the gate of his city, saying, "No, my lord, hear me. The field I give unto you, and the cave that is therein, I give it to you; in the presence of the sons of my people, I give it to you. Bury your dead. I give it to you as a gift. I want nothing in return for it. In the presence of all my people, all these witnesses, I'm going to give you the cave of Machpelah to bury your dead."

And Abraham bowed down before the people of the land, and he spoke unto Ephron in the hearing of the people of the land, saying, "If you will, I pray thee, hear me. I will give you the price of the field. Take it of me and I will bury my dead."

And Ephron answered Abraham, saying unto him, "My lord, why don't you listen unto me? The piece of land is worth four hundred shekels of silver. But let me give you the land. Bury, therefore, your dead. Don't worry about the money."

This was a very high price to pay for a piece of land. But Abraham, trusting the LORD, listened unto Ephron. Then Abraham weighed to Ephron the silver which he had named—four hundred shekels of silver, current money with the merchant. Abraham weighed it out to him in silver and gave it to him.

He did this to ensure a covenant relationship. And it became a field forever for the possession of Abraham and his descendants. Nobody could ever say, 'We gave it to you as a gift, but now we have a new government, a new premier, and we're going to take it back." Abraham had paid them for it. They were bound by a covenant that was agreed upon in front of all the elders in the gate of the city.

So, the field of Ephron, which was in Machpelah, which was before Mamre, the field, and the cave, which was therein, and all the trees that were in the field, that were in all the borders round about, were made sure. When the Hebrew says that something was "made sure," it means that it was guaranteed as a surety forever to Abraham and his descendants.

And after this, Abraham buried Sarah, his wife, in the cave of the field of Machpelah before Mamre; the same is Hebron in the land of Canaan. And the field, and the cave that is therein, were made sure unto Abraham for a possession of a burying place by the sons of Heth. It's still there today.

The field has been in Moslem hands for the last eight hundred years. And up until 1971, even though it belonged to Abraham, no Jew was allowed to go past the first seven of the steps leading to it. Abraham is also the father of the Ishmaelites, the Arabs. And since the Arabs had control and possession of the land, they also took control of the Dome of the Rock where Abraham laid Isaac to sacrifice him, and they took control of the cave of Machpelah.

But recently, year by year, the signs in Arabic have been replaced by signs in Hebrew. And when you go in, you have to cover your head, because the signs in Hebrew say you are upon holy ground. And instead of Arab guards, there are Israeli guards. Today, all Jews can go in past the first landing of steps, and they can look down and see where Abraham is buried, where Sarah is buried, Isaac, Jacob, Leah, and Rebekah. Rachel is buried on the road to Bethlehem.

And Abraham was old, well stricken in age, and the LORD had kept His promise to bless him in all things, spiritually, physically, mentally, financially.

And Abraham said unto his eldest servant of his house, the one who ruled over all that he had, "Put, I pray thee, your hand under my thigh—" that was the Jewish custom in taking an oath—"and I will make you swear by the LORD, the God of heaven, the God of the earth, that you will not take a wife for my son of the daughters of the Canaanites among whom I dwell. But you shall go unto my country, to my kindred, and take a wife for my son, even Isaac. I will not have him mixing with the heathen, with their idolatries, and the abominations that are round about them. Swear to me by the God of heaven, and the God of earth, that you will go back to my family, to my kindred, and bring back a bride for my son."

And the servant, Eliezer, said unto him, "Perhaps the woman will not be willing to follow me into this land. Must I needs bring your son back unto the land from where you came? If I go there and I can't find a woman who will go back with me into the land of Canaan, can I come back and bring your son Isaac back to your homeland?"

Abraham said unto him, "Beware. Beware that you bring not my son back there. He is the son of the promise. This land has been promised to him. He will never leave the land of the promise. Beware that you do not take him back there.

"The LORD God of heaven, who took me from my father's house, and from the land of my nativity, who spoke unto me and who swore unto me, saying, 'Unto your seed will I give this land,' He will send His angel before you, and you shall take a wife for my son from my homeland.

"You don't have to worry, Eliezer. The LORD is going before you, to prepare the way. Any crooked path that you are going to run into will be straightened out. Everything will be just fine. You just remain obedient unto me and unto the LORD. And if the woman is not willing to follow you, then you shall be clear from this, my oath, only you shall not bring my son back there."

The same teaching was embodied in a parable that Jesus taught, about somebody plowing in a field. If you are plowing and planting, sowing seed, and you look behind you, the furrow will be all zigzagged and crooked. Jesus said, "Look straight ahead, don't look behind. I'm your God; I'm your LORD. I'm going before you. Just look at Me and follow Me, and that furrow will be straight. It'll be nice and clean and clear, and I will make sure that it stays that way. Don't look back."

And the servant put his hand under the thigh of Abraham his master, and swore unto him concerning this matter.

And the servant took ten camels of the camels of his master and departed, having all goodly things of his master in his hand, and he arose and he went to Aram-naharaim, unto the city of Nahor, the brother of Abraham. Abraham had settled in Haran after the LORD delivered him from Ur of the Chaldees.

And his servant went back to Aram-naharaim, which means,

"the city of two rivers," the Euphrates and the Tigris, to Haran, the city of Nahor where his family dwelt.

Nahor was an idol worshiper, but once in a while he remembered the Lord. He was like a Yo-Yo. One day he was for the Lord; the next day he was for idolatry. If things were going good and fine and well, the Lord was a good guy, and He was all right. Nahor would trust the Lord. But if something happened that wasn't exactly right with him, or if anything crossed him, or his path, or his family, then he went back to idolatry.

Eliezer went back to the city where the two rivers meet, and he made the camels to kneel down outside the city by the well of water at the time of evening, the time when the women went out to draw water. It was too hot to go out in the afternoon or in the morning.

According to Jewish custom, if the servant was going to bring back a bride, he must bring gifts, not only for the bride, but for her family. Eliezer had ten camels loaded down with gifts, and they'd been traveling many days to leave the land of Canaan to go back to Mesopotamia.

So he made the camels kneel down outside the city by the well of the water at the time of the evening, the time that women went out to get water. He was going to make a fleece, the first fleece we see in the Bible. And Eliezer, the servant of Abraham, the servant of God, prayed to the Lord, saying, "O Lord, the God of my master Abraham, send me, I pray thee, good speed this day, and show kindness unto my master Abraham, as You have promised him. Look Lord, behold, I am standing by the fountain of water, and the daughters of men, the daughters of all kinds of people, are coming out of the city to draw water. Now, Lord, let it come to pass that the damsel to whom I shall say, 'Let down your pitcher, I pray thee, that I may drink,' and she shall say, 'Drink, and I will give your camels drink also,' let her be the same that You have appointed for Your servant Isaac. And thereby shall I know that You have shown kindness unto my master."

He had ten camels with him. A thirsty camel can drink thirty gallons of water—which means that this female was going to have to draw three hundred gallons of water out of that well. Quite a task. The Lord was going to have to answer this prayer and this fleece; it would be in the realm of the miraculous.

Whenever you set a fleece before the Lord, make sure it is in the realm of the miraculous. Then you will know if the Lord has answered it or not.

And it came to pass, that before he had done speaking to the Lord, behold, Rebekah came out, who was born to Bethuel, the son of Milcah, the wife of Nahor, Abraham's brother, with her pitcher upon her shoulder. And the damsel was very fair to look upon, a virgin, Hebrew *bethulah*, neither had any man known her intimately.

Notice that in Genesis 24:16, Rebekah is called a virgin, Hebrew *bethulah*. Later, in Genesis 24:43, she is called a virgin, Hebrew *almah*. And in Isaiah 7:14, the Lord, speaking by the Holy Spirit through the prophet Isaiah, said, "The Lord Himself shall give you a sign: Behold, a virgin *(almah)* shall conceive and shall bear a son and shall call his name Immanuel."

What's the difference between an *almah* and a *bethulah*? Why am I taking the trouble to even discuss it?

Two thousand years after Christ was born to the Virgin Mary, people would stand up and say that *almah* doesn't mean virgin—that it means a young woman, not necessarily a virgin.

They would say it was all poppycock that God by His Holy Spirit spoke through Isaiah saying, "The LORD Himself shall give you a sign—a virgin *(almah)* shall conceive." But the LORD had already set a precedent, a witness, and a testimony for Himself, and for Jesus Christ, and for Mary, right here in this chapter in Genesis.

Rebekah, when she appeared at the fountain in the afternoon before she drew the water was a virgin, a *bethulah*. A few hours later, she was still a virgin, but she was called an *almah*, the only difference being that she now had a ring in her nose, she was betrothed, she was espoused. She had consented to marriage. And the LORD, speaking through Isaiah, had specified that the woman who would conceive and bear a son Immanuel would be a virgin—an espoused, engaged, betrothed virgin. And Hebrew words used in the account of Rebekah's engagement to Isaac make it absolutely, incontrovertibly clear.

And the damsel went down to the fountain, and filled her pitcher, and came up. And the servant ran to meet her and said, "Give me to drink, I pray thee, a little water out of your pitcher."

And she said, "Drink, my lord." And she hasted, and she let down her pitcher upon her hand, and gave him drink. And when she had done giving him drink, she said, "I will draw for your camels also, until they have all done drinking." The LORD was answering the fleece and the prayer. She said, "I'll not just give them a little sip, I'll draw water until they've all had their fill of water."

Three hundred gallons—that was not an easy task. But she hastened. She emptied her pitcher into the trough, ran again unto the well to draw, and drew for all the camels.

And the man just stood there and looked upon her, very steadily. He was not going to help her. He was going to let the LORD answer the prayer. He looked steadfastly upon her, holding his peace, to know whether the LORD has made his journey prosperous or not. He was standing still to see the salvation of the LORD. He would not know until the last camel had his belly full of water whether she would quit or not. If she quit in the middle of the task, then the LORD had not answered the fleece, but if she continued no matter how tired she got, until every camel had had his fill, he would know the LORD had answered his prayer and honored the fleece.

And it came to pass as the camels had done drinking, had had their fill, the man took a golden earring of half a shekel weight, and two bracelets for her hands of ten shekels weight of gold and said, "Whose daughter art thou? Tell me, I pray you, who you are. Is there room in your father's house for us to lodge in?"

And she said unto him, "I am the daughter of Bethuel, the son of Milcah, whom she bore unto Nahor." She said moreover unto him, "We have both straw and provender enough, and room to lodge in."

And the man bowed his head and prostrated himself before the LORD. That was the Hebrew way to worship, and still is today. Jews prostrate themselves before the LORD, and then they stand up and lift up their hands in song and praise and thanksgiving unto the LORD. They never bend their knees to anybody, because that's idolatry. And Eliezer prostrated himself before the LORD.

The ring that he gave Rebekah was a nose ring. This was to

indicate his intentions and impress Laban with Abraham's wealth.

So Eliezer put the ring in her nose, he blessed the LORD and prostrated himself before the LORD, and he said, "Blessed be the LORD, the God of my master, Abraham, who has not forsaken His mercy and His truth toward my master, who has kept every promise He has given him. As for me, the LORD has led me in the way to the house of my master's brethren."

And the damsel ran and told her mother's house according to these words.

And Rebekah had a brother, and his name was Laban, and Laban ran out unto the man, unto the fountain. And it came to pass when he saw the ring and the bracelets upon his sister's hands, and when he heard the words of Rebekah his sister, saying, "Thus spoke the man unto me," that he came unto the man. And, behold, Eliezer stood by the camels at the fountain.

And Laban said, "Come in, thou blessed of the LORD. How come you're standing outside already yet? With all that gold and silver that you have, come into the house. For I have cleared the house and made room even for the camels."

And Eliezer came into the house. Laban ungirded the camels and gave straw and provender for the camels, and water to wash his feet and the feet of the men that were with him. And there was set food before him to eat, but he said, "I will not eat until I have told of my mission."

And Laban said, "Speak on."

And he said, "I am Abraham's servant. And the LORD has blessed my master greatly, and he has become great. He has given him flocks, herds, silver, gold, menservants, maidservants, camels, and asses. And Sarah, my master's wife, bore a son to my master when she was old, and unto him hath he given all that he hath.

"And my master made me swear, saying, 'You shall not take a wife to my son of the daughters of the Canaanites, in whose land I dwell. But you shall go unto my father's house, to my kindred, and take a wife for my son.'

"And I said unto my master, 'Perhaps the woman will not follow me.'

"And he said unto me, 'The LORD, before whom I walk, will send His angel with you, and He will prosper your way. And you shall take a wife for my son of my kindred of my father's house.' "

Notice the faith that Abraham had in the LORD. He said, "The LORD before whom I walk will—" not perhaps, not might —"He will send His angel with you. He will prosper your way, and you shall take a wife for my son of my family and of my father's house." Abraham had no doubts. When the LORD spoke to him, he believed God. Whatever God told him, he believed. He trusted in Him entirely.

And Eliezer said, "Then my master said, 'If they give her not unto thee, then you shall be cleared from my oath.'

"And I came this day unto the fountain, and I said, 'O LORD—' " he was witnessing to the family—" 'O LORD, the God of my master, Abraham, if now You do prosper my way which I go, behold, take a look, I'm standing by the fountain of water. Let it come to pass that the maid that shall come forth to draw to whom I shall say, "Give me, I pray thee, a little water from your pitcher to drink," and she shall say unto me, "Both drink you, and I will also draw for your camels," let the same be the woman whom the LORD hath appointed for my master's son.'

And before I had finished speaking to my heart—I was praying in my heart to the LORD—behold, Rebekah came forth with her pitcher on her shoulder, and she went down unto the fountain and drew, and I said unto her, 'Let me drink, I pray thee.'

"And she made haste, and let down her pitcher from her shoulder, and said, 'Drink, and I will give your camels drink also.'

"So I drank, and she made the camels drink also. And I asked her, 'Whose daughter are thou?'

"And she said, 'The daughter of Bethuel, Nahor's son, whom Milcah bore unto him.' And I put the ring upon her nose and the bracelets upon her hands. And I bowed my head, and I prostrated myself before the LORD and blessed the LORD, the God of my master Abraham, who had led me in the right way to take my master's brother's daughter for his son.

"And now, if you will deal kindly and truly with my master, tell me. And if not, tell me, that I may turn to the right hand or to the left."

Then Laban and Bethuel answered and said, "The thing proceedeth from the LORD. We cannot speak unto thee good or bad. Behold, Rebekah is before thee. Take her and go, and let her be your master's son's wife as the LORD has spoken."

And it came to pass that when Abraham's servant heard their words, he bowed himself down to the earth before the LORD. He prostrated himself again. And the servant brought forth jewels of silver, jewels of gold, and raiment, and gave them to Rebekah. He gave also to her brother and her mother precious things. And they did eat and drink, he and the men that were with him. They tarried all night. They rose up in the morning and Eliezer said, "Send me away unto my master."

And her brother and her mother said, "Let the damsel abide with us a few days, at the least ten; after that, she shall go."

And he said unto them, "Delay me not, seeing the LORD has prospered my way. Send me away that I may go to my master."

And they said, "We will call the damsel, and inquire at her mouth." And they called Rebekah, and they said unto her, "Will you go with this man?"

And she said, "I will go."

And they sent away Rebekah, their sister, and her nurse, and Abraham's servant, and his men. And they blessed Rebekah and said unto her (this blessing is used to this day at every Hebrew wedding), "Our sister, be thou the mother of thousands of ten thousands, and let your Seed"—singular, not plural—"possess the gate of those that hate them."

And Rebekah arose, and her damsels, and they rode upon the camels, and followed the man. And the servant took Rebekah and went his way.

And Isaac came from the way of the well Lahai-roi, for he dwelt in the land of the south. And Isaac went out to pray in the field at eventide, and he lifted up his eyes, and saw, and behold, there were camels coming.

And Rebekah lifted up her eyes, and when she saw Isaac, she alighted from the camel. And she said unto Eliezer, "What man is that that walketh in the field to meet us?"

And the servant said, "It is my master."

She took her veil and covered herself, and the servant told Isaac all the things that he had done, how the LORD had answered his prayer and his fleece, assuring Isaac that she was the right woman from the LORD.

And Isaac brought her into his mother Sarah's tent. He took

Rebekah, she became his wife, and he loved her, and Isaac was comforted, for his mother had died.

Notice the order of the words in Hebrew—"He took Rebekah, she became his wife, and he loved her."

In our modern society, we would have placed "He loved her" first. "We fell in love, and that was it. And after the first few months of love, we had a falling away, and we ended up in the divorce court." That's why so many of our marriages are ending up in divorce, because we think we fall in love, and then we get married. However important it is that love should precede marriage, it is far more important that it should continue after marriage.

While the modern attitude lays all the stress on romance before the marriage, the old Hebrew view emphasized the lifelong devotion and affection after the marriage, the continuous process of growth and love for the rest of their lives.

In the Talmud, our rabbis say that Rebekah filled the gap caused in Isaac's life by the death of his mother. And our rabbis also explain that on the death of Sarah, the blessings that had attended the household of Abraham, and the pious customs which had distinguished his household came to an end, because there was not a woman in the tent to light the sabbath lamp and the sabbath candles unto the LORD.

When Isaac brought Rebekah into Sarah's tent, all the blessings of the LORD were restored, and the sabbath lamp once more illuminated the home of the patriarch Abraham, and Rebekah continued as well all the other faithfulness and worship to the LORD with which Sarah had demonstrated her worship, praise, and adoration of the living God. Even today, the only public

prayer any Hebrew woman is allowed to pray is when she lights
the sabbath lamp ushering in the holiness of the sabbath.

And Abraham took himself another wife, and her name was
Keturah. He was an old man, but when the LORD promised him
His blessing in all things, He kept His promise. And Keturah
bore him Zimran, Jokshan, Medan, Midian, Ishbak, and Shuah.
And Jokshan begat Sheba and Dedan. And the sons of Dedan
were Asshurim, Letushim, and Leummim. And the sons of
Midian were Ephah, Epher, Hanoch, Abidah, and Eldaah. All
these were the children of Keturah.

And Abraham gave all that he had unto Isaac. But unto the
sons of the concubines—the sons of Hagar, the descendants of
Ishmael, his grandchildren, and the sons of Keturah—Abraham gave gifts. He sent them away from Isaac his son while he
yet lived. He sent them eastward into the east country. Isaac
was the only heir, and the promise and the covenant was
passed through him.

And these are the days of the years of Abraham's life which
he lived, an hundred and threescore and fifteen years—175
years. Then Abraham expired and died in a good old age, an
old man, full of years, and was gathered to his people. And
Isaac and Ishmael, his sons, buried him in the cave of Machpelah, in the field of Ephron, the Hittite, the son of Zohar,
which is before Mamre. In the field which Abraham purchased
of the sons of Heth, there was Abraham buried, and Sarah his
wife.

7
And God Blessed Isaac
(Genesis 25:11—27)

And it came to pass after the death of Abraham, that God blessed his son Isaac, and Isaac dwelt by the well Lahai-roi. He stayed where the blessings of the LORD were to be found. The LORD had appeared there, and he was going to stay there.

Now these are the generations of Ishmael, Abraham's son, whom Hagar the Egyptian, Sarah's handmaid, bare unto Abraham. And these are the names of the sons of Ishmael, by their names, according to their generations: the firstborn of Ishmael, Nebaioth; and Kedar, Adbeel, and Mibsam. And Mishma, Dumah, Massa, Hadad, Tema, Jetur, Naphish, and Kedemah. These are the sons of Ishmael. These are their names by their villages, by their towns, and by their castles—twelve princes according to their nations.

The LORD had made a covenant with Hagar that there would be twelve princes descended from Ishmael, twelve nations. He kept His promise.

And these are the years of the life of Ishmael, 137 years, and he died, and was gathered unto his people.

And they dwelt from Havilah unto Shur, that is before Egypt, as you go toward Assyria over against all his brethren, exactly as the Angel of the LORD told Hagar, "Know for a surety that he will dwell side by side with his brethren." The Jew and the Arab would settle side by side, and this is the way they remain today.

And these are the generations of Isaac, Abraham's son. Abraham begat Isaac. And Isaac was forty years old when he took Rebekah, the daughter of Bethuel, the Aramean of Padan-aram, the sister of Laban, the Aramean, to be his wife. And Isaac entreated the LORD for his wife, because she was barren.

Isaac was a good priest and prophet in his home. When his wife was barren, she did not have to come to him and say, "Go to the LORD," or, "What is wrong that I'm not pregnant?" Isaac had discernment of spirit; he was the son of the promise, and as prophet and priest in his home, he entreated the LORD for his wife. He prayed, "LORD, You kept Your promise to my father, Abraham. You gave me a promise, and I am counting on You to keep it."

The LORD kept His promise. He let Himself be entreated of Isaac by his intercessory prayer. And Rebekah, his wife, conceived.

And the children within her struggled together, and she said, "If it be so, wherefore do I live?" Life was unbearable for her, and she willed to die.

There wasn't a day that went by without a struggle taking place within her. Jake and Esau were fighting already yet. And Jakie was saying, "I want that birthright and the blessing. I'm going to come out first so I can get it. It's strictly one hundred percent kosher—I want it, and if I can't get it any other way, I'll get it by conniving." The struggle between Jacob and Esau began even before the children were born.

And Rebekah went to inquire of the LORD. She said, "Hey God, what's happening? How come You gave me a problem?"

And the LORD said unto her after she inquired of Him, "There are two nations in your womb, and two people shall be separated from your bowels. And one people shall be stronger than the other people, and the elder shall serve the younger."

God let Rebekah in on His revealed will, that the elder would serve the younger. And as her days to be delivered were fulfilled, behold, there were twins in her womb. And the first came forth red all over like an hairy mantle, and they called his name Esau. And after that came forth his brother, and his hand held firm on Esau's heel, and his name was called Jacob. Jacob was holding onto Esau, trying to get out first. And Isaac was threescore years old—sixty years—when Jacob and Esau were born.

And the boys grew; and Esau was a cunning hunter, a man of the field; and Jacob was a quiet man, dwelling in tents. Naturally, Isaac related to Esau, the hunter. He was a man's man. Jakie, little Jakie, stayed in the tent with his mother. Jacob was a mama's boy.

Now Isaac loved Esau because he did eat of his venison, but Rebekah loved Jacob. He stayed with her in the tent, and he hung onto her apron strings. And Rebekah loved him because he stuck close by her and because the LORD had revealed to her that the elder would serve the younger.

And Jacob sod pottage—he was boiling a lentil stew—and

Esau came in from the field, and he was faint. And Esau said to Jacob, "Let me swallow, I pray thee, some of your red pottage, for I am faint." Therefore was his name called Edom, meaning red.

And Jacob said, "Sell me first your birthright." The conniving was coming out.

And Esau said "Behold, I am at the point of death; and what profit shall my birthright be to me?"

And Jacob said, "Swear to me first." And he swore unto him. And he sold his birthright unto Jacob.

Then Jacob gave Esau bread and pottage of lentils, and he did eat and drink. Then Esau rose up and went his way, and Esau despised his birthright.

Both of them were connivers. Esau figured that the birthright by itself was no good. The blessing had to go with the birthright to make it valid, to make it kosher. So even if Jacob had the birthright, before Isaac died, Esau, being the eldest, would receive the blessing. And with the blessing would go the inheritance and the promises of God. Esau figured he could outwit Jacob and still receive the blessing, even though he had sold his birthright. So he despised his birthright, he treated it as nothing, he was weak enough to sell it for a bowl of lentils and rice.

Now, there was famine in the land, another famine in addition to the first famine that was in the days of Abraham. And Isaac went unto Abimelech, the king of the Philistines, unto Gerar. Abimelech was an old man; he was king in the days of Abraham, and he was still king.

And the LORD appeared unto Isaac and said, "Do not go down into Egypt. Dwell in the land which I shall tell you of.

Sojourn in this land, and I will be with you. I will bless you, for unto you and unto your seed, I will give all these lands, and I will establish the oath which I swore unto Abraham, your father. I will multiply your seed as the stars of the heavens, and I will give unto your seed all these lands, and by your Seed—" singular, meaning Jesus Christ—"shall all the nations of the earth bless themselves."

God gave Isaac the same Abrahamic covenant that you and I receive today through Jesus Christ. And He told him why: "Because that Abraham listened to My voice, he kept My charge, he kept My commandments, he kept My statutes and My laws."

And Isaac dwelt in Gerar. And the men of the place asked him of his wife, and he said, "She's my sister." She was really his cousin, the daughter of his father's brother.

Isaac had heard from his father Abraham how he had told the king of Egypt and the king of Gerar, Abimelech, that Sarah was his sister, and how he, Abraham, had become very wealthy because of this deception.

The LORD just got through giving Isaac every promise in the book. But when the men of Gerar asked him of his wife, he said, "She's my sister," because he feared to say, "She is my wife," lest the men of the place should kill him, for Rebekah was fair to look upon. He didn't trust the LORD.

And it came to pass that when Isaac had been there a long time, that Abimelech, the king of the Philistines, looked out a window and saw Isaac sporting with Rebekah, his wife. He was petting her, caressing her.

And Abimelech called to Isaac and said, "Behold, of a surety, she is your wife, so why did you say she was your sister?"

And Isaac said to him, "Because I said, 'Lest I die because of her.' I didn't want to die because of her."

And Abimelech said, "What is this that you have done unto us? One of my people might have lain with your wife, and you would have brought guiltiness upon us." And Abimelech charged all the people, saying, "He that toucheth this man or his wife shall surely be put to death." He remembered what the LORD had done to him when he had taken Sarah for his harem.

And Isaac sowed in that land and received in the same year an hundredfold, and the LORD blessed him. And the man waxed great and even more and more, until he became very great. And he had possession of flocks, possession of herds, a great household, and the Philistines envied him.

All the wells which his father's servants had dug in the days of Abraham, his father, the Philistines had stopped and filled with earth. And Abimelech said unto Isaac, "Go from us, for you are much mightier than we."

Isaac departed from there to camp in the valley of Gerar, and dwelt there. And Isaac dug again the wells of water, which they had dug in the days of Abraham, his father, for the Philistines had stopped them after the death of Abraham. And he called their names after the names by which his father had called them. And Isaac's servants digged in the valley, and found there a well of living water. Living water is the opposite of stagnant water; it was spring water, living water.

And the herdsmen of Gerar strove with Isaac's herdsmen, saying, "The water is ours." And he called the name of the well Esek which in Hebrew means "contention," because there they contended with him.

And they dug another well, and they strove for that one also,

139

and he called the name of it Sitnah. And he removed from there, and he dug another well, and for that they strove not, and he called the name of it Rehoboth, meaning "room" or "latitude," broad places. And he said, "For now the LORD has made room for us, and we shall be fruitful in the land."

And he went up from thence to Beer-sheba, the well where the oath was made. And the LORD appeared unto him in person the same night, and He said, "I am the God of Abraham, your father. Fear not, for I am with thee, and I will bless thee, and I will multiply your seed for My servant Abraham's sake."

And he built an altar there, and he called upon the name of the LORD. He pitched his tent there, and there Isaac's servants dug a well.

Then Abimelech went to him from Gerar, and Ahuzzath, his friend, and Phichol, the captain of his host. And Isaac said unto them, "Wherefore are you come unto me, seeing that you hate me, and you have sent me away from you?"

And they said, "We saw, very plainly, that the LORD was with you, and we said, 'Let there now be an oath between us, even between us and you, and let us make a covenant with you, that you will do us no hurt, as we have not touched you, and as we have done nothing unto you but good, and we have sent you away in peace, and now you are blessed of the LORD.'" They saw the LORD's blessing, and the love, and the grace, and the mercy of God, and the favor of God in his life. They knew he was blessed of the LORD.

They had hated him, but he did not return evil for evil. He did not return hatred for hatred. He returned peace, kindness for hatred. They asked him to leave the land. He was obedient unto the people of the land that was rightfully given to him by the LORD.

And he made them a feast, and they did eat and drink. They rose up in the morning and swore one to another, and Isaac sent them away, and they departed from him in peace.

And it came to pass the same day, that Isaac's servants came and told him concerning the well which they had dug, and said unto him, "We have found water." And he called it *Sheba*, meaning, in the Hebrew, "good fortune," as well as "oath." Therefore, the name of the city is till today Beer-sheba, just as it was called when Abraham made a covenant there.

When Esau was forty years old, he took to wife Judith, the daughter of Beeri, the Hittite, and Basemath, the daughter of Elon, the Hittite. And they were a bitterness of spirit to Isaac and to Rebekah. Esau had married into idolatry. His wife was a daughter of the land, who did not know the living God, who did not want to know the living God.

And Isaac was getting old, but Esau still expected to get the blessing from him. Jacob had the birthright, but the birthright was no good without the blessing.

And it came to pass, that when Isaac was old and his eyes were dim, so that he could not see, he called Esau, his elder son, and said unto him, "My son."

And he said unto him, "Here am I," just as his father, Isaac, had answered *his* father, Abraham, saying, "Here am I." "Here am I" means, "I am here to do your bidding and to do your will." When the LORD spoke to Abraham, Abraham had said, "Here am I, obedient, ready to move out on Your word."

And Isaac said, "Behold now, I am old. I know not the day of my death. Therefore, now take, I pray thee, your weapons, your quiver, your bow, and go out to the field and take me venison and make me savory food such as I love, and bring it to me, that I may eat, that my soul may bless thee before I die." He knew he was about to die, and he wanted to bless his beloved favorite son, Esau.

The Jewish woman has a very good habit of always eavesdropping. And Rebekah heard when Isaac spoke to Esau, *his* son. The Scripture doesn't say "*her* son," or "*our* son," it says "*his* son," because Esau was really the old man's favorite.

And Esau went to the field to hunt for venison and to bring it.

And Rebekah spoke unto Jacob, *her* son saying, "Behold, I heard your father speak unto Esau, your brother, saying, 'Bring me venison, and make me savory meat, that I may eat, and bless thee before the Lord before my death.' Now, therefore, my son, listen to my voice. Hearken to my voice according to that which I command thee. Go now to the flock and fetch me from there two good kids of the goats. I will make them savory food for your father, such as he loves, and you shall bring it to your father so that he may eat, so that he may bless *thee* before his death, so that you'll receive the blessing instead of Esau."

And Jacob said to Rebekah, his mother, "Behold, Esau, my brother, is a hairy man, and I am a smooth man. What are we going to do now, Mom? My father is no dumb-dumb. Perhaps he will feel me, and I will seem to him as one who mocks him, and I will bring a curse upon me and not a blessing."

And his mother said unto him, "Upon me be thy curse, my son. Only listen to my voice and go fetch me them." She just cursed herself, and after this deceiving of Isaac, she would have to send Jacob away. He would flee for his life from his brother Esau, because Esau would be out to kill him. She would never see Jacob, her son, again alive, and he would never see his mother again. And she brought that curse upon herself.

And Jacob went, and he fetched, and he brought the kids to his mother, and his mother made savory food, such as his father loved.

And Rebekah took the choicest garments of Esau, her elder son, which were with her in the house, and put them upon Jacob, her younger son. Isaac was nearly blind, but he could still smell. And Esau's garments had the smell of the field upon them, and they smelled like Esau. Jacob's garments smelled entirely different, because he stayed in the tent with mama.

Rebekah took Esau's choicest garments, and placed them upon Jacob, her younger son, and then she put the skins of the kids of the goats upon his hands and upon the smooth of his neck, and upon his arms, right up to the elbows. That was just in case his father would say, "My son, come close to me that I may kiss you." If he felt the hair upon the smooth of Jacob's neck, he would say, "It's Esau." Rebekah was prepared for every eventuality, in the deception of Isaac.

So she put the skins of the kids of the goats upon Jacob's hands and upon the smooth of his neck. And she gave the savory food and the bread which she had prepared into the hand of her son, Jacob.

And he came unto his father and said, "My father."

And he said, "Here am I; who art thou, my son? Who are you?" Isaac was nearly blind, and he didn't know who it was.

And Jacob said unto his father, "I am Esau, your firstborn." He just told an out-and-out lie. "I am Esau, your firstborn son. I have done according as you have commanded me. Arise,

I pray thee, sit and eat of my venison, that your soul may bless me."

And Isaac said unto his son, "How is it that you have found it so quickly, my son?"

And Jacob said, "Because the LORD *your* God sent me good speed." He was afraid at this point to say, "the LORD *our* God," or "the LORD *my* God," because he knew he was transgressing the commandment of the LORD in the deception, in the lie.

And Isaac said unto Jacob, "Come near, I pray thee, that I may feel thee, my son, whether you be my very son Esau or not." Rebekah knew this was going to happen, and she had made preparation for it. And Jacob went near unto Isaac, his father, and he felt him, and he said, "The voice is the voice of Jacob, but the hands are the hands of Esau."

Hebrew oral tradition handed down to us from this time says that Satan is always out to destroy God's people. And Satan was talking one day with his demons, with his angels, and he asked them, "How can I go about destroying Israel? How can I cause them to sin so that God will bring judgment upon them?" And the answer came forth from his lieutenant, saying, "If you happen to be passing by the house of the worship of the LORD, and you don't hear any children there praising and worshiping God, know that the hands are the hands of Esau, and you can go in and attack. But if you happen to be passing by and you hear the little children singing praises unto the LORD and worshiping the LORD, know that that is the voice of Jacob, and you cannot attack because they are praising the LORD. As long as they are praising the LORD, you will never attack Israel. You'll never attack any of God's people as long as they're worshiping and praising God."

How do we get out from under the attack of the enemy? We continue to praise God in every circumstance. We thank Jesus for everything that happens to us.

And Isaac discerned him not. He had lost his discernment of spirit. He had been moving in the Holy Spirit, since the LORD gave him wisdom, knowledge, and discernment. He recognized the voice of Jacob. He felt the hands, and the hands were the hands of Esau. But Isaac did not discern him because God's will, God's purpose, God's plan, was in action. The LORD took away Isaac's discernment of spirit at this particular time so that the blessing could be passed on to Jacob. This was God's will in the first place, that the elder would serve the younger.

And the Scripture says, "He discerned him not because his hands were hairy, as his brother Esau's hands, so he blessed him."

This is a lesson to you and me as Christians. Do we look upon the surface? Or do we ask the LORD, "LORD, give me Your discernment of spirit, and then I will make a move. When You tell me to move, I will move. I'm not going to go by the surface, by what I feel. I'm not going to move by the hands of Esau, but I'm going to move by Your Spirit. Give me discernment showing me which way I should go." When you ask, you can know God will give it to you. He always will. He'll give you a peace that passes all understanding. No matter where you intend to go, or where you think you intend to go, if He does not want you to go, He will shut a door. If He shuts that door, know you are not to go. You'll have turmoil if you go. You will not have the peace that passes all understanding. If you are to go, you will have perfect peace. And it will stay with you if you stay in the LORD's will.

And Isaac asked Jacob one more time, "Are you really my son Esau?"

And he said, "I am," making it twice that he had lied to his father.

And now Isaac said, "Bring it near to me, and I will eat of my son's venison that my soul may bless you." And he brought it near to him, and he did eat, and he brought him wine, and he drank. And his father Isaac said unto him, "Come near now, and kiss me, my son," exactly as Rebekah had suspected he would do.

And Jacob came near, and he kissed him upon the neck. He felt the hair upon his neck, and he also smelled his garment. And as Isaac smelled the smell of his raiment, he blessed him, saying, "See, the smell of my son is as the smell of a field which the LORD hath blessed. So God give thee of the dew of heaven, and of the fat places of the earth, and plenty of corn and wine. Let peoples serve thee, and nations bow down to thee. Be lord over your brethren, and let your mother's sons bow down to thee. Cursed be every one that curseth thee, and blessed be everyone that blesses thee." That was the same promise that God gave to Abraham and to Isaac, and now it was given to Jacob. "Whoever curses you will be cursed; whoever blesses you will be blessed."

And it came to pass as soon as Isaac had made an end of blessing Jacob, and Jacob was yet scarcely gone from the presence of Isaac, his father, that Esau, his brother, came in from his hunting. And he also made savory food, and he brought it unto his father, and he said unto his father, "Let my father arise, and eat of his son's venison that your soul may bless me."

And Isaac, his father, said unto him, "Who art thou? Who are you?"

And he said, "I am your son, your firstborn, Esau."

And Isaac trembled very exceedingly and said, "Who then is he that has taken venison and brought it to me, and I have eaten of all before you came, and I have blessed him? Yes, and he *shall* be blessed."

When Esau heard the words of his father, he cried with an exceedingly great and a bitter cry and said unto his father, "Bless me, even me also, my father."

And he said, "Your brother came with guile and has taken away your blessing."

And Esau said, "Is he not rightly named Jacob—a supplanter, conniver, and cheat? He has supplanted me these two times. He took away my birthright, and behold, he has taken away my blessing." And he said, "Father, have you not reserved a blessing for me?"

And Isaac answered and said unto Esau, "Behold, I have made him your lord, and all his brethren have I given to him for servants; and with corn and wine have I sustained him. And what then shall I do for you, my son?"

And Esau said unto his father, "Have you but just one blessing for me, my father? Bless me, even me also, my father." And Esau lifted up his voice and wept.

And Isaac, his father, answered and said unto him, "Behold, the fat places of the earth, they shall be your dwelling, and of the dew of heaven from above. By your sword shall you live, and you shall serve your brother, and it shall come to pass that when you shall break loose, you shall break the yoke off your neck."

Esau, the sensuous, wild, impulsive man—his cry was almost like the cry of a trapped creature, as he begged his father, "Father, don't you have even one blessing reserved for me?" His tears are among the most pathetic tears we see in the Bible. In the Talmud, our rabbis declare that this crying, this weeping, of Esau, was so pitiful that bitter retribution in later years was exacted from Jacob by the LORD for having caused these tears. The LORD does forgive us of our sin, but there's always the consequence of the sin itself. And Jacob paid for these tears that his brother shed in the twenty years that he spent with Laban.

And Esau hated Jacob because of the blessing wherewith his father had blessed him. And Esau said in his heart, "Let the days of mourning for my father be at hand, then will I slay my brother Jacob. My father is about to die, and as soon as the mourning period is over, I will kill my brother Jacob."

And the words of Esau, her elder son, were told to Rebekah, and she sent and called Jacob, her younger son, and said unto him, "Behold, your brother Esau, as touching thee, doth comfort himself, purposing to kill you. Now, therefore, my son, listen to me one more time. Arise, flee to Laban, my brother, to Haran. Stay with him a few days until your brother's fury is abated, until his anger is calmed down and is turned away from you, and he forgets that which you have done to him. Then I will send and bring you back from there. After all, why should I be bereaved of both of you in one day? Why should I go in mourning for my husband and my son on the same day? As soon as my husband dies, Esau's going to kill you, and I'm going to lose my husband and my son."

And Rebekah needed to give Isaac a reason for Jacob's absence. The old man was sick, about to die, and Rebekah went to him and said, "I am weary of my life because of the daughters of Heth that Esau has married. And now if Jacob takes a wife of the daughters of Heth, such as these of the daughters of the land, what good shall my life be unto me?"

8
And Isaac Blessed Jacob
(Genesis 28—32:24)

Isaac called Jacob, and he blessed him. He charged him, "You shall not take a wife of the daughters of Canaan." Notice the obedience of Isaac to his wife. He died to himself first and submitted to her in perfect love, just as he submitted to the LORD.

This is what submission is all about. This is what Christian marriage is all about. It's not a fifty-fifty proposition, it's a hundred-hundred proposition, each person dying utterly to himself in love of the other, Christ being the head of the house.

And Isaac said to Jacob, "Arise, go to Padan-aram to the house of Bethuel, your mother's father, and take thee a wife there from the daughters of Laban, your mother's brother. And God Almighty bless thee."

Isaac said, "May El Shaddai bless thee, make thee fruitful, multiply thee that you may be a congregation of people. And give thee the blessing of Abraham and to your seed with thee, that you may inherit the land where you sojourn, which God gave unto Abraham."

And Isaac sent away Jacob. He went to Padan-aram unto Laban, son of Bethuel, the Aramean, the brother of Rebekah, Jacob's and Esau's mother.

When Esau saw that Isaac had blessed Jacob and sent him away to Padan-aram, which is Syria, to take him a wife from there, and that as he blessed him, he gave him a charge, saying, "You shall not take a wife of the daughters of Canaan," Esau was angry. He saw that Jacob listened to his father and his mother and went to Padan-aram. And Esau saw that the daughters of Canaan did not please Isaac, his father, so Esau went unto Ishmael and took unto the wives that he had, Mahalath, the daughter of Ishmael, Abraham's son, the sister of Nebaioth, to be his wife. He was slapping the old man in the face another time by taking on another wife, making three wives. Two were the daughters of Canaan, one was the daughter of Ishmael.

So Jacob went out from Beer-sheba, headed toward Haran. And he lighted upon a place, and he tarried there all night, because the sun was set. And he took one of the stones of the place and put it under his head as he lay down in that place to sleep. And he dreamed and beheld a ladder set up on the earth, and the top of it reached to heaven, and he beheld the angels of God ascending and descending on it.

And behold, the Lord stood above it and said, "I am the Lord, the God of Abraham, your father, the God of Isaac. The land whereon you lie, to thee will I give it, and to your seed. Your seed shall be as the dust of the earth. You shall spread abroad to the west, to the east, to the north, to the south, and in you and your seed shall all the families of the earth be blessed."

And then He said, "Jake, I want you to take a good look." The LORD was speaking to him in his own language. He said, "Jakie, behold, I am with you. I will keep you wherever you go, and I will bring you back to this land, for I will not leave you until I have done that which I have spoken to you of."

And Jacob awakened out of his sleep, and he said, "Surely the LORD is in this place and I knew it not." He found the LORD out in the field in the middle of the night, as he lay there with his head upon a rock. And today, the Jewish people worship the LORD seven days a week after sundown because Jacob found the LORD after sundown in the dark.

And he was afraid and said, "How full of awe is this place! This is none other than the house of God, and this is the gate of heaven."

And Jacob rose up early in the morning, and he took the stone that he had put under his head, and he set it up for a pillar, and he poured oil upon the top of it. And he called the name of that place *Beth-el*, meaning "house of God," but the name of the city was Luz at first. And Jacob vowed a vow, saying, "If God will be with me, and He will keep me in this way that I go, and He will give me bread to eat and raiment to put on, so that I come back to my father's house in peace, then shall the LORD be my God. And this stone which I have set up for a pillar shall be God's house, and of all that You shall give me, LORD, I will surely give a tenth unto You."

He made a pledge, a vow, when he said, "Of all that You give me, I will give You a tenth." This was a greater vow than just vowing and pledging a tenth of his income. He had appropriated the promise that God was going to increase him. "Of all the increase that You give me, I'm going to give You ten percent. And I know You're going to increase it, so I will make this vow and this pledge unto You, and I will praise the LORD for the increase."

If we want an increase in our finances, let us start praising the LORD. Let us start paying a tithe on the increase we want, and see what happens. The LORD will give you the increase. Praise the LORD.

And Jacob went on his journey, and he came to the land of the children of the east. This is a term in the Hebrew which denotes the Arab tribes located east and northeast of Palestine. And he looked and beheld a well in the field, and three flocks of sheep lying there by it. Out of that well, they watered the flocks, and the stone upon the well's mouth was very great.

And there were all the flocks gathered, and they rolled the stone away from the well's mouth and watered the sheep and put the stone back upon the well's mouth in its place.

And Jacob said unto them, "My brethren, where do you come from?"

And they said, "Of Haran are we."

And he said unto them, "Do you perhaps know Laban, the son of Nahor?"

And they said, "We know him."

And he said unto them, "Is it well with him? Or is he having problems?"

And they said, "It is well with him. Behold, Rachel, his daughter, is now coming with the sheep."

And he said, "Lo, it is yet high day, neither is it time that the cattle should be gathered together. Water ye the sheep; go and feed them."

And they said, "We cannot, until all the flocks be gathered together, and they roll the stone from the well's mouth. Then we will water the sheep. It's a big stone, and it takes quite a few people to roll the stone off the top of the well. It's so heavy that we have to wait until all the men are together."

And while he was yet speaking, Rachel came with her father's sheep, for she tended the sheep.

And it came to pass that when Jacob saw Rachel, the daughter of Laban, his mother's brother, and the sheep of Laban, his mother's brother, that Jacob went near and by superhuman effort that the LORD gave him at that particular moment, he rolled the stone from the well's mouth. It usually took perhaps ten to twenty men to roll that stone off the mouth of that well, but Jacob rolled it off by himself, and he watered the flock of Laban, his mother's brother.

And Jacob kissed Rachel, and lifted up his voice and wept. He did not kiss her upon the lips. In Hebrew custom, it would be that he kissed her hand as a sign of respect. And he wept because he felt a kindred spirit with Rachel. He was a fugitive, fleeing, but he felt a love that he did not understand being returned to him, and he wept with joy.

Jacob told Rachel that he was her father's kinsman, and that he was Rebekah's son, and she ran and told her father. And it came to pass that when Laban heard the tidings of Jacob, his sister's son, that he ran to meet him. He embraced him, he kissed him, and he brought him to his house. And Jacob told Laban all these things. And Laban said to him, "Surely you are my bone and my flesh. You are my sister's boy.

I'm your uncle, you're my nephew. So now, after all, you know, family's family." And he abode with him the space of a month.

And after the month, Laban said unto Jacob, "Just because you are my kinsman, do you think it's right that you should work for nothing? At least, let me give you a little salary. Tell me what your wages should be. Jake, tell me how much I should pay you."

Now Laban had two daughters; the name of the elder was Leah, the name of the younger was Rachel. And Leah's eyes were weak, but Rachel was a beautiful form and fair to look upon. Now both girls were veiled, and the only thing that Jacob could see was their eyes. And Rachel had big beautiful brown eyes, and he looked at those eyes and fell in love with Rachel the first time he saw her. But Leah had weak eyes, and she squinted, and Jacob couldn't stomach her—he really couldn't stand her. And Jacob loved Rachel, and he said to Laban, "These are my wages. I will work for you, I will serve you, seven years for Rachel, your younger daughter."

And Laban said, "It is far better that I give her to you than to another man. Abide with me, stay with me for the seven years. We have an agreement, we have a bargain. You will work for Rachel for seven years." And Jacob served seven years for Rachel, and they seemed unto him but a few days, for the love that he had for her.

And Jacob said unto Laban, "Seven years have gone by, now give me my wife." (The minute they became promised to each other she was his wife, but the marriage was not consummated.) "Give me my betrothed, the one I am engaged to, the one who is promised to me, for my days are fulfilled. Give me

155

my wife that I may go in unto her and consummate the marriage."

And Laban gathered together all the men of the place, and he made a feast. And it came to pass in the evening, that Laban took Leah, his older daughter, and brought her to Jacob, and he went in unto her. It was dark out on the desert, Leah was veiled, and Jacob didn't realize that Laban had deceived him. And he went in unto her; he consummated the marriage.

And Laban gave Zilpah, his maidservant, unto his daughter Leah for a handmaid. And it came to pass that in the morning, behold, it was Leah instead of Rachel. And Jacob ran to Laban, and he said, "What is this that you have done to me? Did I not serve you for Rachel? Why did you trick me?"

And Laban said, "It must not be so done in our country, to give the younger before the firstborn. Fulfill the week of her honeymoon, and we will give you the other also for the service which you shall still yet serve me another seven years. You've established good credit with us, Jake, and if you will fulfill this week of Leah's honeymoon, we'll give you Rachel on credit if you promise to work another seven years for Rachel after the week is up."

And Jacob did so. He fulfilled Leah's week, and Laban gave him Rachel his daughter to wife also. And Laban gave to Rachel his daughter, Bilhah, his handmaid, to be her handmaid.

And Jacob went in also unto Rachel, and he loved Rachel more than Leah. And he served with Laban yet another seven years—fourteen years in all.

And the LORD saw that Leah was hated, and because she was hated, He opened her womb, but Rachel, the loved one, was barren. And Leah conceived and bore a son, and she called his name Reuben, which in the Hebrew means, "Behold, a son," for she said, "Surely the LORD hath looked upon my affliction; now, therefore, my husband will love me."

And she conceived again, and bore a son, and said, "Because the LORD hath heard that I am hated, He hath therefore given me this son also," and she called his name Simeon, meaning in the Hebrew, "hearing."

And she conceived again, and bore a son, and said, "Now this time will my husband be joined unto me, because I have borne him three sons." Therefore was his name called Levi, meaning "joined." The priestly tribe was the tribe of Levi.

And Leah conceived again, and bore a son, and she said, "This time will I praise the LORD." Therefore, she called his name Judah, and she left off bearing. All the praises of the LORD of all the face of the earth would come through and from the Lion of Judah, who is Jesus the Christ.

And when Rachel saw that she bore Jacob no children, Rachel envied her sister. And she said unto Jacob, "Jake, if you don't give me children, I'm going to die." When Rebekah was barren, Isaac was obedient unto the LORD, and he entreated the LORD for Rebekah his wife because she was barren. And the LORD permitted Himself to be entreated of Isaac's prayer, and Rebekah conceived, and she gave birth.

But Jacob was still a conniver, still arrogant. When Rachel came to him and said, "Give me children or else I die," Jacob's anger was kindled against Rachel, and he said, "What do you think I am? God? Am I the one who has withheld from you the fruit of the womb?"

And she said, "Take a look at my maid, Bilhah. Go in unto

her, that she may bear upon my knees, that I also may be builded up through her."

So she gave him Bilhah, her handmaid, to wife, and Jacob went in unto her. And Bilhah conceived and bore Jacob a son. And Rachel said, "God hath judged me, and has also heard my voice and has given me a son." Therefore, she called his name Dan. The name *Dan* in Hebrew means "judge." One of the judges in Israel, Samson, would come from the tribe of Dan. The emblem of the tribe of Dan was a serpent, a snake in the grass who bit his horse's heel as his rider fell backward. Judas Iscariot would be coming from the tribe of Dan, from this handmaid, Bilhah. That's why he's not mentioned in the Book of Revelation as one of the twelve tribes of Israel.

And Bilhah, Rachel's handmaid, conceived again, and bore Jacob a second son. And Rachel said, "With mighty wrestlings have I wrestled with my sister, and I have prevailed against my sister," and she called his name Naphtali, meaning "wrestling."

And when Leah saw that she had left off bearing, she took Zilpah, her handmaid, and she gave her to Jacob to wife. Now he had four wives, and none of them could stand the others. So Leah gave him Zilpah, her handmaid, to wife, and Zilpah, Leah's handmaid, bore Jacob a son. And Leah said, "A fortune is come. God has rewarded me," and she called his name Gad, meaning "fortune."

And Zilpah, Leah's handmaid, bore Jacob a second son. And Leah said, "Happy am I, for the daughters will call me happy." She called his name Asher, meaning "happy."

And Reuben went out in the day of wheat harvest, and he found mandrakes in the field, and he brought them unto his mother, Leah, Mandrakes are love apples, found in the Middle East. The fruit is about the size of a large plum. It's round and yellow, full of soft pulp, and the fruit in the Middle East even today is considered to be a love charm, a love potion.

In the meantime, the four wives were fighting over Jacob. One said, "It's my turn tonight." Another one said, "No, it's my turn. You're not keeping good track."

And Reuben brought the mandrakes to his mother, Leah. Then Rachel said to Leah, "Give me, I pray thee, some of your son's mandrakes." She was anxious to get them to use them as a love potion with Jacob.

But Leah said to Rachel, "Is it a small thing that you've taken away my husband, and now, would you take away my son's mandrakes also?"

And Rachel said, "He shall lie with you tonight for your son's mandrakes—you give me the mandrakes, and you can have him for tonight."

When Jacob came in from the field in the evening and Leah went out to meet him, she said, "You must come in unto me, for I have surely hired you for the night with my son's mandrakes." And he lay with her that night.

And God hearkened unto Leah, and she conceived, and bore Jacob a fifth son. And Leah said, "God has given me my reward for giving my handmaid to my husband," and she called his name Issachar, meaning "he who is hired."

And Leah conceived again, and bore a sixth son to Jacob. And Leah said, "God has endowed me with a good dowry. Now my husband will dwell with me, because I have borne him six sons." And she called his name Zebulun, which means "dwelling."

And afterward she bore a daughter and called her name Dinah.

And God remembered Rachel, and God hearkened to her. He listened and answered her prayer. Instead of going to Jacob again, and instead of saying to Jacob, "Give me children or else I die," she went to the LORD, and as she prayed to the LORD, the LORD answered her prayers. He opened her womb, and she conceived and bore a son, and she said, "God has taken away my reproach of being childless." She called his name Joseph. The name Joseph in Hebrew means "increaser." And Rachel said, "The LORD will add to me another son."

And it came to pass when Rachel had borne Joseph, that Jacob said unto Laban, "Send me away, that I may go unto my own place and to my country. Give me my wives and my children, for whom I have served thee, and let me go, for thou knowest my service which I have done thee."

But Laban said unto him, "If now I have found favor in your eyes, stay: for I have learned by experience that the LORD hath blessed me for thy sake."

And he said, "Appoint me thy wages, and I will give it. Jake, tell me what you want. I'll give you your wages. Whatever you ask, I'll give it."

And Jacob answered Laban, "You know how I have served thee, and how your cattle have fared with me, for it was little that you had before I came, and it has increased abundantly. And the LORD has blessed me wherever I have turned." The LORD had promised Jacob, "Wherever you go, I'll be with you." And Jacob was acknowledging the blessing of the LORD.

And he said to Laban, "When shall I provide for my own household? I have a big family—four wives and a bunch of kids. I've got to provide for them. I can't wait for social security and welfare."

And Laban said, "What shall I give you?"

And Jacob said, "You shall not give me anything. But if you will do this one thing for me, I will again feed your flock, and I will keep it. Let me pass through all your flock today, removing from your flock every speckled, every spotted one, every dark one from among the sheep, the spotted, and the speckled among the goats. Of such shall be my hire."

The sheep in Syria are white, and the goats are black. Now Jacob asked as his wages the sheep which were not white and the goats which were not black, the freaks. He was asking for the black sheep, and for the goats which were speckled and spotted.

Laban considered Jacob's request fair, and he figured, "Well, I just out-connived that dummy again. He's taking the weakest, those that he cannot possibly sell because they are spotted, speckled, and streaked. Who would want a sheep unless it was perfectly white? If it's got spots on it, it's blemished."

But the LORD had spoken to Jacob and told him, "This is what I want you to do. And if you are obedient unto Me, and do what I tell you to do, I will bless you."

And Jacob said, "So shall my righteousness witness against me hereafter, that when you shall come to look over my hire that is before you, every one that is not speckled, every one that is not spotted among the goats and dark among the sheep, that is found with me shall be counted stolen. If you find a white sheep in my flock, know that I have stolen it from you. I'll have all the black sheep, all the spotted, all the speckled.

Let the LORD be your witness and my witness, whether it is mine or not."

And Laban said, "Behold let it be according to your word." But Laban removed that day the he goats that were streaked and spotted, all the she goats that were speckled and spotted, every one that had white in it, and all the dark ones among the sheep. He took out all the black sheep, and he gave them into the hand of his sons. And he set three days' journey between himself and Jacob, and Jacob fed the rest of Laban's flocks.

In the meantime, the LORD told Jacob, "Here is what I want you to do, Jake. If you'll be obedient, I'll bless you." Jacob took himself rods of fresh poplar, of the almond, and of the plane tree, and he peeled white streaks in them, making the white appear which was in the rod. He set the rods which he had peeled over against the flocks in the gutters in the watering troughs where the flocks came to drink, and they conceived when they came to drink. That was the miracle the LORD promised him, that when they came to drink, they would conceive, and conceiving in the sight of the rods which were streaked, they would bring forth that which was streaked. This was the LORD, working a miracle.

And they conceived when they came to drink, in the sight of the rods, and the flocks brought forth streaked, spotted, and speckled. And Jacob separated the lambs and set the faces of the flocks toward the streaked and all the dark in the flock of Laban, and he put his own droves apart, and put them not unto Laban's flock. And it came to pass that whenever the stronger of the flock did conceive, Jacob laid the rods before the eyes of the flock in the gutters that they might conceive among the rods. But when the flock was feeble, he did not put them in. So Jacob was getting the strongest of the flock, and the feeble were going unto Laban.

And the man increased exceedingly, and he had large flocks, maidservants, menservants, camels, and asses. The LORD was blessing him as he was following the LORD's plan.

Laban was getting poorer by the day. Jacob was getting richer by the day, following the LORD's plan. And Jacob heard the words of Laban's sons, saying, "Jacob has taken away all of that which was our father's, and by that which was our father's has he gotten all this wealth." And Jacob beheld the countenance of Laban, and it was not toward him as before.

And the LORD said unto Jacob, "You have been obedient unto Me. Now I want you to return unto the land of your father, to your own family, and I will be with you. Don't be afraid to go back. I will never leave you nor forsake you."

And Jacob sent and called Rachel and Leah to the field unto his flock. And he said unto them, "I see your father's face, his countenance, is not toward me as before. His attitude has changed. There's no love between us any longer. But the God of my father Isaac has been with me, and you know that with all my power I have served your father. But your father has deceived me. He has changed my wages ten times, but God suffered him not to hurt me. If he said, 'The speckled shall be thy wages,' then all the flock bare speckled. And if he said, 'The streaked shall be your wages,' then all the flock bare streaked. Thus God hath taken away the cattle of your father, and he has given them unto me.

"And it came to pass at the time that the flock conceived, that I lifted up my eyes, and saw in a vision, and, behold, the

JESUS IN GENESIS

he goats which leaped upon the flock were streaked, speckled, and grizzled. And the Angel of the Lord said unto me in the vision, 'Jacob,' and I said, 'Here am I.' "

The Angel of the Lord, Jesus Christ Himself, appeared unto him. He's the one who gave him the plan, saying, "Lift up your eyes, and see that all the he goats which leap upon the flock are streaked, speckled, and grizzled, for I have seen all that Laban has done unto you. I am the God of Beth-el." The Angel of the Lord revealed His true identity when He said, "I am the God of Beth-el. Remember when you laid your head upon that rock? I am the God of Abraham and Isaac, and now I am your God. I am the God of Beth-el, where you did anoint a pillar, where you did make a vow unto Me. Now arise, get yourself up from this land, and return unto the land of your nativity."

And Rachel and Leah answered and said unto him, "Is there still yet any inheritance or portion for us in our father's house?" Some of Jacob's connivance had rubbed off on the two women. "Do we still have any portion or inheritance with our father? Does he not treat us as strangers? For he has sold us, and he had also quite devoured our price. He has sold us to you for seven years apiece of work, and he has taken our price. For all the riches which God hath taken away from our father, that is ours and our children's. Now then, whatsoever God hath said unto you, do. We will go with you wherever the Lord says to go." The girls were going to be obedient unto the Lord.

Then Jacob rose up and set his sons and his wives upon camels. And he carried away all his cattle, all the substance which he had gathered, the cattle of his getting, which he had gathered in Padan-aram, to go to Isaac, his father, into the land of Canaan.

When Laban had gone to shear his sheep, Rachel stole the idols that were her father's. She was not an idol worshiper. She loved the LORD, and she worshiped the LORD. But the custom of the land was that whoever had the idols, the household idols of the father, could go into the court upon the father's death, present the idols, and receive the inheritance. Rachel was out to cheat her brothers from their inheritance by taking the idols to give to Jake so that when Laban died, good old Jakie could go in the court with the idols and say, "I am the rightful heir. Give me all that belongs to Laban."

And Jacob outwitted Laban, the Aramean, the Syrian, in that he told him not that he fled. He had no reason to flee. The LORD had told him, "Go back home, I am with you. You don't have to run." He could have told his father-in-law very nicely, "I'm leaving. My God has spoken to me, and I'm going back home. He says He's with me. You've seen the evidence that He's been with me all these twenty years that I have been with you. He's blessed you because He has blessed me, so now, let's make a covenant together of peace, and I'll take your grandchildren, my children, my wives, and go home. And we can bless the LORD together." But instead of leaving in that manner, Jacob fled with all that he had. And he rose up and passed over the river, and he set his face toward the mountain of Gilead.

And it was told Laban on the third day that Jacob had fled. And he took his brethren with him, and pursued after him seven days' journey, and he overtook him in the mountain of Gilead. And God came to Laban, the Aramean, in a dream of the night and said unto him, "Laban, take heed to yourself that you speak not to Jacob either good or bad. You better cool it. You're walking on eggshells. Be careful what you say."

And Laban came up to Jacob. Now Jacob had pitched his tent in the mountain. Laban, with his brethren, pitched in the mountain of Gilead. And Laban said to Jacob, "What is this you have done, that you have outwitted me? Why have you carried away my daughters as though they were captives of the sword? Why did you have to escape? Wherefore did you flee secretly and outwit me, and you did not tell me, that I might have sent you away with mirth, with songs, with tabret, with harp? And you didn't even suffer me to kiss my sons and my daughters. You have done very foolishly. At least you could have let me give you a going-away party. These children that you have are my children; I'm the grandfather."

Laban was claiming everything—his daughters, the children. "Everything that you have belongs to me. You have done very foolishly. And it is in the power of my hand to do you hurt, but the God of your father, Isaac, spoke unto me last night, saying, 'Take heed unto yourself that you speak not to Jacob either good or bad.' And now that you are surely gone, because you long after your father's house, why have you stolen my gods?

"Your God spoke to me, so why did you take my gods? Your God is with you always, but if you take my gods, who am I going to worship? You're going to put me to a lot of trouble. I'm going to have to sit down and start carving new gods for me to worship. That's an awful lot of work—it may take two months for me to make a god that I can like. What am I going to do?"

And Jacob answered and said to Laban, "I fled because I was afraid."

Can you imagine this? Can you actually believe it? The LORD

had spoken to him and said, "Go back home. It is now time. I'll be with you every step of the way. I'll go with you wherever you go. You don't have to worry. Have no fear." And yet Jacob said, "The reason I fled was because I was afraid lest you should take your daughters, my wives, from me by force." Jacob had no reason to be afraid, because the LORD was with him and no one could be against him.

And Jacob said, "With whomsoever you find your gods, he shall not live. Before our brethren, discern what is thine with me and take it to thee."

Jacob opened his mouth when he should have kept his mouth shut. He should not have said, "With whomsoever you find your gods, he shall not live." In saying that, he cursed the person who had those gods, for Jacob did not know that Rachel had stolen the idols.

And Laban went into Jacob's tent, into Leah's tent, into the tent of the two maidservants, but he didn't find his idols. And he went out of Leah's tent, and he entered into Rachel's tent. Rachel had taken the idols and put them in the saddle of the camel and sat upon them.

Laban felt about all the tent, but he did not find the idols, and Rachel said to her father, "Let not my LORD be angry, that I cannot rise up before thee, but the manner of women is upon me. I can't get up, because I'm having my period, but forgive me, daddy." She had put the idols in the saddlebags of the camel, and she was sitting upon the camel, preventing Laban from searching there. And he searched the tent, but he found not the idols.

Notice the lying and the connivance on Rachel's part. She was out to get whatever she could of the inheritance that was left. She felt there was still an inheritance due her from her father.

And Jacob was very angry, and he strove with Laban. And Jacob answered and said to Laban, "What is my trespass? What did I do that was wrong? What is my sin that you have so hotly pursued after me? You have searched, but have you found anything that is yours? Set it here before my brethren that they may judge between us two.

"These twenty years I have been with you. Your ewes, your she goats, they have not miscarried their young, and the rams of your flocks I have not eaten. That which was torn of beasts I brought not unto you. I bore the loss of it. Of my hand did you require it, whether stolen by day, or stolen by night." In keeping the flocks of Laban, if a mountain lion or other animal consumed or killed a sheep, or anything that belonged to Laban, Jacob did not have to replace it, but he did. In other words, he fulfilled his responsibilities in an excellent manner. Whatever Laban trusted him with, he accounted for to Laban. Jacob reminded Laban, "You required it of me. I did not eat of your flocks. I ate what the LORD supplied. Anything that was hurt, I replaced it myself. In the day, the drought consumed me, and in the night, the frost consumed me, and my sleep fled from my eyes.

"These twenty years have I been in your house. I served you fourteen years for your two daughters and six years for your flock, and you have changed my wages ten times. Every time, you came up with a new law to out-connive me. I used to be the champion conniver, but in you I have met my match." Notice to whom Jacob gave the praise, and the glory, and the honor. He said, "Except the God of my father, the God of

Abraham, and the fear of Isaac had been on my side, surely now you would have sent me away empty. God has seen my affliction and the labor of my hands, and He gave judgment last night when He appeared to you in the dream and said, 'Be very careful what you say to Jacob. Don't speak to him either good or bad.' The LORD passed judgment last night. He vindicated me that I have served you well, and I have served the LORD well. Even though I've been a conniver, I've been learning, I've been growing."

But Laban was still arrogant, and he said unto Jacob, "These daughters are my daughters; the children are my children; the flocks are my flocks. All that you see is mine."

Then, suddenly, the LORD intervened, and Laban changed his tune entirely, asking, "What can I do for you this day?" All at once, total arrogance was replaced by total love. "What can I do for you, and for these, my daughters, or for their children whom they have borne?" They were no longer claimed by him, instead, he wanted to do all he could for them.

And Laban said, "Come, let us make a covenant, you and me. And let it be a witness between thee and me." And Jacob took a stone and set it for a pillar. The LORD had stopped Laban from committing spiritual suicide. The LORD had warned him to be very careful what he said, and when he started speaking in total arrogance, the LORD divinely intervened, and his language was changed.

So Jacob took a stone, and he set it up for a pillar. And Jacob said unto his brethren, "Gather stones." They took stones, and they made a heap, and they did eat there by the heap as they made the covenant. And Laban called it Jegar-sahadutha, which is Aramaic. Jacob called it Galeed (heap of witness), and Laban said, "This heap is a witness between me and thee this day." Jacob also called it Mizpah (watchtower), and said, "The LORD watch between us, that there should be peace between you and me when we are absent one from another." Today, this is called the Mizpah benediction.

Then Laban said to Jacob, "If you shall afflict my daughters, if you shall take wives besides my daughters, though no man is witness, God will be a witness between me and thee."

And Laban said to Jacob, "Behold this heap, behold the pillar, which I have set up between me and thee. This heap be witness, and this pillar be witness that I will not pass over this heap unto you, and you shall not pass over this heap and this pillar unto me for harm. If we come in peace, that's fine, but if we come for harm, the LORD will be the witness between you and me. If we come to this heap which we set in the name of the LORD, making a covenant in His name, if we pass this line, this border, with the intent of doing one another harm, the LORD will stop us from passing over that boundary line."

And Laban said, "The God of Abraham, and the god of Nahor, and the gods of their father, judge between us." Laban was swearing by the living God—the God of Abraham—and by the gods of idolatry, in case one of them happened to be right. He hadn't made up his mind yet.

Jacob swore by the fear of his father, Isaac, by the seeing and the reverential and the respectful awe of the living God of his father, Isaac. And Jacob offered a sacrifice in the mountain, and called his brethren to eat bread. They did eat bread, and they tarried all night in the mountain.

Early in the morning, Laban rose up, and he kissed his sons

and his daughters, and he blessed them. And Laban departed and returned unto his place.

And Jacob went on his way. The angels who had accompanied him twenty years earlier when he left the land of Canaan were still with him, the ones who were ascending and descending the ladder in his vision at Beth-el. And the angels of God met him, Jacob saw them again, and he said, "This is God's host." And he called the name of that place Mahanaim (two camps), because he saw an encampment of angels beside his own.

Would you be afraid, if you saw God's angels standing physically next to you, each one holding on to one of your arms, helping you go back home? What could you be afraid of? Nothing could harm you. But Jacob was afraid.

He sent messengers before him to Esau, his brother, unto the land of Seir, the field of Edom. He commanded them, saying, "Thus shall you say unto my lord Esau: 'Thus saith your servant Jacob, "I have sojourned with Laban and stayed until now. I really didn't go to Laban to escape from you. I went as a sojourner and a stranger just to stay for a few months, but I got outwitted and out-connived, and I've been gone these twenty years. I was a stranger in a strange land. I had no intent on my part to stay away this long. I have oxen, asses, flocks, and maidservants. I have sent to tell you all the good news of every blessing that I have received, to tell you of everything that has happened to me, that I might find favor in your eyes." ' "

And the messengers returned to Jacob, saying, "We came to your brother Esau, and moreover, he's coming to meet you, and he's got four hundred men with him!"

171

Jacob had just seen the angels of the LORD, and the LORD had promised to be with him, to protect him, but Jacob didn't say, "LORD, I'm going to trust You in all things. I'm going to praise You, I'm going to thank You that my brother Esau is coming with four hundred men to greet me, and I'm going to surrender the whole thing in Your hands." No. He was scared stiff. He was greatly distressed, sore afraid.

And Jacob divided his people that were with him, and the flocks, the herds, and the camels, into two camps. He figured if Esau and his men attacked one of the camps, those in the other camp would be able to get away.

When Jacob had divided his camp, then he turned to the LORD and said, "LORD, I want You to okay what I have done. I want Your approval.

"O God of my father Abraham, and God of my father Isaac, O LORD, You're the One who said unto me, 'Return unto your country, unto your family, and I will do you good.' I am not worthy of all the mercies that You have shown me, of all the truths that You have revealed to me, which you have shown unto Your servant, for with my staff I have passed over this Jordan, and now I have become two camps, and it's Your fault, LORD. Why didn't You stop me from becoming two camps? Why did You let me do my will instead of Your will?"

And Jacob continued to complain, "LORD, I did what You told me to do, but now I'm finding myself as two camps." The LORD never told him to become two camps. He had said, "Go back home, and I'll be with you. I'll do you good all the way. My angels are with you. You have nothing to fear, nothing to worry about."

And then Jacob turned around in a prayer of petition, intercessory prayer for himself, and he said, "I know I have done the wrong thing. Deliver me, I pray Thee, from the hand of my brother, from the hand of Esau, for I fear him, lest he come and smite me, and the mother with the children. And You, LORD, You surely did say, 'I will surely do thee good and make your seed as the sand of the sea which cannot be numbered for multitude.' You made a covenant with me, LORD, and now I'm holding You to Your covenant and to Your promise." Jacob finally did what he should have done in the first place.

So he lodged there that night and took of that which he had with him, a present for Esau his brother: two hundred she goats, twenty he goats, two hundred ewes, twenty rams, thirty milch camels and their colts, forty kine, ten bulls, twenty she asses, and ten foals. He delivered them into the hand of his servants, every drove by itself, and he said unto his servants, "Pass over before me, and put a space between drove and drove." And he commanded the foremost, saying, "When Esau my brother meets you, and asks you, saying, 'Whose are these and where do you go and whose are these before thee?' then you shall say, 'They are your servant Jacob's. It is a present sent unto my lord Esau. And behold, he also is behind us.' "

And he commanded also the second and the third and all that followed the droves, saying, "In this manner shall you speak unto Esau, when you find him. You shall say, moreover, 'Behold, your servant Jacob is behind us.' " And Jacob said, "I will appease him with the present that goes before me, and afterward, I will see his face. Perhaps he will accept me."

So the present passed over before him, and he himself lodged that night in the camp. And he rose up that night, and took his two wives, and his two handmaids, his eleven children, and he passed over the ford of the river Jabbok. He took them, and sent them over the stream, and sent over that which he had.

And Jacob was left alone.

9
No More Jacob, but Israel
(Genesis 32:25—36)

Jacob was left alone, and there wrestled a Man with him until the breaking of the day. And when the Man saw that He prevailed not against Jacob, He touched the hollow of his thigh, and the hollow of Jacob's thigh was strained out of joint as he wrestled with Him. From that day forth, Jacob walked with a limp. He forever remembered his encounter with the living God.

And the Man said, "Let Me go, for the day breaketh."

And Jacob said, "I will not let You go, unless You bless me."

And the Man said unto him, "What is your name?"

And he said, "My name is Jacob."

And He said, "Your name shall be called no more Jacob, but Israel, for you have striven with God and with men, and you have prevailed."

And Jacob asked Him, and said, "Tell Me, I pray thee, Your name."

And He said, "Wherefore is it that you do ask after My name?" And He blessed him there. Jacob received the blessing of God right there. And Jacob called the name of the place Peniel, which means, "the face of God." For he said, "I have seen God face to face, and my life is still preserved."

And the sun rose upon him as he passed over Peniel, and he forever limped upon his thigh, reminding him that he did meet the LORD face to face.

Therefore, the children of Israel today eat not of the sinew of the thigh vein which is upon the hollow of the thigh, because He, the LORD, touched the hollow of Jacob's thigh. So we're not allowed to eat Porterhouse steak, T-bone steak, or New York steak, because the LORD touched Jacob right there.

This passage represents the crisis in Jacob's spiritual history. It records his meeting with *the* heavenly Being. This is as close as a rabbi could come to saying, "Jesus Christ."

The Talmud and the rabbis say, in effect, that Jacob had a born-again experience. There was the change of his name to Israel, the blessing of the Being that wrestled with him, and the consequent transformation of his character. Moses Maimonides is of the opinion that the whole incident was a prophetic vision. And other commentators likewise regard the contest as being symbolic, the outward manifestation of the struggle within the patriarch himself as every mortal struggles within himself between his baser passions and his nobler ideals. Modern theologians would like to have us believe that it was not really the Angel of the LORD, Jesus Christ, *the* heavenly

Being who wrestled with him, but that Jacob was only wrestling with his conscience.

Some of our denominational churches don't believe that Jesus was led by the Holy Spirit into the wilderness to be tempted by the devil. They take the word "devil" and change it to "ego." And they say His ego spoke unto Him and said, "Worship me." And His ego said unto Him, "Command these stones to be turned into bread." And that Jesus turned to His ego and said, "Man shall not live by bread alone, but by every word that proceedeth out of the mouth of God." Such teachers would like to take God out of the Bible if they could.

Most rabbis agree that in the dead of night, Jacob sent his wives and his sons and all that he had across the river, and that Jacob was left alone with God. There in the darkness, given over to anxious fears, Jacob was confronted by God's messenger, the Angel of the LORD. He and Jacob wrestled—Jacob, who had so very often wrestled with men and won by sheer energy, persistence, and superior wit. Jacob struggled with the Angel of the LORD, and he prevailed, and Jacob wept and made supplication unto the LORD. That supplication for mercy, forgiveness, and divine protection was heard by the Angel of the LORD. And Jacob received all that he asked for. Jacob, the supplanter, the conniver, the deceiver, became Israel, the prince of God!

Even after you and I have our born-again experience, and we are transformed, because Christ is still in the business of transforming people's lives, we have a tendency to backslide, to take one step back for every two steps forward.

So, it's a constant born-again experience, a whole lifetime of day-by-day dying to ourselves and being born again, trans-

formed and made into the image, into the likeness, of Jesus Christ.

And Jacob lifted up his eyes and looked, and behold, Esau came, and with him four hundred armed men. Jake had his four wives and his eleven children and as far as he was concerned, he was totally helpless. But really, he had the majority, because Jesus was with him. And Jacob, who was now Israel, was a majority with the LORD, believing Him for His word.

And Jacob divided the children unto Leah. He said, "Leah, take your kids," and he told Rachel and the two handmaids to do the same thing. And he separated them into four camps. He was still not willing to trust the LORD. Although he'd had his born-again experience, he was still scared stiff, not willing to trust God for who God says He is.

And he put the handmaids and children foremost, up front, Bilhah and her kids first, then Zilpah and her kids. Next came Leah and her children, and he put Rachel and Joseph in the rear echelon, the safest place of all. The others were expendable, but not Rachel and Joseph.

And Jacob himself passed over before them, and he bowed himself to the ground seven times, eating humble dirt, until he came near his brother.

And Esau ran to meet him. He embraced him, and fell on his neck, and kissed him, and they wept. Instead of killing Jacob as he had planned, Esau was demonstrating the divine intervention of the LORD. The LORD kept His promise to Jacob: "I am your divine protection. You have nothing to fear. I am with you. If I am with you, who could be against you? Could any Esau stand against you? No way."

Esau ran to meet Jacob. He embraced him. He kissed him,

and he wept for his brother—even though he had come with four hundred men to destroy Jacob. The LORD divinely intervened. Esau lifted up his eyes, and he saw the women and the children, and he said, "Whose are these? Who are they that are with you?"

And Jacob said, "The children whom God has graciously given your servant." Then the handmaidens came near, they and their children, and they bowed down to Esau. And Leah also, and her children came near and bowed down, and afterward came Joseph and Rachel, and they bowed down.

And Esau said, "What do you mean by all this camp which I met?"

And Jacob said, "To find favor in the sight of my lord, Esau."

And Esau said, "I have enough, my brother. You don't have to give me anything. You are my brother. Let that which you have be yours."

And Jacob said, "No, I pray thee. If now I have found favor in your sight, then receive my present at my hand, forasmuch as I have seen your face as one sees the face of God." Jacob had just kissed the Jewish blarney stone. He said, "Esau, looking upon your face is almost like looking upon the face of God. Take my present, that you would find me pleasing in your eyes. Take, I pray thee, my gift that is brought to thee, because God has dealt graciously with me, and because I have enough." And he urged him, and Esau took it.

And Esau said, "Let us take our journey. Let us go, and I will go before thee. Okay, Jake, let's get going. I have four hundred men. We'll lead the way back into Canaan."

But Jacob said unto him, "My lord knows that the children

are tender, they're young, they're small kids. And the flocks and herds are giving suck. They're still very young and tender, and they are a care to me, and if we overdrive them even one day, all the flocks will die. So why bother yourself, Esau? I'm stuck with a bunch of kids and women, and cattle and young herds. Why don't you just take your men and go back home, and just let me travel at a very slow pace? I know you've got a lot of things to do. You're a busy man—a great lord. Let my lord, I pray thee, pass over before his servant, and I will journey on very slowly and gently according to the pace of the cattle that are before me, and according to the pace of the children. We have to stop and change their diapers once in a while, and we don't want to bother you with all this stuff. Until I come unto my lord, unto Seir, you just go ahead, and I will follow you into the land of Seir."

The LORD had not told Jacob to go back to Seir, but to go back into the land of Canaan, to go back to his kindred, to the land of his father, Isaac. But he had reverted from Israel to Jacob, telling Esau that he would follow him to Seir. Of course, he had no intention of meeting his brother in Seir. All he wanted to do was to let his brother get away from him, because he still didn't trust him at all. Even though he had seen the mighty miracle of the LORD, he still had no trust.

And Esau said to Jacob, "Well, if you insist, but let me leave with you some of my men that are with me. I don't need all four hundred. I'll leave two hundred of them with you."

But that again scared the daylights out of Jacob, and he said, "What need is there of it? Let me find favor in the sight of my lord." So Esau returned that day with all of his men on his way to Seir.

And Jacob journeyed to Succoth, and he built him a house, and made booths for his cattle. Therefore the name of the place is called Succoth. And we still have a Jewish feast which is called Succoth. During this feast, we live in a booth as Jacob lived in a booth for seven days and seven nights.

And Jacob came in peace to the city of Shechem which is in the land of Canaan, when he came from Padan-aram, which is Syria, and he encamped before the city. And he bought the parcel of land where he had spread his tent at the hand of the children of Hamor, Shechem's father, for an hundred pieces of money. And he erected there an altar unto the LORD, and he called it El-Elohe-Israel, meaning, "God, the God of Israel."

As he dedicated that altar unto the God of Israel, he said, "You are my God, LORD, the God of Abraham, the God of Isaac, and now the God of Jacob."

Now Jacob had one daughter, and her name was Dinah, the daughter of Leah. And Jacob was remiss in his duties as a father. He permitted Dinah to go out to see the daughters of the land. She had no need to go out to see the daughters of the land—her father should not have let her go out in a strange land, in a land of heathen people, unprotected, by herself, to mix with the natives. But Jacob let her go. And she went out to see and to be seen, showing herself off. That is what the Hebrew denotes.

As she went out by herself, Shechem, the son of Hamor the Hivite, the prince of the land, saw her. He took her, and he lay with her, and he humbled her—he raped her. And his soul did cleave unto Dinah, the daughter of Jacob—he loved the damsel and spoke comfortably unto the damsel. He spoke to the heart of the girl, and he tried to console her by his words of love after he raped her, and he declared his wish to her to make her his wife.

So Shechem spoke to his father, Hamor, saying, "Get me this damsel to wife." Now Jacob heard that he had defiled Dinah, his daughter, and his sons were with his cattle in the field, and Jacob held his peace until they came. He stayed put until he presented it to the brothers of Dinah—who were my father, Judah, Simeon, Levi, and Reuben, the eldest. "Your sister has just been raped. Okay, boys, what do we do now?" Jacob held a family counsel when the boys came in from the field.

And all the men of Israel were grieved. They were very angry because Shechem had wrought a vile deed in Israel in lying with Jacob's daughter, a thing which ought not to be done. The Hebrew word translated "vile deed" means, in the Hebrew, "senseless wickedness," and "total insensibility to moral distinction, a thing which ought not to be done."

The nation of Israel was not yet in existence, but even from the very beginning, the sons of Jacob abhorred senseless wickedness. They knew the difference between right and wrong before they received the Ten Commandments.

And Hamor, the father of Shechem, spoke to Jacob, saying, "The soul of my son, Shechem, longs for your daughter. I pray you, give her unto him to wife. And you make marriages with us—give your daughters unto us, and take our daughters unto you. You shall dwell with us, and the land shall be before you. Dwell and trade you therein, and get you possessions therein."

And Shechem said unto her father and unto her brothers, "Let me find favor in your eyes, and what you shall say, I shall give. Ask of me any amount of dowry and gift, and I will give according as you shall say unto me. But give me the damsel to wife."

And the sons of Jacob answered Shechem and Hamor, his father, with guile. Simeon was the leader of the guile. And Levi was a party to it, but not Judah. Knowing that they were outnumbered by the citizens of Shechem, Simeon resorted to a devious method to carry out his determination to avenge his sister's dishonor.

And the sons of Jacob answered Shechem and Hamor his father with guile, because Shechem had defiled Dinah, their sister, and they said, "We cannot do this thing, to give our sister to one that is uncircumcised. We were commanded by God that we are a people under a covenant, and the sign and seal of the covenant is that we are a people which are circumcised. It would be a reproach unto us to give her unto one who is uncircumcised, but if you will do one thing, under only one condition, we will consent to you. If you will be as we are, that every male of you be circumcised, then we will give our daughters unto you. And we will take your daughters unto us, and we will dwell with you, and we will become one people. But if you will not listen unto us, if you will not agree to be circumcised, then we will take our daughter, and we will be gone."

And their words pleased Hamor and Shechem, Hamor's son, and the young man deferred not to do the thing, because he had delight in Jacob's daughter. And he was honored above all the house of his father. And Hamor and Shechem, his son, came unto the gate of the city and spoke with the men of their city, saying to the elders and the princes sitting there, "Take a look at this guy. All he's asking us now to get this daughter for our prince is that we be circumcised. And just look at the wealth he has! Look at the gold and the silver and the cattle. Shall not all this wealth be ours? All we have to do is get circumcised. What's so tough about that?"

And unto Hamor and unto Shechem, his son, hearkened all that went out of the gate of his city, and every male was circumcised.

And it came to pass on the third day, when they were in severe pain and couldn't possibly go to battle, that two of the sons of Jacob, Simeon and Levi, Dinah's brethren, took each man his sword, and came upon the city unaware, and they slew all the males of the city. They slew Hamor and Shechem, his son, with the edge of the sword, and they took Dinah out of Shechem's house—she had stayed with him voluntarily after he had raped her—and went forth. Simeon and Levi had used the covenant of God to perform an act of treachery and murder.

Dinah would never again in the Bible be referred to as Dinah. She would be referred to as "that Gentile woman, that heathen woman."

Then the sons of Jacob came upon the slain, and it was bad enough that they had committed murder, but then they spoiled the city because Shechem had defiled their sister. They put the entire city in ruin. They destroyed every house, every dwelling. They burned, they pillaged, they raped. They took their flocks, their herds, their asses, and that which was in the city, and that which was in the field, all their wealth. They took all their little ones, they took their wives, they took them captives, and they spoiled even everything that was in every house.

Jacob did not forgive them to his dying day. And Jacob said to Simeon and Levi when he found out about it, "You've made my name stink among the inhabitants of the land for what you've done. You've made me odious to the Canaanites and the Perizzites. And I, being few in number, now they will gather themselves together against me. They will slay me, and I will be destroyed, I and my house."

Jacob had no faith that God would protect him, but Simeon and Levi rationalized the whole thing. They said "Should he deal with our sister as with a harlot?"

And the LORD spoke unto Jacob, and He said, "Arise, get yourself up one more time, and go to Beth-el and dwell there, Beth-el, the place where you built an altar. Make there an altar unto God who appeared unto you when you did flee from the face of Esau, your brother."

And Jacob said unto his household, and to all that were with him, "Put away the strange gods that are among you." They still had the idols that Rachel had stolen from her father, and they had picked up idolatry from the people of the land. He said, "We're going to Beth-el, where the LORD first appeared to me. And we're going to purify ourselves by baptism." They were immersed in water, and they abstained from any act which would come between them and the LORD. They were going to have to focus their mind on the LORD, to come back and be in a covenant relationship with God in Spirit and in truth. So Jacob said, "Put away the strange gods that are among you, purify yourselves, and change your garments. And let us arise and go up to Beth-el, and I will make there an altar unto God, who answered me in the day of my distress. When I called upon Him, He answered me in my day of my distress, and was with me in the way which I went. The way that I went was not always the right way, but even so, He was with me in the way that I went, every step of the way."

185

So they gave unto Jacob all the foreign gods which were in their hands, the rings which were in their ears, and Jacob hid them under the terebinth, the oak tree, which was by Shechem.

And they journeyed, and the terror of God was upon the cities that were round about them. The LORD was keeping His promise to Jacob, saying, "You go back, and I'll be with you, I'm your divine protection. I'll protect you from your enemies."

So Jacob came to Luz, which is in the land of Canaan, the same as Beth-el today, he and all the people that were with him. And he built there an altar, and he called the place El-bethel, "God, the house of God," because there God was revealed unto him when he fled from the face of his brother.

And Deborah, Rebekah's nurse—Jacob's mother's nurse who had been with Jacob the whole twenty years while he was gone —died, and she was buried beneath Beth-el under an oak. And the name of it was called Allon-bachuth, "the oak of weeping."

God—in the form of Jesus Christ—appeared unto Jacob again when he came from Padan-aram, and He blessed him. And God said unto him, "Your name is Jacob. Your name shall not be called anymore Jacob, but Israel shall be your name." And He called his name Israel.

Earlier, when Jacob had wrestled with the angel of the LORD at Peniel, God had appeared to Jacob and said, "I have changed your name from Jacob, and now I'm calling you Israel." And now the LORD was confirming Jacob's new name, and also cleansing him from guilt for the murder, rape, pillage, and spoiling of Shechem. It was as if God was saying to him, "Fear not, Jacob. I have forgiven you your sins. You are still Israel with Me."

And God said unto him, "I am God Almighty, El Shaddai." And He commanded him, saying, "Be fruitful and multiply. A nation and a company of nations shall be of thee, and kings shall come out of your loins. From you, all nations of the earth will come to know me as the living God. And the land which I gave unto Abraham and to Isaac, to thee will I give it and to your seed after thee, will I give the land."

And God went up from him in the place where He spoke with him. And Jacob set up a pillar in the place where He spoke with him, a pillar of stone, and he poured a drink offering thereon, and he poured oil thereon.

The drink offering symbolized the shed blood of Jesus Christ, and the oil symbolized the Holy Spirit, the oil of the Holy Spirit. And Jacob called the name of the place where God spoke with him, Beth-el, "house of God."

And they journeyed from Beth-el, and there was still some way to come to Ephrath, the old biblical name of Bethlehem. And Rachel was pregnant, and she travailed, and she had a very hard labor. And it came to pass when she was in hard labor, that the midwife said unto her, "Fear not, the LORD has answered your prayer. This is also a son for thee." And it came to pass as her soul was in departing—she was dying—that she called his name Ben-oni, "son of my sorrow," because she knew she was going to die. But the Holy Spirit descended upon Jacob immediately, and his father called him Benjamin, "son of my right hand."

From this boy, Benjamin, would be coming the right hand of the living Christ, whom Jesus Himself would choose on the road to Damascus, of the tribe of Benjamin, Saul of Tarsus. God dealt with him in the Arabian desert for three years, putting in him the new, living, loving mind of Christ Jesus. He would be the right hand of Christ Jesus, and he would be the greatest evangelist this world has ever seen. He would preach the Gospel to all the ends of the known civilized world. The LORD would put the tribes of Benjamin and Judah together in a kingdom called the kingdom of Judah, with the capital at Jerusalem. From Judah would come Christ Jesus; from Benjamin would come Saul of Tarsus, Saint Paul. The other ten tribes would establish the kingdom of Israel at Samaria.

So Rachel died and was buried in the way to Ephrath, which is Bethlehem. And the place where she died and was buried is about two miles from where Jesus Christ was born in Bethlehem. And Jacob set up a pillar upon her grave; the same is the pillar of Rachel's grave unto this day.

Later on, the descendants of Esau, particularly Herod, would seek to destroy the Christ child. And he would not be able to find the Christ child, but he would destroy and kill the other infants. And they would be buried just about two miles away from where Rachel was buried, and the Scripture would be fulfilled that a mother's voice was heard crying in the wilderness for her children. Those little babies would be buried in the cave next to the one where Jesus was born.

And Israel continued his journey and spread his tent beyond Migdal-eder. And it came to pass that while Israel dwelt in that land that Reuben went and lay with Bilhah, his father's concubine, and Israel heard of it. His sons, Levi and Simeon had transgressed in the massacre of Shechem, and now Reuben had transgressed, going to bed with his father's concubine. This ruled out Reuben the firstborn from receiving the blessing, and the birthright, and the kingship. Simeon was ruled out because he was the leader in the murder and pillage of Shechem and Hamor, and Levi was ruled out because he had accompanied Simeon.

All this meant that Judah would receive the birthright, the blessing, and the kingship. The Lion of Judah, Jesus the Christ, He would receive the priesthood, the birthright, the blessing, and He would be King of kings and Lord of lords.

Now the sons of Jacob were twelve: The sons of Leah: Reuben, Jacob's firstborn, and Simeon, and Levi, and Judah, and Issachar, and Zebulun. The sons of Rachel: Joseph and Benjamin. And the sons of Bilhah, Rachel's handmaid: Dan and Naphtali. The sons of Zilpah, Leah's handmaid: Gad and Asher. These were the sons of Jacob which were born to him in Padan-aram.

And Jacob came unto Isaac, his father, unto Mamre unto Kiriath-arba, the same as Hebron, where Abraham and Isaac sojourned. And the days of Isaac were an hundred and fourscore years, 180 years. And Isaac died and was gathered unto his people, old and full of days. And Esau and Jacob, his sons, buried him in the cave of Machpelah.

The thirty-sixth chapter of Genesis is the generations of Esau. If we follow the genealogy, we see that most of the wickedness which came upon the face of the earth came through the descendants of Esau. Every problem that Israel had came from Esau. The Israelites had to fight the Amalekites —who were descendants of Esau. Herod slew the innocent children, and he was a descendant of Esau. In his day, he was called an Idumean; he wasn't a Jew. The Romans put him in power because they knew he would treat the Jews very cruelly.

But God promised that through Abraham, through Isaac, through Jacob, all the world would be blessed. He said, "Through you all the nations of the earth shall be blessed, because through you, I am bringing the Messiah."

10
Now Israel Loved Joseph
(Genesis 37—39:20)

And Jacob dwelt in the land of his father's sojournings, in the land of Canaan. And these are the generations of Jacob. Joseph being seventeen years old, was feeding the flock with his brethren, being still a lad. Later on, when God specified to Moses that he was to take a census, He told him not to count anybody as a man until he had reached the age of twenty. Those of twenty years of age and older were considered men, and those beneath the age of twenty were considered to be lads, without the ability to discern between right and wrong, good and evil.

Joseph being seventeen years of age, was feeding the flock with his brethren. Although he was still a lad, his father put him in charge of the sons of the handmaids, even the sons of Bilhah, the sons of Zilpah.

Rachel was dead, and Joseph looked very much like Rachel, with big beautiful brown eyes. And Jacob transferred his affections to Joseph. This was bound to bring problems in his household.

And it did. Joseph brought back an evil report of the sons of the handmaids unto his father.

The Scripture tells us that Israel loved Joseph more than all of his children, because he was the son of his old age, and he made him a coat of many colors. The minute Jacob made him a coat of many colors, he announced his favoritism.

And so Jacob created contention in his family, showing such partiality to Joseph. He already had enough contention. He had four wives who couldn't stand each other. And after Rachel's death, he had three that couldn't stand each other. He had twelve boys and a daughter. None of them got along with each other either. Each one was always spying upon the others. The LORD was still dealing with the conniver. God had given him a born-again experience, changed him, transformed him into a new creature, Israel, but he still had garbage in his life that had to come out, uncleanness that the LORD would bring out by His righteousness.

When his brethren saw that their father loved Joseph more than all his brethren, they hated him. Jacob brought the hate into the family by his actions.

God is no respecter of persons. And we cannot be respecters of persons, particularly with our children. We should never show partiality to one child more than we do to another child, because that's not the way God loves us. He loves each and every one of us equally. He says it over and over again: "I'm no respecter of persons. I love you all the same." So, if we're going to follow our heavenly Father, we have to love each other and our children exactly as God loves us.

Jacob was showing favoritism to one boy, and he was thereby creating hatred in the family. And his brethren hated Joseph, and they couldn't even speak peaceably unto him. They couldn't even say "shalom" unto him, or "good morning," "good night," or "hello." They couldn't say even one word peaceably unto him.

And all of a sudden Joseph dreamed a dream, and he had the nerve to tell it to his brethren, because it was a very good dream.

Joseph said unto them, "Hear, I pray you. Come here and listen. It was not I who invented the dream, but it was the LORD our God who gave me this dream. I want you to listen to this dream which I have dreamed. For behold, all of us were binding sheaves in the field, and lo, my sheaf arose, and stood upright, and behold, your sheaves came round about and bowed down to my sheaf."

And his brethren said to him, "Oh brother! Shall we really bow down to you, and shall you, indeed, reign over us? Shall you indeed have dominion over us?" And then they hated him yet the more for his dream and for his words.

And Joseph dreamed yet another dream, and again, instead of keeping his mouth shut, he flaunted it before his brethren, and he told his brethren the dream. And he said, "Behold, I have dreamed yet another dream. And behold, the sun and the moon and the eleven stars bowed down to me." And he told it to his father and to his brethren.

And his father rebuked him and said unto him, "What is this dream you have dreamed? Shall I and your mother and your brethren indeed come to bow down to thee to the earth?"

And his brethren envied him. And there was hate, jealousy, and envy in the family. Satan was having a field day.

But the father kept the saying in mind, thinking, "LORD, You've just confirmed that I did the right thing. You gave my boy two dreams, and by these two dreams, You've confirmed to me that when I put the coat of many colors upon him, I did the right thing." Joseph's father saw it as a confirmation of his own will, not the will of God. He saw himself, Jacob, as being right in creating hatred, jealousy, and envy in his family with the coat of many colors.

And Joseph's brethren went to feed their father's flock in Shechem. And Israel said unto Joseph, "Do not your brethren feed the flock in Shechem? Come, I will send you to them."

And Joseph said to him, "Here am I."

And Jacob said to Joseph, "Go now. See whether it is well with your brethren, and well with the flock. And bring me back word." So he sent him out of the vale of Hebron, and he came to Shechem.

And a certain man found him, and, behold, he was wandering in the field. And the man asked, saying, "Whom do you seek?"

And he said, "I seek my brethren. Tell me, I pray thee, where they are feeding the flock."

And the man said, "They are departed from here, for I heard them say, 'Let us go to Dothan.' " And Joseph went after his brethren. He found them in Dothan. And when they saw him afar off, even before he came near unto them, they conspired against him to slay him.

And they said, "Here comes that no-good dreamer. Here comes that no-good character with the fancy coat. If we're not careful, he's going to get the inheritance, the birthright, the blessing away from us. Let's get rid of him. Let's kill him before he gets here."

But Reuben was already in hot water with Jacob for going to bed with Bilhah, his father's wife. And he thought maybe he could bail himself out by saving the favorite son, Joseph. If he could save Joseph, and Joseph would go back with him to the old man and say, "It was Reuben who stepped in between the brethren and myself and saved my life," Reuben would be back in very good graces with his father, and he would receive the birthright, the blessing, and the inheritance, and the kingship.

And so Reuben said, "Let us not take his life. Shed no blood, but cast him into this pit that is the wilderness, and lay no hand upon him." He would deliver him out of their hands and restore him to his father. Reuben was hoping later to rescue Joseph and bring him back to Jacob against whom he had so grievously sinned. But in the meantime, he had to leave on some business.

And it came to pass that when Joseph was come unto his brethren, that they stripped Joseph of his coat of many colors that was upon him. And they took him and cast him into a pit. The pit was empty—there was no water in it.

When they put Joseph into the pit, they sat down to eat bread. They were going to have corned beef, pastrami, lox, and bagels—a nice picnic lunch—while Joseph was in the pit, crying for help. And they lifted up their eyes and looked, and behold, a caravan of Ishmaelites coming from Gilead with their camels bearing spicery and balm and myrrh, carrying it down into Egypt.

And Judah intervened, trying to save Joseph. Judah said now to his brethren, "What profit is there in it for us if we slay our brother, and we conceal his blood? Come, let us sell him to the Ishmaelites, which are the Arabs, and let not our hand be upon him, for he is our brother, and he is our flesh." This was the first acknowledgment that Joseph was a brother to any of them.

And his brothers listened unto Judah, and there passed by Midianites, merchantmen. And they drew and lifted up Joseph out of the pit, and they sold Joseph to the Ishmaelites for twenty shekels of silver. And the Ishmaelites brought Joseph into Egypt.

Afterward, Reuben returned unto the pit. And, behold, Joseph was not in the pit, and Reuben tore his garments and he said, "There goes my last chance. I had one chance to get back into the good graces of my father, but now Joseph is gone," and he went into mourning, because he knew he was finished with his dad forever. His father never forgave him, and he never forgave Simeon. He held a grudge against those two.

Reuben tore his garments, and in a Jewish manner, he put on sackcloth and ashes, and he figured that not only Joseph was finished, but he himself was finished. And he returned unto his brothers and he said, "The child is not. The child's not there. And as for me, where shall I go? I'm the eldest brother, but where will I go? How can I go home and tell dad his beloved son is gone? I don't know what happened to him." And they took Joseph's coat, and they killed a he goat and dipped the coat in the blood. And they sent the coat of many colors, and they brought it to their father and they said, "This we have found. Know now whether it is your son's coat or not."

And he knew it, and he said, "It is my son's coat. An evil beast has devoured him. Joseph is without doubt torn in pieces." And Jacob rent his garments and put sackcloth upon his loins and mourned for his son many days. And all his sons and all his daughters rose up to comfort him, but he refused to be comforted. And he said, "No, I will go down to the grave mourning for my son. God had the greatest nerve of all to take Rachel away from me, and now Joseph is taken away from me, and this born-again experience of being Israel is all garbage, and I'll have no part of it."

I said the very same words when the Lord *took my mother from me, and when He took my younger brother from me. I know how Jacob felt.*

He said, "I'm not going to be comforted. I'm going to sit in my little corner with my sackcloth and my ashes. Nobody talk to me. I have a spirit of self-pity within me, and I want to live this way. Just leave me alone. I'm going to go down to the grave mourning for my son for the rest of my days." And his father wept for him for thirteen years.

And the Midianites sold Joseph into Egypt unto Potiphar, an officer of Pharaoh, the captain of his guard.

None of this had happened by accident. It was all by divine appointment. Man has his hand in doing His will, but God's will is what wins out, even without the interference of man. God had told Abraham, "Know for a surety your descendants *will* go into Egypt. They will be in slavery and in bondage for four hundred years. I will deliver them. I will bring them up with a great redemption. I will make of them a people, a nation. Before I take them down into Egypt, your descendants will be twelve brothers who hate each other. But after Egypt, they will become a congregation of peoples, and they will become Israel. They will become a mighty nation that the whole world will recognize, but first I have to put them into that fire, through that refining process."

It was no accident that Joseph was sold to Potiphar, the captain of the guard, who was such a big wheel that he accounted only to Pharaoh.

The Bible never covers up for any of its heroes. It reveals everything about them. They were human beings like you and I are—they sinned, they backslid, they lied, they cheated, they stole. If it was not for the grace of God, none of them, none of us, would ever have found salvation.

And it came to pass at that time that Judah, from whom was coming King David, from whom was coming Jesus the Christ, went down from his brethren and turned in to a certain Adullamite, whose name was Hirah. And Judah saw there a daughter of a certain Canaanite, whose name was Shuah. And he took her, and he went in unto her. Judah was not allowed to marry a Canaanite, or to have any sexual relationship with anybody, much less a Canaanite, a heathen. But Judah saw her, he desired her, he took her, he went in unto her, and she conceived, and she bore a son, and she called his name Er. She conceived again and bore a son and called his name Onan. And she yet again bore a son and called his name Shelah, and he was at Chezib when she bore him. And Judah took a wife for Er his firstborn, and her name was Tamar. And Er, Judah's firstborn, was wicked in the sight of the LORD, and the LORD slew him.

According to a Jewish custom that is still observed today, when Er died, his unmarried brother was to take his brother's wife to be his wife, and any inheritance, any children that were born from this relationship, would be accounted to his brother.

And Judah said unto Onan, his second son, "Go in unto your brother's wife and perform the duty of a husband's brother unto her, and raise up seed for your brother, so that your brother's name will not die."

And Onan knew that the seed, the children, would not be his, and it came to pass that whenever he went in unto his brother's wife, he spilled his semen on the ground, lest he should give seed to his brother. He had a spirit of lust within him, lusting after his brother's wife, and he had a sexual relationship with her, but he spilled his seed upon the ground, and the thing that he did was evil in the sight of the LORD, and the LORD slew him also.

Then said Judah to Tamar, his daughter-in-law, "Remain a widow in your father's house. Go back to your father's house. Get out of my house. You've already cost me two sons. Wait till my youngest son, Shelah, be grown up, lest also he die like his brethren." He blamed Tamar for the death of his sons, failing to see the two boys committing a sin before the LORD. And Tamar went and dwelt in her father's house. In the process of time, Shuah's daughter, the wife of Judah, died, and Judah was comforted and went up unto his sheepshearers to Timnath, he and his friend, Hirah the Adullamite.

And it was told Tamar, "Behold, your father-in-law goes up to Timnath to shear his sheep." Then Tamar took off her garments of her widowhood, and she put on her nice new wig, her eyelashes, and her makeup. She dressed up and covered herself with a veil. And she wrapped herself and sat in the entrance of the gate of Enaim, which is by the way to Timnath, for she saw that Shelah was grown up, but Judah had not given her to him to wife. And when Judah saw her, he thought her to be a harlot, a prostitute, for she had covered her face. He didn't recognize who she was. His wife was dead, and he thought Tamar was a harlot, so he turned unto her by the way and said, "Come, I pray thee, let me come in unto thee." He did not know that she was his daughter-in-law.

And she said, "What will you give me that you may come unto me? What price?"

And he said, "I haven't got anything with me today, but I promise you that I will send you a kid of the goats from the flock."

And she said, "Would you give me a pledge till you send it?"

And he said, "What pledge shall I give you."

And she said, "Your signet, your cord, and your staff that is in your hand."

The signet ring was the ring that classified him as the elder and the prince of the tribe of Judah. The cord showed that he had the birthright and the blessing. The staff was the staff passed on from father to son, recording the genealogy of the family. In effect, she asked for his birthright, his blessing, his inheritance, his genealogy—every spiritual blessing he owned.

And the dumb-dumb gave them to her. And he came in unto her, and she conceived by him, her father-in-law. Afterward, she arose, went away, put off her veil from her, and put on her garments of widowhood again.

And Judah went back home, planning to redeem the pledge right away, because he wanted his signet, his cord, and his staff. God forbid that anybody should find out that he had a relationship with a prostitute—much less that he had given the symbols of his birthright, blessing, kingship, and leadership to some unknown harlot.

And so Judah sent the kid of the goat that he promised her by the hand of his friend, Hirah the Adullamite, to receive the pledge from the woman's hand, but Hirah could not find her. Then he asked the men of her place, saying, "Where is the harlot that was at Enaim by the wayside?"

And they said, "There has been no harlot here."

And he returned to Judah and said, "I couldn't find her. And also, the men of the place said there had not been any harlot there."

And Judah said, "Then let her keep it, lest we be put to shame. If anyone asks, I can always pretend they were stolen from me. Just keep your mouth shut, Hirah. Behold, I have sent this kid as I promised her, but you did not find her."

And it came to pass about three months later, that it was told Judah, saying, "Tamar, your daughter-in-law, has played the harlot, and, moreover, she is with child by harlotry."

And Judah said, "Bring her forth, and let her be burnt at the stake."

When she was brought forth, she said to her father-in-law privately, "By the man whose these are, the cord, the signet, and the staff, discern, I pray thee, by whom I am with child. I beg you, Judah, take a look at these. Do you recognize them? Do they look slightly familiar? By the man whose these are, I am with child."

And Judah acknowledged them and said, "She is much more righteous than I, forasmuch as I gave her not to Shelah my son."

And Judah went publicly before the entire tribe of Judah, and he acknowledged his sin before God and before his tribe. He said, "She is pregnant by me. She is far more righteous than I." He confessed his sin before man and before God.

Any time we let God take a bad situation and surrender the bad situation unto him, He will always make a good situation out of it.

And he knew her no more intimately—he no longer had any sexual relationship with her—but he treated her as his daughter-in-law.

And it came to pass in the time of her travail, that, behold, twins were in her womb. And it came to pass that when she travailed, one put out a hand, and the midwife took and bound upon his hand a scarlet thread, saying, "This one came out first." She wrapped a scarlet thread on his wrist so he would have the right of the firstborn, because the entire inheritance would pass to the firstborn, the kingship, the priesthood, the inheritance, the leadership, the blessing.

And it came to pass, as he drew back his hand, that, behold, his brother came out, and she said, "Wherefore have you made a breach for yourself." Therefore, his name was called Perez. *Perez* in Hebrew means "breach."

And it would be through the line of Perez that King David would come, and it would be through the line of Perez that

Jesus would come and cause a breach in the world. And He would say, "I have not come to bring peace, but to bring a sword. There's coming a time when you're going to have to decide whether you're going to follow your mother and your father, or whether you're going to follow Me. There's going to come a time when you decide whether you fear Me more or you fear man more than you do Me." And He said, "If you're lukewarm, I'll spit you out of My mouth; if you're not for Me, you're against Me." Perez was the line that Solomon and David would come from, and all the kings of Judah until the coming of Christ.

Afterward came out his brother, that had the scarlet thread upon his hand. And his name was called Zerah, meaning, "scarlet."

The only defeat Joshua ever suffered was the fault of Achan, the son of Zerah, who took of the gold and the silver of the city of Jericho, which was not permitted. It was devoted unto the Lord as being holy, but Achan took it and hid it underneath his tent, and sin came into Israel. When nobody would confess to the sin, the Lord told Joshua, "Tomorrow morning, bring forth all the twelve tribes of Israel, and I will show you who the sinner is." And the Lord called them tribe by tribe. And when He arrived at the tribe of Judah, He came to Zerah, and He came to the family of Achan, and He said, "Achan, step forward. You're the sinner." Then Achan confessed his sin, but he and his family were destroyed, stoned to death. Thus was the sin put out of Israel. And nobody ever again stood up against Israel during the days of Joshua or any of his elders. As long as Israel remained obedient to the Lord, they continued to receive victories from His hand.

Now Joseph was sold as a slave into Egypt. Joseph was brought down to Egypt, and Potiphar, an officer of Pharaoh, the captain of the guard, an Egyptian, bought him out of the hands of the Ishmaelites who had brought him down there. And the LORD was with Joseph, and he was a prosperous man. All that he did prospered—spiritually, physically, financially, mentally. Everything that he touched went well. The LORD was with him.

Joseph was in the house of his master, the Egyptian. And his master received discernment from the LORD and saw that the LORD was with Joseph and that the LORD made all that Joseph did to prosper in his hand. And Potiphar said, "Gee, am I lucky! I've got me a good thing here in this guy Joseph." And Joseph found favor in the sight of his master, and he ministered unto him as his personal attendant. And he was advanced to the position of overseer and controller of the household and the estate.

So Joseph's master appointed him overseer over his house, and all that he had, he put into his hand. And it came to pass from the time that he appointed him overseer in his house, and over all that he had, that the LORD blessed the Egyptian's house for Joseph's sake. And the blessing of the LORD was upon all that he had in the house and in the field. And Joseph's master left all that he had in Joseph's hand, and having him, he didn't have to pay attention to anything save the bread which he did eat. Joseph was in charge of everything. The only thing his master knew anything about was the bread that he put in his mouth.

And Joseph was of beautiful form and fair to look upon. And it came to pass after these things, that his master's wife, Potiphar's wife, cast her eyes upon Joseph and she said, "Lie with me."

But he refused and said unto his master's wife, "Behold, my master, having me, knoweth not what is in the house. He has no idea what's in the house, or the estate, or the bank account. He has put all that he has into my trust, into my care, and into my hand. There is none greater in this house than I, neither has he kept back anything from me except you, his wife. How then can I do this great wickedness that you want me to do, and sin against God?"

Joseph put sin in the proper perspective. He did not say, "I cannot sin against my master." He said, "I cannot sin against my God." Sin is always directed against the LORD.

And it came to pass as she spoke to Joseph day by day that he did not listen unto her, to lie with her, or to be with her. And it came to pass on a certain day when he went into the house to do his work, there were none of the men of the house there within the house. She caught him by his garments, saying, "Lie with me." And he left his garment in her hand and fled and got himself out. And it came to pass, when she saw that he had left his garment in her hand, and was fled forth, that she called unto the men of her house and spoke unto them, saying, "Rape! See what my husband did? He has brought a Hebrew in unto us to mock us." This is the first known case of anti-Semitism in the Bible. "He has brought in an Hebrew in unto us to mock us. He came in unto me to lie with me, and I cried with a loud voice. And it came to pass that when he heard I lifted up my voice and cried, that he left his garment by me and fled and got himself out." And she laid up his garment by her until his master came home.

And she spoke unto him according to these words, saying, "The Hebrew servant—" he was no longer controller or overseer, but she brought him down to a servant—"the evil servant, whom you have brought in unto us came in unto me to mock me. And it came to pass as I lifted up my voice and cried, that he left his garment with me, and he fled out."

And it came to pass, when his master heard the words of his wife, which she spoke unto him, saying, "After this manner did your servant do to me," that his anger and his wrath were kindled.

Potiphar had it in his power, if he believed his wife, to do away with Joseph without any questions being asked. But he did not believe his wife. So instead of having Joseph executed, he had him put into prison.

He was angry with his wife, but he had to protect his honor and his wife's honor. She had made a statement, and he had to back her up.

And Joseph's master took him and put him into the prison where the king's prisoners were bound.

11
The Lord Was with Joseph
(Genesis 39:21—47:28)

But the LORD was with Joseph and showed kindness unto him and gave him favor in the sight of the keeper of the prison. And the keeper of the prison committed to Joseph's hand all the prisoners that were in the prison, and whatsoever they did there, he was the doer of it. The keeper of the prison looked not to anything that was under his hand, because the LORD was with Joseph, and that which he did, the LORD made it to prosper.

The keeper of the prison surrendered the entire prison into Joseph's hand. He was the head trusty, in charge of the whole thing. The LORD was with him. And Joseph would say for the rest of his life, always, "You meant it for evil, you meant it for harm, but the LORD meant it for good." And he constantly praised and thanked God for every circumstance in which he found himself.

And it came to pass after these things that the butler of the king of Egypt and his baker offended their lord, the king of Egypt. And Pharaoh was angry against his two officers, against the chief of the butlers, and against the chief of the bakers, and he put them in custody in the house of the captain of the guard, Potiphar. And the captain of the guard charged Joseph to be with them, and he ministered unto them, and they continued a season inward. In the Hebrew, when it says, "a season," it means almost a full year had gone by.

And they dreamed a dream, both of them, each man his dream in one night, each man according to the interpretation of his dream, the butler and the baker of the king of Egypt who were bound in the prison. And Joseph came in unto them in the morning, and saw them and behold, they were sad. And he asked Pharaoh's officers that were with him in the ward of his master's house, saying, "How come you look so sad today?"

And they said, "So why shouldn't we look sad already yet? We have dreamed a dream. There is none that can interpret it."

And Joseph said unto them, "Do not interpretations belong to God? Let me pray, let me seek the LORD's will. Perhaps He will give us the interpretations by His Holy Spirit. Tell it to me, I pray you."

And the chief butler told his dream to Joseph and said to him, "In my dream, behold, a vine was before me. In the vine were three branches. It was budding, its blossoms shot forth, and the clusters thereof brought forth ripe grapes. And Pharaoh's cup was in my hand. I took the grapes, and I pressed them into Pharaoh's cup, and I gave the cup into Pharaoh's hand."

Joseph was praying, and Joseph was ready to give him the

interpretation. Joseph said unto him, "This is the interpretation of it. The three branches are three days. Within yet three days shall Pharaoh lift up your head. He will lift you up, restore you to your original position, to your office, and you shall give Pharaoh's cup into his hand after the former manner when you were his butler."

After Joseph had told the butler the interpretation of his dream, he failed for the first and only time in his life. He took his trust out of the LORD, and he put his trust in man. He said to the butler, "Here is what I want you to do for me. Have me in remembrance when it shall be well with you, and show kindness, I pray thee, unto me. Make mention of me unto Pharaoh, and bring me out of this house. For indeed, I was kidnapped. I was stolen away out of the land of the Hebrews, and here also I have done absolutely nothing that they should put me into the dungeon." Now Joseph should have asked the LORD to get him out of prison instead of asking the butler.

When the chief baker saw that the interpretation was good, he said unto Joseph, "I also saw in my dream, and, behold, three baskets of white bread were on my head. And in the uppermost basket there was all manner of baked foods for Pharaoh, and the birds did eat them out of the basket upon my head."

And Joseph answered and said, "This is the interpretation thereof: The three baskets are three days. Within three days shall Pharaoh lift up your head from off of you. He shall hang you on a tree, and the birds shall eat your flesh from off of you." That was the meaning of the birds eating out of the basket.

And it came to pass on the third day, which was Pharaoh's birthday, that he made a feast unto all his servants. He lifted up the head of the chief butler and the head of the chief baker among his servants. He restored the chief butler back unto his butlership, and he gave the cup unto Pharaoh's hand. But he hanged the chief baker, just as Joseph had interpreted the dream to him.

Yet the chief butler did not remember Joseph but forgot him.

The LORD caused him to forget Joseph, because Joseph took his trust out of the LORD and placed it into the trust of the butler, saying, "Remember me to Pharaoh. You get me out of this dungeon that I'm in." The LORD kept him in prison for another two years to teach him the lesson that he is to trust the LORD—and only the LORD—in every circumstance.

In the twelfth chapter of Hebrews, we see that the Holy Spirit, writing through Saint Paul, says that all of us have been spanked and chastised by the LORD because He does love us. If He didn't love us, He wouldn't spank us, He wouldn't care. He wouldn't even bother. So I say, praise the LORD, that the LORD loves us enough, cares enough for us, that He will chastise us once in a while, that He will put us through a refining fire once in a while. The thing to remember is the message that was given to Moses as Israel stood by the Red Sea: "Stand still and see the salvation of the LORD. For the enemy that you see before you this day, you shall never see again, for the LORD will fight for you, and you shall hold and have your peace from this day forward, and forevermore." That's the message to you and to me. Praise the LORD.

And it came to pass at the end of two full years that Pharaoh dreamed, and, behold, he stood by the river. And behold, there came out of the river seven kine—cows—well-favored and fat-fleshed, and they fed in the reed grass. And, behold, seven other kine came up after them out of the river, ill-favored and leanfleshed, and stood by the other kine upon the brink of the river. And the ill-favored and leanfleshed kine ate up the seven well-favored and fat kine.

If we didn't already know the story, we would be like Pharaoh was. We would awake, and we would be in a puzzle, wondering what the dream meant. So Pharaoh awoke.

And he slept and he dreamed a second time. And behold, seven ears of corn came up upon one stalk, rank and good. And, behold, seven thin ears and blasted with east wind sprang up after them. And the thin ears swallowed up the seven rank and full ears. And Pharaoh awoke and, behold, again it was a dream.

And it came to pass in the morning that his spirit was troubled, so he sent and he called for all the magicians of Egypt, and all the wise men thereof. And Pharaoh told them his dreams, but there was none that could interpret them unto Pharaoh.

And it came to pass that the chief butler spoke unto Pharaoh, saying, "I hate to do this, Pharaoh. I don't want to remind you, but I make mention of my faults this day. Remember the time you were angry with me, Pharaoh? When Pharaoh was very wroth with his servant, he put me in custody in the house of the captain of the guard, me and the chief baker. And we dreamed a dream in one night, I and he. We dreamed each man a dream with a meaning of its own. And there was with us a young man, a Hebrew, a servant to the captain of the guard, who was Potiphar, and we told him, and he interpreted to us our dream. To each man according to his dream, he did interpret. And it came to pass, as he interpreted

211

to us, so it was. I was restored to my office and he, the baker, was hanged."

Then Pharaoh sent and called for Joseph, and they brought him hastily out of the dungeon, he shaved himself, he changed his garments, his prison garb, and he came in unto Pharaoh. That was probably the first shower and shave he'd had in quite a while. And he changed his raiment, and he was brought in unto Pharaoh.

And Pharaoh said unto Joseph, "I have dreamed a dream. There is none that can interpret it, and I have heard some say of you that when you hear a dream, you can interpret it."

This was a chance for Satan to attack Joseph through his ego. Joseph could have boasted, "Oh yes, I've done this in the past. I have healed, I have baptized, I've laid hands, I've interpreted dreams, I've done all these things."

But Joseph answered Pharaoh, saying, "It is not in me, but God will give Pharaoh a favorable answer. It's nothing that I can do, nothing that I will ever be able to do. It is from God." Joseph had already the discernment of spirit to know that the interpretation of the dream would be a favorable answer, but the LORD would give it, not Joseph.

This was a beautiful witness to Pharaoh. Joseph was not taking any honor, or praise, or glory to himself, but he was giving all the honor, all the praise, all the glory to the LORD.

So Pharaoh spoke unto Joseph and he said, "In my dream, behold, I stood on the brink of the river—" and he told Joseph the entire dream. Then he said, "There was none that could declare it unto me. Nobody has been able to tell me the meaning of my dream."

And Joseph said unto Pharaoh, "The dream of Pharaoh is

one dream—both dreams mean the same thing. What God is about to do, He has declared unto Pharaoh. The LORD is showing you in advance, so you can prepare. Here's the interpretation: The seven good kine are seven years; the seven good ears are seven years. The seven lean and ill-favored kine that came up after them are seven years, and the seven empty ears blasted with the east wind, they shall be seven years of famine. What God is about to do, He has shown unto Pharaoh. Behold, there are coming seven years of great plenty throughout all the land of Egypt, and there shall arise after them seven years of famine. And all of the plenty shall be forgotten in the land of Egypt. And famine shall consume the land."

In the dream, the lean, ill-favored cattle ate up the well-fleshed cattle, and there was nothing remaining. And the corn was blasted by the east wind. In the Middle East, there is a very hot east wind that destroys everything in its path and usually blows for fifty days. And the temperature can rise anywhere from 140 to 160°.

And Joseph said, "In the seven years of famine, everything that was of plenty will be forgotten. The famine will be so bad that nobody will be able to remember the time when they had enough to eat. Famine shall consume the land, and it shall be very grievous."

God's plan was in action. The LORD was about to fulfill the promise that He gave to Abraham and Isaac when He said, "Know for a surety that your descendants will go and dwell and sojourn in a strange land, but I will bring them up with a great deliverance, with a great judgment, with miracles, with power." The LORD was about to bring the people of Israel down into Egypt, because the famine would be not only in Egypt, but it would be in the land of Canaan also, and in all lands. There would be only one place where they could go and buy food, and that would be in the land of Egypt.

Joseph, still speaking to Pharaoh, said, "That dream was doubled unto Pharaoh twice because the thing is established by God, and God will shortly bring it to pass. Don't try to pray an intercessory prayer, asking the LORD to change His mind. God's will is in action already, right now, and God will shortly bring it to pass."

Then the Holy Spirit descended upon Joseph, and he spoke to Pharaoh, saying, "Now, therefore, let Pharaoh look out for a man of discretion and wisdom, and set him over the land of Egypt. Let Pharaoh do this, and let him appoint overseers over the land, and take up the fifth part of the land of Egypt in the seven years of plenty. Tax the people twenty percent of that which they produce in the time of plenty, because there's going to be plenty, a superabundant harvest. They'll never miss it. Let them gather all the food of those good years that come, and lay up corn under the hand of Pharaoh, and let them keep food in the cities. And the food shall be for a store to the land against the seven years of famine, which shall be in the land of Egypt, that the land shall not perish through the famine."

And the thing was good in the eyes of Pharaoh and in the eyes of all his servants. This Pharaoh was related to the Hebrews. He was a Semitic Pharaoh, of the Hyksos dynasty which came in from the land of Canaan and took control of the land of Egypt. This Pharaoh could see that Joseph was speaking in and through the power of the Holy Spirit. God gave Pharaoh discernment to receive the advice as to what he should do, how he should conduct his kingdom, how he should conduct Egypt. And Pharaoh turned around and said to his servants, "Can we find such a one as this, a man in whom the Spirit of God is?" He saw the Holy Spirit of God in Joseph right then and there.

And Pharaoh said unto Joseph, "Forasmuch as God has shown you all of this, there is none that has discernment and wisdom as you. You shall be over my house, and according to your word shall all my people be ruled. Only in the throne will I be greater than you. See, I have set you over all of the land of Egypt."

And Pharaoh took off his signet ring from his hand, and he put it upon Joseph's hand, and he arrayed him in vestures of fine linen, and put a gold chain about his neck. And he made Joseph to ride in the second chariot behind him, and they all cried before him "Abrech," which means "Bow the knee." The entire population of Egypt would bow down to Joseph because Pharaoh set him over all the land of Egypt.

And Pharaoh said unto Joseph, "I am Pharaoh, and without you shall no man lift up his hand or his foot in the land of Egypt. Nobody can do anything without your permission. The only one you're responsible to is me, and from this point on, you'll run the entire nation of Egypt."

The mercy of the LORD was brought into focus. Joseph was sold into slavery, but Joseph always said, "You meant it for harm, but the LORD meant it for good. I can praise God in all things, in all circumstances. I am rejoicing in the fact that I have spent all these years in prison." Joseph was seventeen years of age when he was sold into slavery. He spent some time in the house of Potiphar and the rest of the time in prison. He was thirty years old when he started his ministry of ruling Egypt. And Jesus began His ministry when He was thirty years old.

Joseph would come the closest of all the people in the Old Testament to being Christlike. He would always turn the other cheek, always praise God no matter what happened to him, no matter who despitefully used him.

And Pharaoh changed Joseph's name to Zaphenath-paneah. Zaphenath-paneah comes from *Zaphenath* meaning, "food man," and *paneah*, "of the life." Joseph's new name was "food man of the life." All in Egypt who wanted to buy food had to go to the food man to receive life.

All those who want everlasting life, all those who want to eat of the bread of life, must receive life from Jesus. He said, "I am the bread of life. All who eat of Me shall never perish, and shall never hunger, shall never thirst."

And Pharaoh said to Joseph, "I want to give you a little gift." And he gave him to wife Asenath, the daughter of Poti-pherah, the priest of On.

And Joseph went out from the presence of Pharaoh, and he went throughout all the land of Egypt. And in the seven years of plenty, the earth brought forth in heaps. He gathered up all the food of the seven years, which were in the land of Egypt. He laid up the food in the cities. The food of the field, which was round about every city, he laid up the same. And Joseph laid up corn as the sand of the sea, very much, until they left off numbering, for it was without number.

And unto Joseph were born two sons before the years of the famine came, which Asenath, the daughter of Poti-pherah, the priest of On, bore unto him. And Joseph called the name of the firstborn Manasseh—in the Hebrew meaning, "one who causes to forget," for he said, "God has made me forget all my toil, and all my father's house." And the name of the second he called Ephraim, meaning, "to be fruitful," and he said, "God has caused me to be fruitful in the land of my affliction."

And the seven years of plenty that was in the land of Egypt came to an end. Joseph was thirty-seven. It had been twenty years since he was sold into slavery, twenty years since he had seen his brethren.

And the seven years of famine began to come, according to the interpretation that Joseph was given, and there was famine, not just in Egypt, but in all lands. But in the land of Egypt, there was bread. And when all the land of Egypt was famished, the people cried unto Pharaoh for bread, and Pharaoh said unto all the Egyptians, "Go see Zaphenath-paneah. He's in charge. Go unto Joseph, and what he says unto you, do."

And the famine was over all the face of the earth, and Joseph opened all the storehouses. He sold unto the Egyptians, and the famine was sore in the land of Egypt, and all countries came unto Egypt to buy corn, because the famine was sore in all the earth.

In the meantime, back in the Promised Land, when Jacob saw that there was corn in Egypt, he said unto his sons, "Look, you dummies, what are you doing already yet? Why do you look one upon another? Why aren't you doing something constructive? Behold, I have heard that there is corn in Egypt. Get yourselves down there and buy for us from thence, that we may live and not die."

And Joseph's ten brethren went down to buy corn from Egypt. But Benjamin, Joseph's brother, Jacob sent not with

217

his brethren because he said, "Perhaps harm would befall Benjamin, and I might lose him like I lost Joseph, and he's the only one that faintly reminds me of my beloved Rachel. Rachel is gone. Joseph is gone. I only have one son remaining by my beloved Rachel, and that's Benjamin, and if I send him down to Egypt, something might happen to him, and that would be the finish for me."

So the sons of Israel came to buy corn among those that came, for the famine was in the land of Canaan. And Joseph was the governor over all the land, and it was he that sold to all the people of the land. He made the final decision as to who could buy corn from Egypt and who could not, as all nations came to buy from Egypt.

And Joseph's brethren came and bowed down to him with their faces to the earth just as they had long ago in Joseph's dream. And Joseph saw his brethren, and he knew them, but he made himself strange unto them and spoke roughly unto them, and he said unto them, "Where do you come from?"

And they said, "From the land of Canaan to buy food." And Joseph knew his brethren, but they knew him not; they didn't recognize him.

They couldn't recognize him because he was dressed as an Egyptian, speaking in Egyptian, through an interpreter. His head was shaved, just like Pharaoh. They remembered him with the long, brown, curly hair of the tribe of Joseph. And they hadn't seen him for twenty years, and certainly weren't expecting to see him whom they had sold into slavery as the chief officer of Pharaoh's court.

Joseph could have taken this opportunity for revenge. After all, he had been shamefully treated and sold into slavery. But he remembered what he had learned as a child: before God gave it to Israel, the LORD gave it to all the people, saying, "Vengeance is Mine. You're never to take revenge. If you trust Me, the LORD your God, I will avenge you."

And Joseph tested his brethren, holding his own natural feelings in check, because he wanted to be convinced of their devotion to their father and his father. And he wanted to be convinced of their love for Benjamin, his brother. And he wanted to know if they were repentant, if they had contrite hearts for their crime toward him. So he spoke roughly to them. "You are spies. You have come to see the nakedness of the land."

And they said unto him, "No, my lord, we came to buy food, and this is the only reason your servants came, to buy food. We are all one man's sons; we are upright men. Your servants are not spies."

And he said unto them, "No, to see the nakedness of the land are you come." In other words, he was accusing them of coming to see the defenses of the land. If an attack would ever take place against Egypt, it would have to come in through Israel or the land of Canaan.

And they said to him again, "We, your servants, are twelve brothers, the sons of one man in the land of Canaan, and behold, the youngest is this day with our father, and one is not."

And Joseph said unto them, "This is what I spoke to you about, saying, 'You are spies,' and hereby, you're going to have to prove yourselves. By the life of Pharaoh, you shall not go forth from here except that your youngest brother come here."

How in the world could they get Benjamin away from the

old man back in the Promised Land and bring him down into Egypt? It would be impossible.

But Joseph said, "You are not going to leave here except your youngest brother comes here. Send one of you, let him fetch your brother, and you shall be bound that your words may be proved, whether there be truth in you, or else, as Pharaoh lives, surely you *are* spies." And he put all of them together in the guardhouse for three days. And Joseph said unto them the third day, "This do and live, for I fear God."

They had professed with their lips that they were upright, honest men. But he told them that profession was not enough. They had to bring their youngest brother to verify their words, to save their lives. Joseph said, "I fear God, and since I fear God, I am unwilling to treat you with unnecessary severity on just mere suspicion. I will keep one of you as a hostage, and the rest shall convey food to your families.

"If you are upright men, let one of your brothers be bound in your prison house, but you go, carry corn for the famine of your houses, and bring your youngest brother unto me. So shall your words be verified, and you shall not die." And they did so.

And they said one to another, "We are verily guilty concerning our brother." This is the first time in twenty years they have admitted their sin. Now they were saying, "We are guilty concerning our brother, in that we saw the distress of his soul when he besought us. Remember we cast him into that pit? He was only seventeen years old, and he was screaming at the top of his lungs. He beseeched us, and we did not hear. We did not want to hear him, therefore is this distress brought upon us."

220

And Reuben answered them and said, "I told you so. Did I not speak unto you, saying, 'Do not sin against this child'? But you would not hear me. Therefore, also behold, his blood is now required of us." And they knew not that Joseph understood them, because he had spoken to them through an interpreter. But Joseph hadn't forgotten Hebrew, and he understood every word.

And Joseph turned himself about from them, and he wept. And he returned unto them, and he spoke unto them, and he took Simeon from among them, and he bound him before their very eyes. Simeon was the one who had taken vengeance in his own hands and destroyed Shechem and Hamor and the entire city of Shechem. And Joseph took Simeon from them, and he bound him and placed him in the prison before their eyes.

Then Joseph commanded to fill their vessels with corn, and to restore every man's money into his sack, and to give them provision for the way, and thus it was done unto them. They loaded their asses with corn, and they departed thence. And as one of them opened his sack to give his ass provender in the lodging place, he saw his money. And, behold, it was in the mouth of his sack, and he said unto his brethren, "My money is restored, and lo, it is even in my sack." And their hearts failed them, and they said, turning one to another, saying, "What is this that God has done unto us?"

And they came unto Jacob, their father, unto the land of Canaan and told him all that had befallen them, saying, "The man who is the lord of the land spoke roughly with us. He took us for spies of the country, and we said unto him, 'We are upright men. We are not spies. We are twelve brethren, sons of our father. One is not, and the youngest is this day with our father in the land of Canaan.' And the man, the lord of the land, said unto us, 'There's only one way that I will know you are upright men. Leave one of your brothers with me, take corn for the famine of your house, and go your way. But bring your youngest brother unto me. Then I shall know that you are not spies, but that you are upright men. So I shall deliver you your brother, and you shall traffic in the land. You'll be able to buy, sell, and trade in the land.' "

And it came to pass as they emptied their sacks, that behold, every man's bundle of money was in his sack, and they said, "Now we've really got a problem!" And when they and their father saw their bundles of money, they were afraid, and Jacob, their father, said unto them, "Boy, you're really a fine bunch of kids. Me have you bereaved of my children. Joseph is not. Simeon is not, and now you want to take Benjamin away. All these things are against me."

And Reuben spoke unto his father, saying, "You shall slay my two sons if I bring him—Benjamin—not unto you. Deliver him into my hand, and I will bring him back to you."

And Jacob said, "My son will *not* go down with you, for his brother is dead, and he only is left. If harm befalls him by the way in which you go, then you will bring down my gray hairs with sorrow to the grave."

Reuben's impetuous nature was brought to light when he said, "You can slay my two sons, one for Benjamin and one for Joseph, if I don't bring Benjamin back to you." He felt he shared the guilt with his brothers, and he had an ulterior motive—he was still trying to buy his way back into his father's graces so he could receive the birthright, the blessing, and the inheritance. But Jacob would not have any part of it. And the famine was still sore in the land.

And it came to pass when they had eaten up the corn which they had brought out of Egypt that their father said unto them, "Go again and buy us a little food."

And Judah spoke unto him, saying, "The man did earnestly warn us, saying, 'You shall not see my face except that your brother Benjamin be with you.' If you will send our brother with us—" This was the first time Benjamin was called "*our* brother." Usually, he had been referred to as "*your* son." There was a difference. And Judah said, "If you will send our brother with us, we will go down, and we will buy you food. But if you will not send him, we will not go down, for the man did say unto us, 'You shall not see my face except your brother be with you.' "

And Israel said, "Wherefore have you dealt so ill with me? Why didn't you keep your big, fat Jewish mouth shut? Did you have to tell him you were twelve brothers, that you had another brother back there? Couldn't you say you were eleven and one was not? Did you have to say you were twelve sons? Why have you dealt so ill with me as to tell him that you still had a brother back with his father?"

And they said, "The man asked us straitly concerning ourselves, concerning our family, saying, 'Is your father yet alive?' " If they had been sharp enough, Joseph's questioning them about their father could have been the tip-off to them as to who he was. Joseph loved his father very much. That was why he asked the question in the first place.

"And he asked, 'Have you another brother?' And we answered him according to the tenor of these words. Could we have known that he would say, 'Bring your brother down'? We had no idea."

And Judah said unto Israel, his father, "Send the lad with me. We will arise and go, that we may live and not die, both we and you, and also our little ones. I will be surety for him. Of my hand shall you require him. If I bring him not before you and set him before you, then let me bear the blame forever."

The Lion of Judah, Jesus Christ, would be coming through Judah. And Jesus would say to our heavenly Father, in regard to you and me, "I will be the surety for him. I will be the guarantee for him, because I will go to the cross for him. Of My hand shall you require him. If I don't bring him unto You, Father, and set him before You, then let Me bear the blame forever." Judah's words were symbolic of the coming of Jesus Christ.

And Judah reminded the old man, "All this talk! We're wasting time! Except that we have been lingering, surely we would have been gone down into Egypt, and we would have returned the second time already."

And their father, Israel, said unto them, "If it must be so now, do this." All of a sudden, he was being referred to as Israel instead of Jacob, because the anointing of the LORD was upon him. He was moving in the Spirit of the LORD, and once again he was Israel, because he was going to trust the LORD with Benjamin.

There comes a time in your life and in my life when we have to trust the LORD with our children, with our wives. They are a gift to us from God. They do not belong to us. They belong to Him. They are a trust from the LORD. We need never worry

about our children if we know that we have committed them
unto the LORD, *and we say,* "LORD, *Your will be done.*"

And Israel said unto them, "If it must be so now, do this.
Take of the choice fruits of the land in your vessels. Carry
down the man a present, a little balm, a little honey, spices, and
myrrh, nuts, and almonds. Take double money in your hand,
and the money that was returned in the mouths of your sacks,
carry it back in your hand. Perhaps it was an oversight. Take
also your brother, and arise and go unto the man. And God
Almighty—" he called upon the revelation of God that he
knew, El Shaddai—"and El Shaddai give you mercy before the
man, that he release unto you the other brother and Benjamin."
He didn't even mention the other brother by name, because he
said, "My spirit will have no part with the spirit of Simeon."
He held a grudge against Simeon till his dying day. And Jacob
said, "As for me, if I'm going to be bereaved of my children, I
am bereaved." Notice his faith, as he passed from Jacob to
Israel. He was saying, "LORD, I'm trusting You all the way now
with my kids. If I'm going to be bereaved, and this is Your will,
let it be Your will. I am going to be bereaved. Praise the LORD."

So the men took the present, they took double money in
their hand, and they took Benjamin and rose up. They went
down to Egypt, and they stood before Joseph. And when
Joseph saw Benjamin with them, he said to the steward of his
house, "Bring the men into the house, kill the beast, and prepare the meat, for these men shall dine with me at noon." And
the man did as Joseph bade; and the man brought the men into
Joseph's house.

And the brethren were afraid because they were brought into
Joseph's house. They knew that Hebrews were not allowed to

225

eat with Egyptians, and they knew that Egyptians were not allowed to eat with Hebrews. It was an abomination for an Egyptian to sit down and have dinner with a Hebrew.

But they were brought into the house of Joseph, and they said, "This is happening because of the money that was returned in our sacks at the first time. Maybe he is seeking occasion against us, to fall upon us, and take us for slaves, and our asses."

And they came near to the steward of Joseph's house, and they spoke unto him at the door of the house, saying, "O my lord, we came indeed down at the first time to buy food. It came to pass when we came to the lodging place, that we opened our sacks, and we took a look, and every man's money was in the mouth of his sack, our money in full weight, and we have brought it back in our hands. And other money have we brought down in our hands to buy food. We know not who put our money in our sacks."

And the steward said, "Shalom, peace be unto you. Fear not. Your God and the God of your father has given you treasure in your sacks. I had your money. Don't worry. It's all right. We were paid in full." And he brought Simeon out to them.

And the steward brought the men into Joseph's house. He gave them water, and they washed their feet. He gave their asses provender. And they made ready the present for Joseph's coming at noon, for they heard that they should eat bread there together.

And when Joseph came home, they brought him the present which was in their hand into the house, and they bowed down to him to the earth, just as they had in both of Joseph's dreams long ago. And he asked them of their welfare, and again, he asked the question, "Is your father well, the old man of whom you spoke? Is he yet alive?"

And they said, "Your servant, our father, is well and he is yet alive." And they bowed their heads, and they made obeisance.

And Joseph lifted up his eyes, and he saw Benjamin, his brother, his mother's son, and he said, "Is this your youngest brother of whom you spoke unto me?" And he said, "God be gracious unto you, my son." And Joseph made haste, for his heart yearned toward his brother, and he sought somewhere to weep, and he entered into his chamber, and he wept there. He could not refrain from weeping at this point, just as he did previously when he heard the confession of his brethren. The minute he saw his brother Benjamin, he began weeping for joy.

Then he washed his face, and he came out, and he controlled himself from weeping, and he said, "Set on bread." And they set on for him by himself and for them by themselves and for the Egyptians that did eat with him by themselves, because the Egyptians must not eat bread with the Hebrews.

And they sat before him, the firstborn according to his birthright, and the youngest according to his youth. And the men marveled one with another. They were astounded. He seated them exactly in a Hebrew manner, following the Hebrew custom, the eldest at the right hand, going right around the table, with the youngest sitting at the left hand.

This is the way Jesus seated the disciples. The eldest was Judas Iscariot, who was at His right hand. The youngest, John the Apostle, the Gospel writer, was seated at his left

hand. He was the one who laid his heart upon the heart of Jesus.
And Judas Iscariot was the one dipping the unleavened bread
and bitter herbs in the dish when Jesus turned around and
said, "The hand that dips in the dish with Me is the hand that
will betray Me."

And portions were served unto them all from Joseph's table,
but Benjamin's portion was five times as much as any of theirs.
And they drank, and they were merry with him. "Merry"
means they got loaded. They drank and they got drunk.
Joseph got them drunk to divert their attention from his table
where his goblet that he drank from was about to be removed.
He was going to trap them, to have his steward remove his
goblet from his table.

And Joseph commanded the steward of his house, saying,
"Fill the men's sacks with food, as much as they can carry,
and put every man's money in his sack's mouth. Put my goblet,
the silver goblet, in the sack's mouth of the youngest one,
Benjamin, with his corn money." And he did according to the
word that Joseph had spoken.

As soon as the morning was light, the men were sent their
way, they and their asses. And when they were gone out of the
city, and they were not yet very far off, Joseph said unto his
steward, "Up, follow after the men, and when you overtake
them, say unto the men, 'Wherefore have you rewarded evil for
good? How come you have returned evil for good? I have been
good unto you; you have done nothing but evil. Is not this the
very thing from which my lord drinks, and whereby indeed he
does divine, where he looks to see what is going to happen in
the future? You have done evil in so doing! You shouldn't
have stolen it.' "

And when the steward overtook them, he spoke unto them these words. And they said unto him, "Wherefore and how come does my lord speak words such as these? Far be it from your servants that we would do such a thing. Behold the money, remember the money that we found in the mouth of our sacks? To prove our honesty and our integrity, we brought it back unto you out of the land of Canaan. So why would we steal out of your lord's house silver or gold? Why would we take the goblet?"

Again, they opened their big, fat mouths and said, "With whomsoever of your servants it be found, let him die, and we also will be my lord's bondmen."

And the steward said, "That would be fair enough. But only he with whom it is found shall be my bondman, my slave, and the rest of you shall be blameless." Then they hastened, and took down every man his sack to the ground, and they opened every man his sack. The steward searched, beginning at the eldest, and he left off at the youngest, and the goblet was found in Benjamin's sack. And then they rent their clothes, they tore their garments, they laded every man his ass, and they returned to the city, greatly distressed.

How could they ever go back to Canaan and tell Jacob, "Benjamin is not"?

And now they returned to the city. And Judah and his brethren came to Joseph's house. He was there waiting for them. And they fell before him on the ground. And Joseph said unto them, "What deed is this that you have done? Don't you know that a man such as I can certainly divine? I knew what you had done, and I sent my steward to bring you back."

And Judah said, "What shall we say unto my lord? What

shall we speak? Or how shall we clear ourselves? God hath
found out the iniquity of your servants. Behold, we are your
lord's slaves, both we, and he also in whose hand the cup
is found."

And he said, "Far be it from me that I should do such a thing.
The man in whose hand the goblet is found, he shall be my
slave. But as for you, get you up in peace and go unto your
father."

Then Judah came near unto him and said, "O my lord, let
your servant, I pray thee, speak a word in my lord's ears, and let
not your anger burn against your servant, for you are even as
Pharaoh. You have the same power as Pharaoh. My lord asked
his servants, saying, 'Have you a father or a brother?' And we
said unto my lord, 'We have a father, an old man, and a child
of his old age, a little one. And his brother is dead, and he alone
is left of his mother, and his father loves him.' " This was the
first time he had spoken of the brother as dead; previously,
Joseph had been referred to as "the one who is not."

Judah went on to say, "Then you said unto your servants,
'Bring him down unto me, that I may set mine eyes upon him.'
And we said unto my lord, 'The lad cannot leave his father,
for if he should leave his father, his father would die.' And you
said unto your servants, 'Except your youngest brother come
down with you, you shall not see my face anymore.' And it
came to pass that when we came unto your servant, my father,
we told him the words of my lord. And our father said, 'Go
again and buy us a little food.'

"And we said, 'We cannot go down if our youngest brother
be not with us. If he be with us, we will go down, for we may not
see the man's face, except our youngest brother be with us.'

And your servant, my father, said unto us, 'You know that my wife bore me two sons, Joseph and Benjamin.'" (Again the partiality. Again, the favoritism in the family. He just wiped out all the other ten sons.)

"'And the one went out from me, and I said, "Surely, he is torn in pieces." I have not seen him since, and if you take this one away from me also, and harm befalls him, you will bring my gray hairs down with sorrow to the grave.'

"Now, therefore, when I come to my father, your servant, and the lad is not with us, seeing that his soul is bound up with the lad's soul, it will come to pass that when he sees that the lad is not with us, that he will die, and your servants will bring down the gray hairs of your servant, our father, with sorrow to the grave. For your servant, the one who is speaking to you now, became surety, became guarantee for the lad unto my father, saying, 'If I bring him not unto you, then shall I bear the blame to my father forever.'

"Now, therefore, let your servant, I pray thee, stay instead of the lad a slave to my lord, and let the lad go up to be with his brethren. For how shall I go up to my father if the lad is not with me, lest I look upon the evil that shall come upon my father?"

Joseph was not going to be able to stand much more. He had about reached his breaking point, and Joseph could not refrain himself before all of them that stood by him, and he cried, "Cause every man to go out from me." The repeated references to the misfortunes of his aged father had overwhelmed him. And as he did not wish his court and his retinue to hear of the crime of his brethren, he ordered every man to depart. And he was left alone with his brothers. There was no interpreter present, and Joseph made himself known to his brethren. And he wept aloud, and the Egyptians heard, and the house of Pharaoh heard.

And Joseph said unto his brethren, "I am Joseph. Does my father truly yet live? Is it really true that our father, who is so old, who has been so sorely tried by the LORD in this life, is he still alive? Is the old conniver still going? Or have you lied?"

And his brethren could not answer him. They were standing there with their mouths gaping open. They couldn't answer him with words. They couldn't believe their eyes and ears when he told them, "I am Joseph."

To better convince them, he had to tell them something else. Joseph said unto his brethren, "Come near unto me, I pray you." And they came near. And he said, "I am Joseph, your brother, whom you sold into Egypt. Remember me—the guy you sold into slavery?" Here, Joseph departed from being Christlike. He gave their consciences a little jab with a little knife.

On the day of the resurrection, Jesus told Mary, "Tell the disciples that I will see them in Galilee. And tell Peter also." He never mentioned the fact that Peter had denied him three times. It was a total message of love.

Then Joseph wanted to calm his brothers. He said, "Don't be grieved. Don't be afraid. Don't put yourself under condemnation. I have forgiven you. Don't be angry with yourselves that you sold me here, for God did send me before you to preserve life. You meant it for evil, but the LORD meant it for good. For these two years has the famine been in the land, and there are still five years in which there shall be neither plowing nor harvest. God sent me before you to give you a remnant on the earth, and to save you alive for a great deliverance."

Joseph gave the glory to God. "It was not you who brought me here into Egypt, but God. And He has made me a father to Pharaoh, and the lord of all of his house, and the ruler over all of the land in Egypt. Now, here's what I want you to do. Hurry and go up to my father and say unto him, 'Thus saith your son Joseph. "God has made me lord of all Egypt. Come down unto me and tarry not. Hurry and come down. And you shall dwell in the land of Goshen, you shall be near unto me, you and your children, and your children's children, and your flocks, and your herds, and all that you have. And there I will sustain you, for there are still five years of famine, lest you come into poverty, you and your household and all that you have." ' And behold, your eyes see, and the eyes of my brother Benjamin see that it is my mouth that speaks unto you. I'm not speaking to you through an interpreter, it's my own mouth speaking to you in Hebrew, so you know who I am. There's no doubt in your mind."

So far, the brethren hadn't said one word. They were still standing there with their mouths gaping open. And Joseph said, "And you shall tell my father of all my glory in Egypt and all of that that you have seen, and you shall hurry and bring down my father here."

Then he fell upon his brother Benjamin's neck, and he wept, and Benjamin wept upon his neck. And Joseph kissed all of his brothers and wept upon them. And after that, his brothers talked with him. They wouldn't open their mouths until he had kissed them and wept with them. Then they knew they were forgiven. And after that, they talked to him.

And the report thereof was heard in Pharaoh's house, saying, "Joseph's brothers are come," and it pleased Pharaoh well and his servants.

And Pharaoh said unto Joseph, "Say unto your brethren, 'This do, lade your beasts and go. Get yourself into the land of Canaan. Take your father, your household, and come unto me, and I will give you the good of the land of Egypt, and you shall eat the fat of the land. Take wagons out of the land of Egypt for your little ones, and for your wives, and bring your father, and come into the land of Egypt. Hurry, and do it now. Also, do not regard your stuff—don't concern yourself with all your stuff that you've got there, for the good things of all the land of Egypt are yours.' "

And the sons of Israel did so. Joseph gave them wagons according to the commandment of Pharaoh, and he gave them provisions for the way. And to all of them, to each and every man, he gave changes of raiment, but to Benjamin he gave three hundred shekels of silver and five changes of raiment. And to his father, he sent in like manner, ten asses laden with the good things of Egypt, ten she asses laden with corn and bread and victual for his father by the way. So he sent his brothers away, and they departed. And he said unto them, "See that you fall not out by the way. Don't argue. Don't quarrel. Just get the wagons, get back to dad, get the wagons loaded, and get back into Egypt."

So they went out of Egypt, and they came into the land of Canaan unto Jacob, their father, and they told him saying, "Joseph is yet alive, and he is ruler over all the land of Egypt." His heart fainted, for he believed them not. And they told him all the words of Joseph which he had said unto them, and when he saw the wagons which Joseph had sent to carry him, the spirit of Jacob, their father, revived. He was released from that mourning, that grieving spirit that he had. He was like a newborn creature once again, like he was the night when he met the LORD and wrestled with Him. He was Israel once again.

And Israel said, "It is enough. Joseph, my son, is still alive. I will go and see him before I die."

So Israel took his journey with all that he had, and he came to Beer-sheba, the well of the oath where the covenant was made. And he offered sacrifices unto the God of his father Isaac, unto the living God.

And God spoke unto Israel in the visions of the night and said, "Jacob, Jacob."

And he answered, "Here am I," the same way that Isaac and Abraham had answered. "Here am I, LORD, to do Your will."

And He said, "I am God, the God of your father. Fear not to go down into Egypt." In Hebrew, this means He said, "I am Elohim, the very same LORD who in the beginning, created the heavens and the earth." He did not reveal Himself as Yahweh or El Shaddai at this point, but He said, "I am God, the God of your father. Fear not to go down into Egypt, for I will there make of you a great nation. I will go down with you into Egypt, and I will surely also bring you up again. And Joseph shall put his hand upon your eyes as you sleep the sleep of death. Joseph, your beloved son, will close your eyes as you go to sleep, to come home to be with Me."

And Jacob rose up from Beer-sheba. And the sons of Israel carried Jacob, their father, their little ones, the wives, in the wagons which Joseph had sent to carry them, and which

Pharaoh had given them. They took their cattle, their goods, which they had gotten in the land of Canaan, and came into Egypt, Jacob, and all his seed with him. His sons, his sons' sons with him, his daughters, and his sons' daughters, and all of his seed he brought with him into Egypt.

These are the names of the children of Israel which came into Egypt: Jacob and his sons: Reuben, Jacob's firstborn. The sons of Reuben: Hanoch, Phallu, Hezron, and Carmi.

The sons of Simeon: Jemuel, Jamin, Ohad, Jachin, Zohar, and Shaul the son of the Canaanitish woman, Dinah. Dinah would never again be referred to as a Hebrew woman, because she voluntarily stayed in the house of Shechem after he raped her.

The sons of Levi: Gershon, Kohath, and Merari.

The sons of Judah: Er, Onan, Shelah, Perez, and Zerah. But Er and Onan died in the land of Canaan when they sinned against the LORD. And the sons of Perez were Hezron and Hamul.

And the sons of Issachar: Tola, Puvah, Job, and Shimron.

The sons of Zebulun: Sered, Elon, and Jahleel.

These are the sons of Leah whom she bore unto Jacob in Padan-aram, with his daughter Dinah. All the souls of his sons and his daughters were 33.

The sons of Gad: Ziphion, Haggi, Shuni, Ezbon, Eri, Arodi, and Areli.

The sons of Asher: Jimnah, Ishuah, Isui, Beriah, and Serah, their sister. And the sons of Beriah: Heber and Malchiel.

These are the sons of Zilpah, whom Laban gave to Leah, his daughter, and these she bore unto Jacob, sixteen souls.

The sons of Rachel, Jacob's wife: Joseph and Benjamin.

And unto Joseph in the land of Egypt were born Manasseh and Ephraim, whom Asenath, the daughter of Poti-pherah, the priest of On, bore unto him.

And the sons of Benjamin were Bela, Becher, Ashbel, Gera, Naaman, Ehi, Rosh, Muppim, Huppim, and Ard.

These are the sons of Rachel, who were born to Jacob. All the souls were fourteen.

The sons of Dan: Hushim.

The sons of Naphtali: Jahzeel, Guni, Jezer, and Shillem. These are the sons of Bilhah, whom Laban gave unto Rachel, his daughter. These she bore unto Jacob, and all the souls were seven.

All the souls belonging to Jacob that came into Egypt, that came out of his loins, besides Jacob's sons' wives, all the souls were 66. Now, counting Joseph and his wife, Asenath, and his sons, Ephraim and Manasseh, who were born to him in Egypt, that would make seventy. All the souls of the house of Jacob, which came to Egypt, were threescore and ten, seventy. And from seventy, in the short four hundred years before they left Egypt, there would be close to four and a half million people.

The LORD fulfilled His commandment, "Be fruitful and multiply." And He fulfilled His promise, "I will multiply you as the stars and as the sand." The LORD is faithful to keep His word.

Jacob sent Judah before him into Egypt, to show the way before him unto Goshen, and to establish a house of teaching, to teach the nurture and the admonition of the LORD to the seventy souls who were coming down into Egypt.

And Joseph made ready his chariot, and he went to Goshen to meet Israel, his father. He presented himself unto him, he fell on his neck, and wept on his neck a good while. And Israel said unto Joseph, "Now let me die, since I have seen your face, that you are still alive."

And Joseph said unto his brethren and unto his father's house, "I will go up and tell Pharaoh. I will say unto him, 'My brethren and my father's house, who were in the land of Canaan, are come unto me. The men are shepherds, for they have been keepers of cattle. And they have brought their flocks and all their herds and all that they have.' And it shall come to pass when Pharaoh shall call you and shall ask you, 'What is your occupation?' that you shall say, 'Your servants have been keepers of cattle from our youth even until now, both we, and our fathers.' Say this that you may dwell in the land of Goshen, for every shepherd is an abomination unto the Egyptians."

And Joseph went in, and he said to the Pharaoh, "My father and my brethren and their flocks and their herds, all that they have, are come out of the land of Canaan, and behold, they are in the land of Goshen." And from among his brethren, he took five men and presented them unto Pharaoh.

And Pharaoh said unto his brethren, "What is your occupation? What is it that you do?"

They said unto Pharaoh, "Your servants are shepherds, both we, and our fathers. To sojourn in the land are we come. For there is no pasture for your servants' flocks, for the famine is sore in the land of Canaan. Now, therefore, we pray thee, let your servants dwell in the land of Goshen."

This was a crucial test of Joseph's character. Remember, he was the viceroy of Egypt, the grand vizier, the prime minister, the big man in Egypt. For the viceroy of Egypt to acknowledge as his own brothers the rude Canaanite shepherds, who had given him every reason for having nothing to do with them, called for his highest loyalty and devotion to his lord, to his God, and to his family.

Many men in our day and age, and even past generations, resist the temptations of youth, attain to positions of highest eminence, and fail to pay the debt which they owe to their own humble kinsmen who have helped them to success.

With Joseph, the debt to his brethren—if there was any debt at all—was very small. There was no need for him to reveal their identity, much less invite his uncouth brethren to the land of Egypt. His action showed a simple nobility of character, a simple faith and trust in the LORD, rarely equaled in the past or the present. He firmly trusted the LORD, and he constantly said, "You meant it for evil, you meant it for harm, but the LORD meant it for good. And I'm trusting my God all the way."

When Joseph's brothers told Pharaoh they were shepherds, and that they wanted to dwell in the land of Goshen, Pharaoh spoke unto Joseph, saying, "Your father and your brethren are come unto you. The land of Egypt is before you. In the best of the land make your father and your brethren to dwell. In the land of Goshen, let them dwell." He gave them the best that he had. They were right with the LORD. They were right with their Father. They were right with their brother. And the LORD moved upon Pharaoh and he said, "Let them have the best of everything."

Then Pharaoh turned around and told Joseph, "If you know of any able men among them, make them rulers over my cattle.

239

Put them in charge of my cattle also." Joseph's own brothers would be in charge of all the cattle of Pharaoh.

So Joseph brought in Jacob, his father, and set him before Pharaoh, and Jacob blessed Pharaoh. Joseph presented his father to the king, and the aging patriarch asked the blessings of God for the king who had befriended his beloved son. He knew that the Pharaoh was an instrument, a channel of grace, from the Lord to his beloved son, and he blessed Pharaoh.

And Pharaoh asked Jacob, "How many are the days of the years of your life? How old are you?"

And Jacob said unto Pharaoh, "The days of the years of my sojourning—not the days of my life, but the years of my sojourning, because I am a sojourner in and a stranger on this earth, and I'm looking forward to going to the next world to be with my Lord, with my Redeemer, with my Savior, with my King—the days of the sojourning of my life are 130 years. Few and evil have been the days of my life."

In the original Hebrew, Jacob is not complaining, but he is praising God that with all the trials, the tribulations, the temptations, the circumstances that he'd gone through, he could still say, "The evil in my life has been very little. And my life has not attained unto the days of the years of the life of my fathers in the days of their sojournings preparing for the world to come." And Jacob blessed Pharaoh again, and went out from the presence of Pharaoh.

And Joseph placed his father and his brethren, and gave them a possession in the land of Egypt, in the best of the land, in the land of Rameses, as Pharaoh had commanded. And Joseph sustained his father, and his brethren, all of his father's household, with bread according to the want of their little ones.

And there was no bread in all the land, for the famine was very sore, so that the land of Egypt and all the land of Canaan languished by reason of the famine. And Joseph gathered up all the money that was found in the land of Egypt, and in the land of Canaan, for the corn which they bought. And Joseph brought the money into Pharaoh's house. And when the money was all spent in the land of Egypt, and in the land of Canaan, all the Egyptians came unto Joseph and said, "Give us bread. Our money is gone, our money fails, and why should we die in your presence? Give us bread, Zaphenath-paneah."

And Joseph said, "Give your cattle, and I will give you bread for your cattle, if your money fails."

How could they starve if they had cattle? The same thing would happen later on in the wilderness. The Israelites would complain unto the LORD *that they were starving, but they were still wealthy in cattle. Yet, they would tell the* LORD, *"We have nothing to eat." Israel had picked up the abomination, the idolatry of the Egyptians, when they made the golden calf. The main god that the Egyptians worshiped was the cow.*

People in India today are starving to death, yet they worship the sacred cow, of which the LORD *said, "I have given it to you as a provision to meet your needs. Don't worship it; worship Me."*

So the Egyptians brought their cattle unto Joseph. Joseph gave them bread in exchange for their horses, their flocks, their herds, for their asses. When that year was ended, they came unto him the second year and said unto him, "We will not hide from you my lord, how that our money is all spent, and the herds of cattle are my lord's. There is nothing left in the sight of my lord, but our bodies and our lands.

"Why should we die before your eyes, both we and our land? Buy us and our land, and if you buy us and our land for bread, we and our land will be slaves or bondsmen unto Pharaoh. Give us seed that we may live and not die, and that the land be not desolate."

So Joseph bought all the land of Egypt for Pharaoh, for the Egyptians sold every man his field, because the famine was so upon them, and the land became Pharaoh's.

As for the people, Joseph removed them city by city, from one end of the border of Egypt even to the other end thereof. He scattered them from one border of Egypt to the other border, throughout the whole land. He was going to make share-croppers out of them, and he was not going to leave them in one area. He spread them out, to have the land produce as much as it possibly could.

Only the land of the priests he did not buy, for the priests had a portion from Pharaoh, and they did eat their portion which Pharaoh gave them; therefore, their land was not sold.

Then Joseph said unto the people, "Behold, I have bought you this day and your land for Pharaoh. Here is seed for you. You shall sow the land. And it shall come to pass at the ingathering that you shall give a fifth unto Pharaoh. And four parts shall be your own for the seed of the field, for your food, and for those of your household, and for food for your little ones." He exacted a tax of twenty percent for Pharaoh from the share-croppers. Everything belonged to Pharaoh. And from that time until the revolution in Egypt in our day and age, the land stayed in the possession of the kings of Egypt.

And they said, "You have saved our lives. Let us find favor in the sight of my lord, and we will be Pharaoh's servants."

And Joseph made it a statute concerning the land of Egypt unto this day, that Pharaoh should have the fifth, or the twenty percent. Only the land of the priests alone did not become Pharaoh's.

And Israel dwelt in the land of Egypt, in the land of Goshen. They got themselves possessions therein. They were fruitful and multiplied exceedingly. From seventy people, God would bring forth a nation dedicated unto Him, a nation who would bring forth the Scripture to all the world. He would make a covenant with them forever, an everlasting covenant. Many of us Christians seem to think that the LORD canceled His covenant with Israel, but He did not. In Isaiah 66:8 He said that a land would be born in one day, and Israel came into existence in one day on May 14, 1948, as the LORD promised through the prophet Isaiah 2800 years ago. God keeps His word. He keeps every covenant and every promise that He makes. Israel is still His beloved, still His choice. Paul wrote, "And so shall all Israel be saved." Praise God. Praise the LORD.

And Jacob lived in the land of Egypt seventeen years. So the days of Jacob, the years of his life, were 147 years.

12
Israel Said, "Bury Me Not in Egypt"
(Genesis 47:29—50)

And the time drew near that Israel must die. The Lord had revealed it to him, telling him, "Prepare, get your house in order. You're about to come home to your eternal reward." And Jacob could hardly wait to go home and be with his Lord, and his Savior, his Redeemer, the Redeeming Angel, Jesus, who was with him all the days of his life.

And Israel called for his son Joseph and said unto him, "If now I have found favor in your sight, put, I pray thee, your hand under my thigh, and deal kindly and truly with me. Bury me not, I pray thee, in Egypt. But when I sleep with my fathers, you shall carry me out of Egypt, and bury me in their burying place."

And Joseph said, "I will do as you have said."

And Israel said, "Swear unto me." And he swore unto him. And Israel bowed down upon the bed's head.

Jacob was not afraid to die. He was not afraid to say, "I will sleep with my fathers." He was at peace with God. He would make the statement, "I wait for Thy salvation, Thy Jesus, O LORD." The word "salvation" in Hebrew is the name of Jesus in Hebrew. Jacob knew that he could never travel beyond God's care.

Looking back on the life of Jacob, remembering Esau, Dinah, Joseph, and the strife, the suffering, and anguish each one of these tragedies brought to him, and all the grief which he brought upon himself—in spite of them, he died blessing. He did not die grudging; he died blessing.

He erred, he sinned, he stumbled, he fell, time after time, but he always rose up again. And on the anvil of affliction and chastisement from the LORD, his soul was restored, and on his deathbed, he was ready to meet his Maker.

And it came to pass after these things, that someone came to Joseph and said, "Behold, your father is sick." And he took with him his two sons, Manasseh and Ephraim.

And someone told Jacob, "Behold your son, Joseph, comes unto you." And Israel strengthened himself and sat upon the bed.

And Jacob said unto Joseph, "God Almighty appeared unto me at Luz in the land of Canaan, and blessed me, and said unto me, 'Behold I will make you fruitful and multiply you. I will make of you a company of people. I will give this land to your seed after you for an everlasting possession.' And now your two sons who were born unto you in the land of Egypt before I came unto you into Egypt are mine. Ephraim and Manasseh, even as Reuben and Simeon, shall be mine." And he adopted Ephraim and Manasseh. They would each become half a tribe of Israel because the name of Joseph would be removed from the roll. Eventually, the tribe of Reuben would disappear entirely, and the tribe of Simeon would be absorbed in the tribe of Benjamin and Judah. Reuben and Simeon would disappear, and Ephraim and Manasseh would remain. Reuben sinned against the LORD, and against his father, by going to bed with one of his father's wives. He never repented of it. He never asked forgiveness of his father or of the LORD. And Simeon sinned against the LORD and against his father with the slaughter at Shechem.

So Jacob said, "I will adopt these two boys. And your issue that you shall beget after them shall be yours. They shall be called after the name of their brethren in their inheritance. As for me, when I came from Padan, from Syria, Rachel died by me in the land of Canaan in the way when there was still some way to come into Ephrath. And I buried her there in the way to Ephrath, the same is Bethlehem."

And Israel beheld Joseph's sons and said, "Who are these?"

And Joseph said unto his father, "They are my sons whom God hath given me here."

And Jacob said, "Bring them, I pray thee, unto me, and I will bless them." Joseph's boys had been raised to know the LORD. And Jacob adopted them as two of the sons and two of the tribes of Israel.

Now the eyes of Israel were dimmed from age so that he could not see. He brought them near unto him. He kissed them, and he embraced them. And Israel said unto Joseph, "I had not thought to see your face, and behold, praise the LORD, God has let me see your children also."

And Joseph brought them out from between Israel's knees,

and he fell down on his face to the earth. To place a child upon the knee was a symbol of adoption, and is still so with Orthodox Jews today. If we're going to adopt a child, the child must be placed upon our knee. Joseph's sons had just been placed upon and between the knees of Jacob, and this having been done, Joseph removed them, and he fell upon his face in gratitude to his father for adopting them.

And Jacob wanted to bless the lads. Joseph took them both, Ephraim in his right hand toward Israel's left hand, and Manasseh in his left toward Israel's right hand, and he brought them near unto him. Now Israel stretched out his right hand and laid it upon Ephraim's head, who was the youngest, and his left hand upon Manasseh's head, guiding his hand wittingly, for Manasseh was the firstborn. Jacob crossed his hands, because the Holy Spirit was upon him. If his right hand had been stretched straight out, it would have been upon the head of Manasseh, who was the eldest, and his left hand upon Ephraim, who was the youngest. But he crossed his hands, and his right hand was upon the head of Ephraim, his left hand upon the head of Manasseh. And the Holy Spirit was telling him, "This is what I want you to do." The Holy Spirit doesn't always work by the rules. And he said, "Jacob, you do exactly as I tell you to do."

So Jacob guided his hand wittingly, and he blessed Joseph and said, "The God before whom my fathers, Abraham and Isaac, did walk the God who has been my shepherd all my life long unto this day, the Angel of the LORD who has redeemed me from all evil, the Redeeming Angel, the One who has purchased me, who has bought me, all the days of my life, this very same Angel of the LORD, bless the lads. And let my name be named in them, and the name of my fathers, Abraham and Isaac, and let them grow into a multitude in the midst of the earth."

And when Joseph saw that his father was laying his right hand upon the head of Ephraim, it displeased him. And he held up his father's hand to remove it from Ephraim's head unto Manasseh's head. And Joseph said unto his father, "Not so, my father, for this is the firstborn. Put your right hand upon his head."

But his father refused. He said, "I know it, my son, I know it. But the LORD has spoken to me, and I know exactly what I am doing. He also shall become a people; he also shall be great. However, his younger brother shall be greater than he, and his seed shall become a multitude of nations." And he blessed them that day, saying, "By these shall Israel bless, saying, 'May God make thee as Ephraim and as Manasseh.'"

To this very day, every pious Orthodox Jewish father, on the sabbath evening, places his hand on the head of his son and blesses him in the very same words that the Holy Spirit just stated: "May God make thee as Ephraim and Manasseh."

Ephraim and Manasseh would never barter away their Jewishness for the most exalted social position. They voluntarily gave up their place in the higher Egyptian aristocracy, and they openly identified themselves with their alien kinsmen, the despised shepherd immigrants. It is fitting that every mother and father who know the LORD should pray that their children will show the same loyalty to their father and their father's LORD, Jesus Christ, as did Ephraim and Manasseh.

And Israel said unto Joseph, "Behold, I die, but God will be with you, and He will bring you back unto the land of your fathers. Do not be afraid to stand on the word of the LORD. He spoke to Abraham. He said, 'Know for a surety your descendants will go down into a strange land and sojourn there, and they will be in slavery for four hundred years, but I will bring them up in a great redemption, out of bondage, and out of slavery. I will bring them up.' "

Israel was reminding Joseph, "Remember, God is with you. He will never leave you nor forsake you, and He will bring you back into the land of your fathers." Then he said, "Moreover, I have given you one portion above your brethren, which I took out of the hand of the Amorite with my sword and my bow." He was referring to that extra portion that he bought in Shechem for a hundred pieces of silver. It came under attack, and he had to go and fight for it, and retrieve it, and take it back again. He gave this to Joseph as his extra portion. He was still showing that extra bit of favoritism to the son whom he loved who reminded him so much of Rachel.

And Jacob called unto his sons and said, "Gather yourselves together, that I may tell you that which shall befall you in the end of days. Assemble yourselves and hear, you sons of Jacob, and hearken unto Israel, your father.

"Reuben, you are my firstborn, my might, the first fruit of my strength, the excellency of dignity, and the excellency of power. You are unstable as water. You have not now the excellency, because you went up to your father's bed; you defiled it; you went up to my couch."

He was saying, "Reuben, you have forfeited your natural right of the firstborn. Through being the firstborn, you've had dignity, and you've had opportunity, but you did not have strength of character."

Reuben appeared to be a man who began good actions, but he did not complete them. He planned to save Joseph, and he actually prevented the murder of Joseph, but Joseph was sold, nevertheless, in spite of Reuben.

Reuben's descendants in Jewish history remained true to their ancestral type, unstable as water. When Deborah unfurled the banner of Israel's independence in the days of the judges, all of the tribes rallied round about her, but in the camp of Reuben, there was great deliberation, mighty searchings of heart, and no action. Instead, they appointed half a dozen committees to study whether they should take action.

Subsequently, we see the tribe of Reuben is very rarely mentioned in Israel's history. They begin, but they never finish. They open their big mouth, but they never move any further than that.

Jacob said to Reuben, "You are my might." As the firstborn, Reuben was endowed with a superabundant vitality, the cause of both his preeminence and his undoing. He didn't know how to use what he had wisely, with the wisdom of the LORD. And Jacob said, "You have had the excellency of dignity," which in the Hebrew means, "You have been superior in dignity. You have had this given to you, because it belongs to the firstborn. Reuben, it was provided for you to receive three portions above your brethren. And the three portions are the right of the firstborn, the priesthood, and the kingdom. You should have had all three. But now you're not going to get anything."

The right of the firstborn was given to Joseph. The priesthood was given to Levi. The kingly power and the headship were given to Judah. Judah would be the king of Israel, and the Lion of Judah would be the King of the entire universe.

And Jacob said to Reuben, "You're unstable as water. My son, any breeze can ruffle your surface. You bubble over like water in an uncontrolled vehemence of passion. You're a very emotional person. You've had weakness of will, lack of self-control and firmness of purpose. You've also had a spirit of lust within you that you never overcame. You had the excellency, but now you'll forfeit all your privileges of the firstborn."

The Holy Spirit was speaking through Jacob, because none of the descendants of Reuben ever became judges, prophets, or leaders in Israel. The Scripture very clearly stresses that moral character is more important than hereditary right. The LORD wants us to be moral and to be ethical one with another. In Leviticus 19:18 He says, "I want you to love your neighbor as you love yourself."

And Jacob said, "In violence, Simeon and Levi are a pair. Weapons of violence are their kinship. They are acquainted with weapons of violence—they know about instruments of cruelty, and they will dwell with instruments of cruelty in their possession. Let my soul not come into their counsel, unto their assembly. Let my glory not be united with them, for in their anger they slew man, and in their self-will they hewed oxen. Cursed be their anger, for it is fierce, and their wrath, for it is cruel. I will divide them in Jacob, and I will scatter them in Israel." This was the LORD speaking to them; this was the Holy Spirit speaking.

And Jacob said, "In the past they formed a secret confederacy together when they went out and slaughtered the men of Shechem. They denied the LORD when they took the LORD's everlasting covenant, the circumcision, and profaned it by having every man be circumcised after Dinah was raped, and on the third day, they killed every man in the city."

And he said, "My soul, my glory, shall not be united with them." Jacob was speaking about God's glory in the soul. God breathed His Holy Spirit into man, and man became a living soul. Jacob said his soul should not be united together with theirs.

Jacob also said that they hewed oxen, they were so cruel. They were not content with just getting revenge for the rape of Dinah, but they raped women themselves. Though the LORD constantly says, "Vengeance is Mine and not yours," they took children, they killed the men, they killed other women, and then, they even hamstrung the animals.

And Jacob said, "Cursed be their anger." Jacob did not curse them, but their sin. The LORD curses our sin, He hates our sin, but He still loves the sinner. Otherwise, none of us would be here today.

Then Jacob said, "Cursed be their sin. I will divide them in Jacob, and scatter them in Israel." We see this prophecy being fulfilled by the intermingling of the tribe of Simeon in the inheritance of Judah. The tribe of Judah swallowed them up. You can't find anybody of the tribe of Simeon any longer. And the tribe of Levi was dispersed among all the tribes of Israel, and this prophecy of the Holy Spirit was fulfilled.

Now we come to Judah, the fourth-born son. The Holy Spirit said through the lips of Leah, "This time I will praise the LORD," as she gave birth to Judah. And the Holy Spirit speaking through Jacob, said, "Judah, thee shall your brethren praise. Your hand shall be on the neck of your enemies. Your father's sons shall bow down before you. Judah is a lion's whelp. From the prey, my son, you are gone up. He stooped down, he crouched as a lion, and as a lion, who shall rouse him up? The scepter shall not depart from Judah, nor the rule of staff from between his feet, until Shiloh comes, and unto him, shall all the obedience of the peoples be."

He was describing the coming of Jesus Christ, the coming Messiah, the coming Savior.

"Binding his foal unto the vine, and his ass's colt unto the choice vine, he washed his garments in wine and his vesture in the blood of grapes. His eyes shall be sparkling as if with wine, and his teeth white with milk."

Unlike Reuben, Judah had neither the birthright, nor the dignity, nor the opportunity of the firstborn, but he had strength, and he was consistent in his purpose. Whatever he started, he would follow through. He knew his enemy, and whether it was a person, an evil, or a cause, his hand was upon that enemy's neck, because Jesus Christ defeated Satan upon the cross. He knew His enemy; He took the sting out of death. Praise God.

Judah was capable of falling into grievous error and sin and yet, he was true at heart to himself and to the LORD. Judah's character fitted him to take the lead and the rule. He was the father of the royal tribe, the ancestor of David, Isaiah, Nehemiah, and Jesus Christ. The Lion of David and the Lion of Judah came from Judah. Christ would be called the Lion of David, and He'd also be called the Lion of Judah. Jesus was never called the son of Abraham, the son of Isaac, or the son of Jacob, but he was called the son of David. That's what made David great.

And Jacob said to Judah, "All your brothers will praise you."

He was foretelling Judah's military glory, as he would be the leader of all the tribes of Israel in subduing the enemies of the LORD, the Philistines, and the Edomites.

Then Jacob said a strange thing: "The scepter shall not depart from Judah, nor the ruler's staff from between his feet, until Shiloh comes." The word *Shiloh* in Hebrew means, "the exact image and reflection of God." Not until He comes into the world will the scepter and the ruler's staff depart from the tribe of Judah. And Jesus Christ did come into the world, being the exact image and reflection of God, and He Himself said, "If you have seen Me, you have seen the Father. I and the Father are One."

And Jacob, still speaking by the Holy Spirit, said, "And unto Him shall all the obedience of the people be." Through Him, the world would be made right, as He would take on all the sin, all the transgression and iniquity of the world as He went to the cross. His eyes would be as if sparkling with wine, and yet He would not be drunk. He would always have a sparkle in His eye. His teeth would be whiter than milk. The verses are a description of Christ.

The Holy Spirit spoke through Jacob, saying, "Zebulun shall dwell at the shore of the sea. He shall be a shore for ships, and his flank shall be upon Zidon."

Zebulun settled in the favorable geographical position described here, and his tribe became mariners. The actual territory of Zebulun stretched from the Sea of Galilee to Mount Carmel close unto Tyre and Zidon.

Issachar was described as a large-boned ass couching down between the sheepfolds. For he saw a resting place, that it was good, and the land that it was pleasant. He bowed his shoulder to bear and became a servant under task work—at forced labor. As a large-boned ass, the people of Issachar would have great physical power, and the minute they found a resting place, they would stay right there. They would not become nomads like the rest of the people of Israel, living in tents. They would not like the life of a wandering Jew. If Issachar found a place where he wanted to rest, he would much prefer to pay tribute and to submit to any enemy that came upon him than to leave his plowshare and take up the sword. He would never go to battle. All this was fulfilled.

Dan would judge his people as one of the tribes of Israel. Samson came from the tribe of Dan to be one of the judges of Israel. Dan would also be a serpent in the way, a horned snake in the way that bites the horse's heels so that his rider falls backward. Judas Iscariot would be coming from the tribe of Dan. The Holy Spirit knew who would betray Jesus with a kiss. This is why the tribe of Dan is not mentioned in the Book of Revelation.

And then Jacob said, "Lord, I am waiting for Your salvation. I can hardly wait to come home and be with You, LORD. I'm waiting for Your Jesus. I'm waiting for Your salvation, O LORD."

Then Jacob described Gad and what would befall him in the end days. "Gad, a troop shall troop upon him, but he shall troop upon their heel." There is a play on words here, and the translation should be, "A raiding band raids him, but he will now band himself against their heel." He would always know where to attack in their rear position. Gad succeeded in repelling the Ammonites, the Moabites, and the Arameans, who were constantly raiding his border. And Jepthah, one of the judges of

Israel, came from the tribe of Gad. The LORD used him as an instrument to bring forth His victory. The victory is always the LORD's.

"And as for Asher, his bread shall be fat, and he shall yield royal dainties." The name Asher means "happy," and this meaning is reflected in the blessing that is bestowed upon him. The land of Asher was prosperous and happy, and they lived in and around Arabia and parts of Israel, where they went in business making delicacies fit for the tables of kings. The Holy Spirit is never wrong.

"Naphtali is a hind let loose: and he giveth goodly words." This gives us an image of swiftness and grace in movement. "He gives goodly words" refers to the tribe's reputation for eloquence. The great victory of Barak, who was of the tribe of Naphtali, was followed by the glorious song of Deborah, who was also of the tribe of Naphtali. They would not only follow through where the LORD led them, they would also bring forth words of praise and thanksgiving unto the LORD.

And Jacob said, "Joseph is a fruitful vine by a fountain. Its branches run over the wall. The archers have dealt bitterly with him, praise the LORD, and shot at him and hated him. But his bow abode firm, and the arms of his hands were made supple by the hands of the Mighty One of Jacob, by the Shepherd, by the Stone of Israel, the Rock of Israel, even by the God of your father who shall help you, and by the Almighty, who shall bless you with blessings of heaven above, blessings of the deep that couches beneath, blessings of the breasts and of the womb. The blessings of your father are mighty beyond the blessing of my progenitors, unto the utmost bound of the everlasting hills.

They shall be upon the head of Joseph, and on the crown of the head of the prince among his brethren."

Jacob reserved his softest and his most loving accents for Joseph, who was united with whatever was best and noblest in both Reuben and Judah. Joseph was the man of visions, the man of dreams. But to this he joined moral and spiritual strength in all his circumstances of life. He was the ideal son, the ideal brother, the ideal servant, the ideal administrator. His character and story have from the beginning of time been held to be typical of the character of the people in the story of Israel. Like Joseph, the people of God, if they trust in the LORD, have been the dreamers of the ages. The LORD said, "In the end days, I shall pour out My Spirit upon all flesh." Some of us are going to dream dreams, and see visions—because we trust in the LORD.

As Jacob blessed Joseph, he said that there was a period of exile coming, and like Joseph in that period of exile, the people of Israel were going to be subjected to great temptations to be disloyal to the God of their fathers. But Joseph always remained loyal to the living God, to the true God, to the God of Abraham, Isaac, and Jacob. This was a reminder to the people of Israel to remain loyal despite great temptations even to the point of death.

And we have seen the people of Israel go to the gas chambers, never denying the living God, never denying the living LORD.

Today we're seeing a miracle happening everywhere with the people of Israel. They're coming to know the LORD *Jesus Christ as their Messiah. Praise God for this great miracle of these end times.*

And the Holy Spirit, still speaking through Jacob, said,

257

"Benjamin is a wolf that ravens—that tears. In the morning he devours the prey, and at evening he divides the spoils." The tribe of Benjamin was wolflike. And Saul of Tarsus would come from the tribe of Benjamin. He would walk meekly into a synagogue, and begin preaching the Gospel, and when they took out a whip and began beating him to death, he could say, "I count it a joy." He was like a wolf who persists, and he would go back again and again preaching the Gospel, bringing the message of salvation, until he won them to the LORD.

These were the twelve tribes of Israel, and this is what their father spoke unto them, and blessed them, every one according to his blessing, he blessed them. And he charged them, and said unto them, "I am to be gathered to my people. Bury me with my fathers in the cave that is in the field of Ephron the Hittite, in the cave that is in the field of Machpelah, which is before Mamre, in the land of Canaan, which Abraham bought with the field from Ephron the Hittite, for a possession of a burying place.

"There they buried Abraham and Sarah, his wife. There they buried Isaac and Rebekah, his wife. And there I buried Leah. The field and the cave which is therein was purchased from the children of Heth." And when Jacob made an end of charging his sons, he gathered up his feet into the bed, and he expired and was gathered unto his people.

The LORD had given Jacob time to bless all of his sons, and he told them all what would befall them. When he got through praising the LORD, and blessing all of his sons, he died. He died blessing and not grudging.

The LORD had promised Jacob when he went down into Egypt, "You shall sleep with your fathers, and Joseph will be the one who will close your eyes in death."

And Joseph fell upon his father's face, wept upon him, and kissed him. And Joseph commanded his servants, the physicians, to embalm his father, and the physicians embalmed Israel.

Joseph was standing by his father, and the LORD's promise to him was that Joseph would kiss him, and Joseph would close his eyes. And all the boys kissed their father and wished him farewell.

And forty days were fulfilled for him, for so are fulfilled the days of embalming, and the Egyptians wept for him three-score and ten days, out of respect to Joseph. And the forty days of the embalmment formed part of the seventy days where they wept for him. It took them forty days to prepare him, and thirty days where they wept for him, thirty days of mourning. Because they mourned thirty days, we Jews today mourn for our dead thirty days. If it was good enough for Israel, it's good enough for us.

When the days of weeping for him were past, Joseph spoke unto the house of Pharaoh, saying, "If now I have found favor in your eyes, speak, I pray you, in the ears of Pharaoh, saying, 'My father made me swear, saying, "Lo, I die. In my grave which I have digged for me in the land of Canaan, there shall you bury me." Now therefore, let me go up, I pray thee, and bury my father, and I will come back.' "

And Pharaoh said, "Go up and bury your father, according as he has made you swear."

And Joseph went up to bury his father. And with him went up all the servants of Pharaoh, the elders of his house, and all the elders of the land of Egypt, and all the house of Joseph, and his brethren, and his father's house. Only their little ones, their flocks, and their herds, they left in the land of Goshen.

Joseph assured Pharaoh he intended to return to Egypt when he said, "I will come back." And all the elders went up to show respect to Jacob due to the great position which was occupied by Joseph in Egypt. They went and they brought Jacob to the place where he wanted to be buried. And there went with them many chariots, horsemen, a very great company.

They came to the threshing floor of Atad, which is beyond Jordan, and there they wailed with a very great and sore wailing, and Joseph made a mourning for his father seven days. The place of Atad has not been identified even till today. We don't know where it is.

Because they made a wailing period of seven days, we still today do it for seven days. We sit on the floor for seven days and seven nights, and we wail. Now, if it's a small family and there are not enough wailers, we are allowed to hire professional mourners, who will wail with us. Notice that this was what *they* did, not what Jacob did. Jacob was saying, "LORD, I can hardly wait to come home to be with You. I'm eager to see Your salvation, to see Your Savior, Your Jesus, my Redeemer, my Angel who has been with me my whole life. I'm eager to see You, face to face."

When the inhabitants of the land, the Canaanites, saw the mourning in the floor of Atad, they said, "This is a grievous mourning to the Egyptians." Wherefore, they called it Abelmizraim, which in Hebrew means, "the mourning of Egypt."

And his sons did unto him according as he commanded them. For his sons carried him into the land of Canaan, and buried him in the cave of the field of Machpelah, which Abraham bought with the field for a possession of a burying place of Ephron the Hittite, in front of Mamre.

And Joseph returned into Egypt, he, and his brethren, and all that went up with him to bury his father, after he had buried his father.

And when Joseph's brethren saw that their father was dead, they said, "Now what? It may be that Joseph will hate us, and he will fully requite us of all the evil which we did unto him."

Jacob knew what they did to Joseph, because they had admitted it to him. They had confessed it to him. They are scared stiff at this point— "The old man is dead; we're going back into Egypt; he is the viceroy of Egypt, the ruling power in Egypt. Perhaps he will hate us. Perhaps he will seek vengeance against us, and he will fully requite of us that which we did unto him."

So they sent a message to Joseph through a messenger, saying, "*Your* father"—not *our* father, but *your* father—"did command before he died, saying, 'So shall you say to Joseph upon my death, "Forgive I pray thee now, the transgression of your brethren and their sin for what they did unto you evil."' " And now we pray you, forgive the transgression of the servants of the God of your father."

"Though your *father* is dead," they are saying, "the *God* of your father lives. He's not our God. He's the God of *your* father." So they asked for his forgiveness, basing their plea and their petition on the claims of the brotherhood of faith, that they belonged to the same LORD.

It would have sounded much better if they'd said, "Forgive the servants of the God of *our* father," but they said, "the God of *your* father." This hurt Joseph very much, and he wept.

And his brethren went and fell down before his face, and they said, "Behold, we are your slaves. We are your bondsmen."

And Joseph said unto them, "Fear not, for am I in the place of God? Can I possibly judge you? Can I find fault with you, I, who have had so many faults? Can I criticize? Can I judge? Am I in the place of God?"

Jesus said, "Judge not, lest you be judged." When we start judging, we've moved Christ off the throne and we've sat upon it. Joseph knew his place. "Am I in the place of God?" He said, "No, I'm not."

And Joseph said to them, "As for you, you meant evil against me, but God meant it for good, to bring to pass, as it is this day, to save very much people alive. Now therefore, fear you not. Don't be afraid. I will sustain you and your little ones." And he comforted them and spoke kindly unto them.

And Joseph dwelt in Egypt, he, and his father's house. And Joseph lived to be 110 years of age. And Joseph saw Ephraim's children of the third generation; the children also of Machir, the son of Manasseh, who were born upon Joseph's knees.

And Joseph said unto his brethren, "I die, but God will surely remember you and bring you up out of this land unto the land which He swore to Abraham, to Isaac, and to Jacob. Do not fear. Do not be afraid. No matter what happens to you, God made a promise. He will keep His promise. He's putting you in this furnace to make a nation out of you, a congregation of people. He will bring forth a mighty nation who will be a witness for all the world.

"But," he said, "God will surely remember His covenant with you, and He will bring you up in a great deliverance, in a great miracle." And then he said, "I want something from you, my brethren." He took an oath of the children of Israel, saying, "God will surely remember you." He reminded them again of His everlasting covenant. And then he said, "You shall surely carry up my bones from here." He didn't say, *"Perhaps* when the LORD remembers you," but "God *will* remember His covenant, and when the time comes, take my bones with you."

So Joseph died, being 110 years old, and they embalmed him, and he was put in a coffin in Egypt.

At the appointed time, exactly four hundred years to the day, to the minute, to the hour, from the time they went into slavery, God brought forth the people of Israel out of bondage and out of slavery. And Moses carried up the bones of Joseph (Exod. 13:19).

And when Moses died, Joshua, who was a son of Ephraim, who was a son of Joseph, who received the blessing, took the bones of Joseph back to Shechem where he was sold into slavery. His bones were buried in the very same spot in that extra parcel of land that Jacob gave him (Josh. 24:32).

According to Hebrew custom, the completion of any of the five books of the Pentateuch or the Torah must be signified by exclaiming or making some sort of a remark. Since we have just finished the first book of the Pentateuch, as a former Jewish rabbi, I have to tell you, "Be strong, be strong, and let us strengthen one another by holding one another up in prayer. Praise God."

Any counseling requests, comments, inquiries for speaking engagements, or orders for tapes should be directed to Dr. Michael Esses, P.O. Box 3397, Orange, California 92665.